# Best Hikes Near
## Colorado Springs

# Best Hikes Near
## Colorado Springs

### STEWART M. GREEN

**FALCON**GUIDES

GUILFORD, CONNECTICUT
HELENA, MONTANA

AN IMPRINT OF ROWMAN & LITTLEFIELD

# FALCONGUIDES®

An imprint of Rowman & Littlefield
Falcon, FalconGuides, and Outfit Your Mind are registered trademarks of Roman & Littlefield.

Distributed by NATIONAL BOOK NETWORK

Copyright © 2014 by Rowman & Littlefield

Photographs by Stewart M. Green except pages 134 and 166 by Susan Joy Paul.
Maps: Trailhead Graphics © Rowman & Littlefield

British Library Cataloguing-in-Publication Information is available.

Library of Congress Cataloging-in-Publication Data is available on file.
ISBN: 978-0-7627-8077-8 (paperback)

∞™ The paper used in this publication meets the minimum requirements of American National Standard for Information Sciences—Permanence of Paper for Printed Library Materials, ANSI/NISO Z39.48-1992.

The author and Rowman & Littlefield assume no liability for accidents happening to, or injuries sustained by, readers who engage in the activities described in this book.

# Contents

HELEN HUNT FALLS ✓ FRIDAY

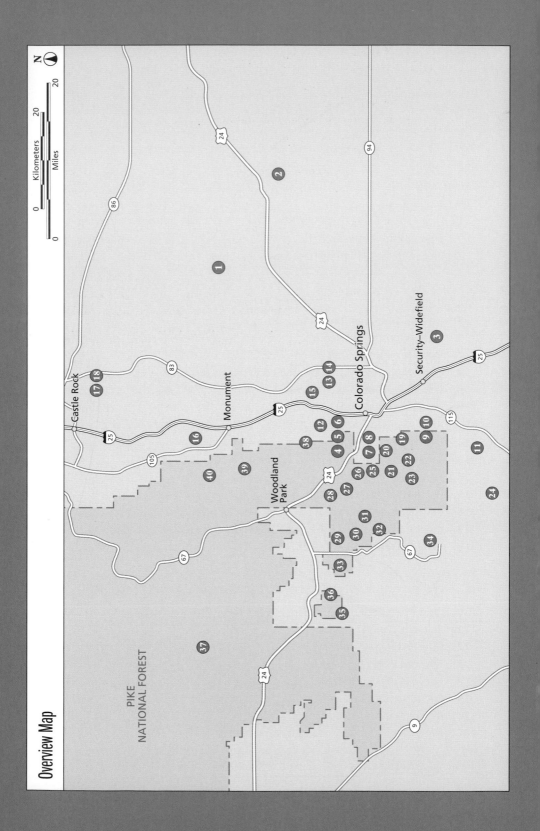

# Overview Map

# Acknowledgments

*Best Hikes Near Colorado Springs* is an exploration of the wild lands surrounding my hometown. Almost every day in summer when I grew up near North Cheyenne Cañon, I would pack a lunch, fill my steel army canteen with water, and shoulder an Austrian rucksack for the day's adventure.

I would walk in the cool morning to the pine forests at the canyon entrance. Some days I puttered along the creek, taking off shoes and wading in glassy water. Other days I watched 10th Mountain Division soldiers give climbing exhibitions at an amphitheater below the Pinnacle. But usually I logged miles on my boots, hiking Columbine Trail, then branching to St. Mary's Falls and the summit of Mount Rosa or hoofing it up to Captain Jack's, Tenney Crags, and Mount Arthur. I would arrive back home in the evening—footsore, tired, but always happy.

This book details those hikes I did as a boy and more. There is no shortage of great hikes near Colorado Springs. The city park system is simply one of the best in the United States. There aren't many cities that offer so much hiking on public lands. The Springs was fortunate to have General William Jackson Palmer, its forward-thinking founder, donate natural areas as parks but also to have a wealth of undeveloped land for recreation, including El Paso County parklands, Colorado state parks, and Pike National Forest. My thanks to the general, as well as other residents who love Pikes Peak Country and work to preserve and protect its natural values and diverse trails.

Thanks to all of my trail companions over the years as well as other hiking experts, FalconGuides editors, and park staff at state and city parks who reviewed the manuscript, offered advice, proofread sections, and added their ten cents, including Deb Acord, Chris Baddams, Kevin Baker, Katie Benoit, Howard Brooks, John Burbidge, Bob D'Antonio, Jimmie Dunn, Dave Golec, Brett Green, Ian Green, Isaac Hamilton, Doug Hatfield, Mike and Sherry Heinrichs, Bob Hostetler, Dennis Jackson, Jewels Johnson, Dennis Jump, Mitch Martin, Cindy McCaffrey, Martha Morris, Susan Joy Paul, Max Phelps, Brian Shelton, Nancy Spencer, Bill Springer, Spencer Swanger, Autumn Thorpe, and Jeff Wolin.

# Introduction

Walking is one of the most basic human activities. Walking is physical exercise that any able-bodied person can do, yet all too often we get in the car and drive somewhere when we could walk instead. There is great joy in walking or hiking for pleasure—in putting on lightweight boots, shouldering a pack, and setting off on foot into the world and into the wild.

The way of the trail is a great American tradition. The Native Americans followed ancient worn paths across Colorado's mountains, plateaus, and plains. Later trappers, traders, miners, and settlers trod the Santa Fe Trail, Smoky Hill Trail, and Cherokee Trail into this vast untrammeled land, taking to heart the words of the great nineteenth-century poet Walt Whitman: "Afoot and light-hearted I take to the open road. Healthy, free, the world before me. The long brown path before me leading me wherever I choose."

One of the best ways to enjoy, understand, and appreciate the beauty and diversity of the Pikes Peak region is by hiking across its varied landscapes. Footpaths take you away from highways, roads, and suburbs and into ancient places preserved in the rarefied air, past lakes ringed by windswept grass and in the shadow of shining mountains. Anyone interested in Colorado's different ecosystems, from plains to peaks, can learn much by hiking the area's many trails.

A hiker crosses a broad meadow on the Aiken Canyon Trail (hike 11).

## Hiking Pikes Peak Country

The Pikes Peak region, including the city of Colorado Springs, is simply one of America's best areas for hiking and trails. Over a thousand trail miles thread across prairie, peak, and canyon, climbing to cloud-scraping summits, ending at tumbling waterfalls, crossing wildflower-strewn meadows, and finding silence and solitude on wild lands within sight of a major city.

It is hard to decide what are the best hikes in Pikes Peak country and the best within an hour's drive of Colorado Springs, since there is no shortage of great hikes. There are no objective criteria that can be used to determine the best hikes, but the forty hiking adventures in *Best Hikes Near Colorado Springs* offer outdoor rewards for hikers of every ability, from beginners seeking an easy 2-hour day trip to intrepid trekkers who want to hike to the back of beyond.

You will find amazing hikes that wind among the soaring sandstone formations at the Garden of the Gods, follow tumbling creeks in Lost Creek Wilderness Area and North Cheyenne Cañon, and reach lofty summits like Mount Herman and Pikes Peak.

The hikes are divided among the region's three geographic provinces: prairie, foothills, and mountains. The mostly easy prairie hikes traverse open plains and climb bluffs with views of distant mountains. The foothills hikes, including the city of Colorado Springs, lie in a long strip of land sandwiched between the plains and the mountains. These hikes are easily accessible for year-round expeditions. The mountain hikes, the largest number in the book, explore the rugged Front Range peaks and valleys. These diverse hikes, taking you to scenic vistas and through gorgeous terrain, are of varied distances, difficulty, and steepness.

## America the Beautiful

When you stand atop Pikes Peak after hiking up, a vault of sky and clouds fills the heavens above. Far below to the east, cloud shadows trail across shimmering Colorado Springs and the distant prairie horizon edges the world. Beneath the open sky, you feel on top of the world and sense the ancient eternal Earth, the original Colorado.

In the summer of 1893, that same primeval Colorado prompted Katherine Lee Bates, a young English professor at Wellesley College, to write "America the Beautiful," the country's unofficial anthem, after riding to the top in a wagon and then a mule. On the summit she penned, "O beautiful for spacious skies, for amber waves of grain, for purple mountain majesties above the fruited plain."

"The opening lines of the hymn floated into my mind," Bates later recalled, "as I was looking out over the sealike expanse of fertile country spreading away so far under those ample skies."

## Pikes Peak Region Trails

Colorado Springs, the forty-first-most populous city in the United States with a 2012 population of 431,834, spreads across plains and valleys beneath a looming escarpment of mountains. The city's park system, run by the City of Colorado Springs Parks, Recreation, and Cultural Services Department, is simply one of the best and largest in the United States.

There just aren't many major American cities that offer so much hiking on public lands and trails. The Springs was fortunate to have many benefactors who donated scenic gems to the city as public parkland. General William Jackson Palmer, the city's forward-thinking founder, in 1871 donated some of its best natural parks, including Palmer Park and North Cheyenne Cañon Park.

Charles Eliot Perkins, a friend of General Palmer and fellow railroad man, bought 480 acres at the Garden of the Gods and wished to give it to the city but died before it was included in his will. His six children honored his wishes and conveyed those acres in 1909 to Colorado Springs as the seed of today's Garden of the Gods Park with the stipulation that it would always remain free to the public.

There is a wealth of undeveloped public land in Pikes Peak country that is available for recreation and hiking, including El Paso County parks, Colorado state parks, Pike National Forest, and BLM lands. There are also many urban trails and trail corridors that follow old rail beds and abandoned right-of-ways, including the Santa Fe Trail or Pikes Peak Greenway. This multiuse 30-mile trail, not included in this book, runs from Fountain Creek Nature Center south of Colorado Springs to Palmer Lake along the old Santa Fe Railroad bed and provides branches and link-ups to other urban trails in Colorado Springs.

The city parks are also dog friendly with lots of off-leash areas for Fido to romp unfettered; the best dog areas are at Red Rock Canyon Open Space, Garden of the Gods Park, Palmer Park Dog Park, and the very popular Bear Creek Dog Park. Remember, however, to keep your dog under voice control to avoid unpleasant contact with other dogs and hikers and to always pick up and dispose of your dog's waste. It's the polite thing to do.

## Pikes Peak Defines Geography

The Pikes Peak region is roughly bounded by the short-grass prairie east of Colorado Springs, the Arkansas River and Cañon City to the south, the Puma Hills and South Park to the west, and the South Platte River and Palmer Divide to the north. Geography dictates the landscape, a place of textbook geological formations including billion-year-old bedrock granite, thick layers of Mesozoic sandstone uplifted into soaring hogbacks, and coarse gravels deposited by runoff during recent ice ages.

Geography, geology, and the huge range of elevations from below 6,000 feet to 14,115 feet conspire to make Pikes Peak country an ecological melting pot. The diversity of animal habitats and plant communities are molded by variable temperatures, precipitation patterns, and elevation. Indeed, traveling from the arid desert south of Colorado Springs to the frigid ice-bound summit of Pikes Peak is like taking a telescoped journey from Mexico to beyond the Arctic Circle in less than 30 miles and in over 8,000 feet of elevation difference.

The region is, of course, dominated by Pikes Peak, Colorado's thirty-first-highest mountain. From everywhere within 50 miles, the great Peak dominates the central Colorado landscape and the skyline of Colorado Springs, etching its snowcapped crown against a blue sky horizon. Pikes Peak stands alone as a silent granite sentinel, proudly rising above the tawny eastern plains and the lower forested mountains and valleys that surround it.

The storied mountain shapes more than the land and its natural history—it also exerts a powerful influence on the region's history, culture, and economics. The Peak is always there—serene, eternal, and a constant reminder of the wild out there beyond the city limits.

Pikes Peak is sacred to the native Ute Indians, who called it *Tava* (sun) as well as *Tavakiev* (sun mountain). The Utes, calling themselves *Tabeguache* (people of the sun), revered the mountain and lingered at the "boiling springs" at its base

Looking across East and West Beaver Creek Canyons from high on the Powerline Trail (hike 24)

and camped among the sculptured sandstone formations at the Garden of the Gods. Even still the Ute Indians come and leave ritual offerings at sacred sites and twisted prayer trees, some hundreds of years old.

Later, during the 1859 gold rush to the diggings at Central City, west of Denver, the famous mountain was a slogan—"Pikes Peak or Bust!"—for fortune seekers who marched across the Great Plains, including over 100,000 in a three-month period. The *St. Louis News* documented the peak obsession in a March 13, 1859, article: "Now they hear of nothing, dream of nothing, but Pike's Peak. It is the magnet to the mountains, toward which everybody and everything is tending. It seems that every man, woman and child, who is going anywhere at all, is moving Pikes's Peakward."

## The Ten Essentials

The Ten Essentials are easy to carry and will help you survive. The purpose of carrying the Ten Essentials is twofold: to allow you to respond positively to an accident or emergency situation and to allow you to survive one or more nights outside. It's best to carry most of the Ten Essentials in your hiking pack on a major trek like Pikes Peak, even though the highway parallels half of the trail.

These are the essential items to carry:

1. **Navigation.** Bring a map, compass, GPS unit, and extra batteries.
2. **Sun protection.** Sunscreen is essential to protect from the burning rays of the high-altitude sun as well as lip balm and either baby powder or Gold Bond powder for chafing.
3. **Insulation.** Bring plenty of clothing and dress in layers. Waterproof outer gear is essential.
4. **Illumination.** Bring a headlamp and extra batteries if you have to hike down in the dark.
5. **First-aid supplies.** A small first-aid kit with bandages, Band-Aids, and basic medical supplies is important.
6. **Fire.** Bring a lighter and box of matches to start a fire for warmth if you are benighted.
7. **Repair kit and tools.** A multiuse tool or pocket knife along with some duct tape can repair torn gear.
8. **Nutrition.** Pack plenty of food. Bring extra energy bars to stash in your pack. You may need them if you get lost.
9. **Hydration.** Bring plenty of water. In summer bring a minimum of three quarts of water. You can substitute a sports drink for one of them or bring powder to mix in water. You can refill your water bottles or Camelbak at the Summit House or at many area parks.
10. **Emergency shelter.** It's easy to pack a lightweight space blanket or ultralight tarp for shelter from the storm.

## Pikes Peak Country Trails and Hikes

*Best Hikes Near Colorado Springs* describes forty of the area's best hikes with an informative text, GPS coordinates, and detailed maps within 50 miles of the city and Pikes Peak. It is difficult to narrow down all the wonderful trails in the region to only the select few, which were handpicked by the author, a native Colorado Springs resident, climber, and hiker.

There are some significant omissions, including Barr Trail, an arduous 12.6-mile trail up Pikes Peak's east side, and the fabulous Captain Jack's hike above North Cheyenne Cañon. Barr Trail was not included due to its length and difficulty and simply because the Devils Playground Trail is a better way to hike the Peak. The Captain Jack's hike was omitted because the Bear Creek area has been closed indefinitely by the USDA Forest Service to protect the endangered greenback cutthroat trout, the Colorado state fish. A 4-mile stretch of the creek southwest of Colorado Springs is the only remaining place with a genetically pure greenback population, and hikers using the creek area put those surviving fish at risk for extinction.

Also, the Waldo Canyon Trail had to be excluded because that trail has been closed until further notice, perhaps even permanently, as a result of the Waldo Canyon Fire in 2012.

The hikes in this book are of varying lengths and difficulties so it is easy to pick out fun strolls for families, nature walks for kids, and barrier-free trails that are wheelchair accessible, as well as long, difficult hikes on rough terrain and in wilderness areas teeming with wildlife.

All of the trailheads are easily reached by driving, have parking lots, and often have facilities including water and restrooms. GPS coordinates are given for all of the parking areas and trailheads as well as in the Miles and Directions section for each hike's important trail junctions, points of interest, overlooks, and turnaround locations. The hikes are also rated by difficulty from easy to challenging so you can find trails for your ability and interest.

*Best Hikes Near Colorado Springs* is all about getting outside, walking for pleasure, and having a great adventure. So pick a trail, put on your boots, and go hiking. If you put one foot in front of the other, you can go just about everywhere.

## Practice Zero-Impact Philosophy

Colorado Springs is an outdoors-oriented city. The US Olympic Committee is headquartered in downtown Colorado Springs. World-class runners, Olympic speed skaters, triathletes, and mountain bikers train on Colorado Springs' trails. One of the region's biggest sporting events is the famed Pikes Peak Marathon—26 miles and 8,000 vertical feet up and down America's most famous mountain. In 2009 *Outside* magazine rated Colorado Springs the "Best Place to Live," while *Men's Fitness* magazine ranked it the #2 "Fittest City in America," and

*Women's Health* magazine ranked it the #10 "Best Place to be a Woman." Colorado Springs and the Pikes Peak region is simply a wonderful place to go outside and enjoy wild nature.

With all the hikers and outdoors enthusiasts in the Pikes Peak region, it's important to practice a zero-impact philosophy so that the area's natural resources and its trails are protected from overuse and to maintain a positive outdoor experience for all backcountry visitors. Use the following zero-impact suggestions to make both your own as well as everyone else's visit enjoyable and to protect our spectacular natural world.

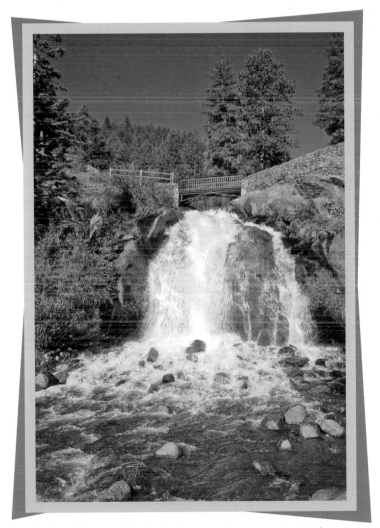

Helen Hunt Falls, named for the famed nineteenth-century writer, is at the western end of Columbine Trail (hike 20).

Zero-impact is about responsible outdoor ethics, including staying on the trail, not cutting switchbacks, packing out litter, keeping your dog leashed and picking up its poop, disposing properly of human waste, and leaving the environment as pristine as possible. Mountain and prairie ecosystems and environments are fragile and sensitive to human use. The marks of man, including social trails and damage from ATVs and motorcycles, linger for years on this dry landscape.

Every hiker should adopt the zero-impact ethic to minimize his or her impact on this beautiful land. It's our responsibility to pay attention to our effect on the environment so that we can ensure that all these fabulous trails will remain as wild refuges from the urban environment.

### FalconGuide Principles of Zero Impact

Always stay on the trail. Cutting switchbacks or traveling cross-country causes erosion and destroys plants. Often an area, like Garden of the Gods, is braided with social trails from careless hikers. Try to always follow the main route whenever possible. The mountains, especially steep slopes, are susceptible to erosion caused by unthinking off-trail hiking.

Pack it in—pack it out. Everything you carry and use, including food wrappers, orange peels, cigarette butts, plastic bottoms, and energy-bar wrappers, needs to come out with you and be deposited in a trash can. Carry a plastic bag for picking up other trash along the trail. Also remember to pick up your dog's

Evening light on the Garden of the Gods in Colorado Springs, Colorado (hike 4)

waste and pack it out in a plastic bag. Too many bad dog owners leave their pet's feces in the middle of the trail. That's just gross.

Respect public and private property, livestock fences, and mining claims. Federal laws protect all archaeological and historic antiquities, including Indian artifacts, projectile points, old ruins, petroglyphs, fossilized bone and petrified wood, and historic sites. Don't carve your name in a rock surface or on a tree. Leave all natural features, like flowers and rocks, where you found them. Enjoy their beauty, but leave them for the next hiker.

Properly dispose of human waste. Dig a hole 4 to 6 inches deep and at least 300 feet from water sources and dry washes. Do not burn or bury toilet paper. Instead, pack it out in a plastic baggie. The best thing to do, of course, is to use the public restrooms that are found at many of the trailheads.

Take only photographs and memories. We can easily avoid leaving any evidence of our passage across this lovely and delicate mountain environment. With care and sensitivity, we can all do our part to keep the Pikes Peak region beautiful, clean, and pristine. Don't pick flowers, pick up rocks, or take anything with you when you leave. If everyone took just one item, it wouldn't be long before nothing special was left. Leave your souvenirs for other hikers to enjoy.

## Be Prepared

Hiking, while immensely rewarding, also comes with hazards and inherent risks, especially for those who come unprepared. Respect the mountain environment and be prepared and you'll be safe. Remember that many dangers are found in the greater Colorado Springs area.

You must assume responsibility for your own actions and for your safety. Be aware of your surroundings and of dangers, including drop-offs, cliffs, and loose rock; the weather; and the physical condition of both your party and yourself. Never be afraid to turn around if conditions aren't right. Pay attention to those bad feelings—they keep you alive.

Here are a few suggestions to be prepared for emergency situations on your hike:

- Bring extra clothes and a raincoat, especially in the mountains. The weather can change in an instant. Heavy thunderstorms regularly occur on summer afternoons and cold wet clothing can lead to hypothermia.
- Colorado's Front Range has more lightning strikes than almost anywhere else in the United States. Pay attention to the weather and get off high places before a storm arrives. If you can hear thunder, you're probably not safe.
- The air is thin and the sun is bright. Summer temperatures can be hot. Use sunscreen to avoid damaging sunburns, and wear a hat.
- Carry plenty of water and sports drinks for electrolyte replacement due to sweating. Don't drink any water from streams unless you treat and purify it.

- If you're coming from a lower elevation, watch for symptoms of altitude sickness, including headache, nausea, and loss of appetite. The best cure is to lose elevation.
- Allow enough time for your hike. If you start in late afternoon, bring a head-lamp or flashlight so you can see the trail in the dark.
- Bring plenty of high-energy snacks for the trail and treats for the youngsters.
- Wear comfortable hiking shoes and good socks. Your feet will thank you for that. To avoid blisters, break in your shoes before wearing them in the backcountry.
- Enjoy wildlife you see along the trail, but keep your distance and treat the animals with respect. Cute little animals can bite and spread diseases like rabies. Watchful mother animals, including deer and black bears, are protective of their babies. Rattlesnakes are found on low-elevation trails. Watch were you place your hands and feet. Don't feed wildlife to avoid disrupting their natural eating habits.
- Carry a day pack to tote all your trail needs, including a raincoat, food, water bottle, first-aid kit, flashlight, matches, and extra clothes. A whistle, GPS unit, topo map, binoculars, camera, pocket knife, and FalconGuide identification book for plants and animals are all handy additions. And don't forget your *Best Hikes Near Colorado Springs* book!

The upper section of the Mount Manitou Incline Trail reaches grades steeper than 60 degrees (hike 26).

# How to Use This Guide

Take a close enough look, and you'll find that this guide contains just about everything you need to choose and enjoy a hike near Colorado Springs. Here's an outline of the book's major components.

Each hike starts with a short summary of the hike's highlights. These quick overviews give you a taste of the hiking adventures to follow. You'll learn about the trail terrain and what surprises each route has to offer.

Following the overview you'll find the hike specs: quick, nitty-gritty details of the hike. Most are self-explanatory, but here are some details on others:

**Distance:** The total distance of the recommended route—one-way for loop hikes, the round-trip on an out-and-back or lollipop hike, point-to-point for a shuttle. Options are additional.

**Hiking time:** The average time it will take to cover the route. It is based on the total distance, elevation gain, and condition and difficulty of the trail. Your fitness level will also affect your time.

**Difficulty:** Each hike has been assigned a level of difficulty. The rating system was developed from several sources and personal experience. These levels are meant to be a guideline only and may prove easier or harder for different people depending on ability and physical fitness.

*Easy*—Five miles or less total trip distance in one day, with minimal elevation gain, and paved or smooth-surfaced dirt trail.

*Moderate*—Up to 10 miles total trip distance in one day, with moderate elevation gain and potentially rough terrain.

*Strenuous*—More than 10 miles total trip distance in one day, strenuous elevation gains, and/or rough or rocky terrain.

**Trail surface:** General information about what to expect underfoot.

**Seasons:** General information on the best time of year to hike.

**Schedule:** Days and hours the trail and visitor center, offices, etc. are open to the public. Unless restrictions are stated, the trail is open 24 hours, and if the park is open, the trails are open.

**Other trail users:** Such as horseback riders, mountain bikers, inline skaters, etc.

**Canine compatibility:** Know the trail regulations before you take your dog hiking with you. Dogs are not allowed on several trails in this book.

**Land status:** National forest, county open space, national park wilderness, etc.

**Fees and permits:** Whether you need to carry any money with you for park entrance fees and permits.

**Maps:** This is a list of other maps to supplement the maps in this book. USGS maps are the best source for accurate topographical information, but the local park map may show more recent trails. Use both.

**Trail contacts:** This is the location, phone number, and website URL for the local land manager(s) in charge of all the trails within the selected hike. Before you head out, get trail access information, or contact the land manager after your visit if you see problems with trail erosion, damage, or misuse.

**Other:** Other information that will enhance your hike.

**Special considerations:** This section calls your attention to specific trail hazards, like hunting seasons or a lack of water, and other safety information.

The **Finding the trailhead** section gives you dependable driving directions to where you'll want to park, as well as GPS coordinates for the start of the hike. **The Hike** is the meat of the chapter. Detailed and honest, it's a carefully researched impression of the trail. It also often includes lots of area history, both natural and human. Under **Miles and Directions,** mileage cues identify all turns and trail name changes, as well as points of interest. **Options** are also given for many hikes to make your journey shorter or longer depending on the amount of time you have.

Don't feel restricted to the routes and trails that are mapped here. Be adventurous and use this guide as a platform to discover new routes for yourself.

## How to Use the Maps

**Overview map:** This map shows the location of each hike in the Colorado Springs area by hike number.

**Route map:** This is your primary guide to each hike. It shows all of the accessible roads and trails, points of interest, water, landmarks, and geographical features. It also distinguishes trails from roads, and paved roads from unpaved roads. The selected route is highlighted, and directional arrows point the way.

# Trail Finder

**Best Hikes for Views**

6. Perkins Central Garden Trail
7. Red Rock Canyon Trail
22. Gray Back Peak Trail
31. Devils Playground Trail (Pikes Peak)
32. Pancake Rocks and Horsethief Falls Trails
37. Goose Creek Trail

**Best Hikes for Waterfalls**

20. Columbine Trail
21. St. Mary's Falls Trail
32. Pancake Rocks and Horsethief Falls Trails

**Best Hikes for Kids**

6. Perkins Central Garden Trail
9. Coyote Run Trail
18. Canyon View Nature Trail
35. Florissant Fossil Beds National Monument Trails

**Best Hikes for Wildlife**

11. Aiken Canyon Trail
24. Beaver Creek Loop Trail
33. Mueller State Park Trails
35. Florissant Fossil Beds National Monument Trails

**Best Hikes for Photography**

2. Calhan Paint Mines Trail
6. Perkins Central Garden Trail
30. Crags Trail
31. Devils Playground Trail
32. Pancake Rocks and Horsethief Falls Trails
37. Goose Creek Trail

**Best Summit Hikes**

22. Gray Back Peak Trail
29. Raspberry Mountain Trail
31. Devils Playground Trail
39. Mount Herman Trail
40. Palmer Reservoirs and Cap Rock Trails

**Best Hikes for Solitude**

11. Aiken Canyon Trail
22. Gray Back Peak Trail
24. Beaver Creek Loop Trail
27. Heizer Trail
31. Devils Playground Trail

# Map Legend

## Transportation
- 25 Interstate Highway
- 24 U.S. Highway
- 67 State Highway
- 621 Forest/Paved/Improved Road
- Unpaved Road
- Railroad

## Trails
- Selected Route
- Trail/Fire Road
- → Direction of Route

## Water Features
- Body of Water
- River or Creek
- Intermittent Creek
- Spring
- Waterfall

## Symbols
- 20 Trailhead
- ■ Building/Point of Interest
- P Parking
- Restroom
- Scenic View/Overlook
- ? Visitor Center
- Picnic Area
- ▲ Campground
- Gate
- Bench
- ○ Towns and Cities
- × Spot Elevation
- ▲ Mountain/Peak
- ∩ Cave
- — Dam

## Land Management
- National Park/Forest
- State/Local Park
- Wilderness Area

# The Prairie

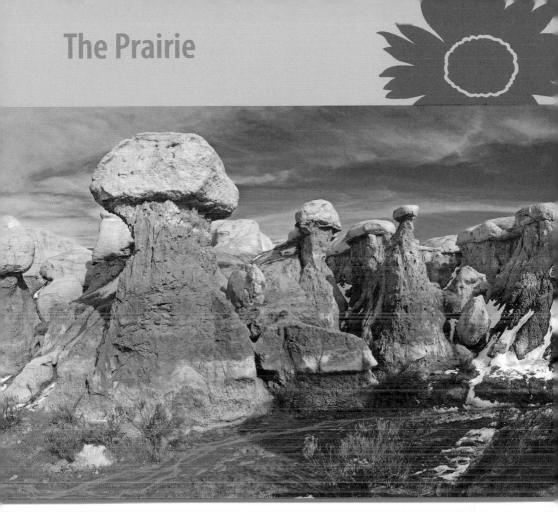

Colorful sandstone hoodoos stand above a dry wash at the Calhan Paint Mines (hike 2)

The wide, expansive prairie, stretching east from Colorado Springs to the Kansas border, is a Great Plains landscape of undulating hills broken by rocky bluffs and cottonwood-lined water courses. Much of the short-grass prairie near the Springs, once populated by vast herds of bison and migrating Native Americans, is now privately owned and divided into 5-acre ranchettes. Some exquisite pockets of prairie, however, offer scenic and unusual trails in both county and city parklands.

*The Homestead Ranch Trail is composed of two loops that form a 3.4-mile hike through pine woods and grasslands on a high plains bluff northwest of Colorado Springs.*

**Start:** Trailhead next to a building with restrooms at the northwest corner of the loop drive and parking lots

**Distance:** 3.3-mile double loop

**Hiking time:** About 2 hours

**Difficulty:** Easy

**Elevation gain:** 180 feet

**Trail surface:** Doubletrack dirt trail

**Seasons:** Year-round. Trail can be snowy and icy in winter.

**Schedule:** Open daily sunrise to sunset

**Other trail users:** Horseback riders, mountain bikers

**Canine compatibility:** Leashed dogs only

**Land status:** El Paso County Park

**Fees and permits:** None

**Maps:** USGS Eastonville; El Paso County Park Map

**Trail contact:** El Paso County Parks, 2002 Creek Crossing, Colorado Springs, CO 80906; (719) 520-7529; http://adm.elpasoco.com/CommunityServices/Park Operations/Pages/default.aspx

**Finding the trailhead:** Drive east from Colorado Springs on US 24. Before reaching Peyton, turn left (north) on Elbert Road and drive 5 miles. Make a sharp right (east) turn on Sweet Road and drive 2.5 miles to Gollihar Road. Turn left on gravel Gollihar and drive a half mile to the park. Turn left into the park on Person Drive and drive to a loop with several parking areas. Park at the northwest end of the loop in front of a building with restrooms. The trailhead is to the right of the building. The park's address is 16444 Gollihar Road (**GPS:** 39.074583, -104.523505).

## THE HIKE

Homestead Ranch Regional Park, a 450-acre El Paso County regional parkland, protects a gorgeous slice of a high plains ecosystem northwest of Colorado Springs. The area includes pine-covered bluffs lined with sandstone cliff bands and broad meadows blanketed with tall grass and wildflowers. The park also offers expansive views toward Pikes Peak and the Front Range and distant views south to the ragged Sangre de Cristo Range and the Spanish Peaks.

The Homestead Ranch Trail makes two loops, an east loop and a west loop, connected by a short trail segment. Either loop can be hiked separately for a shorter outing or together for full value. The recommended and described hike is to do the east loop first and then the west.

The hike begins at the trailhead on the north side of the park building at the west side of the parking area. Walk up the doubletrack road past a playground on the left and continue through a broad meadow fringed with woods, passing a left turn and a short trail that descends down to a spring-fed pond. The small pond, stocked with bluegills and small bass, is a great fishing hole, especially for youngsters learning the art of fishing.

After almost 0.2 mile you reach a major trail junction. Keep right and continue hiking uphill toward the forested bluff ahead. The trail coming in from the left is on the west loop trail. After hiking the two loops, you will return to this point on the west loop.

Low broken cliffs rim bluffs along the trail at Homestead Ranch Regional Park.

The trail heads northwest and enters the ponderosa pine forest. Tall trees cast dappled shadows across the wide trail and thick grass on the forest floor. The final section of uphill trail climbs steeply and, after climbing 195 vertical feet from the parking lot, reaches the top of the bluff. Continue hiking and after 0.5 mile reach a trail junction. Go right to start the east loop trail. The west loop goes left at this junction.

The sandy trail hooks right and heads northeast through a meadow above a wooded draw. At 0.55 mile the trail passes a spinning windmill with a water tank for horses, a hitching rack, picnic table, and a stone marker with a brass plaque placed by the El Paso County Horseman's Council. One of the quotes on the plaque reads "There's nothing better for the inside of a person than the outside of a horse." Continue hiking east to a Y-shaped trail junction and the start of the east loop trail at 0.6 mile.

Go left at the junction so that you will get the best mountain views as you hike along the bluff edge on your return to this spot. The trail swings below a low-browed hill rimmed with broken rock and scattered pines. It slowly climbs east to the top of a flat hill and continues across an open meadow to a trail junction at the northeast corner of the park. Go right on the main loop trail. The trail that goes straight east travels 0.1 mile to the park boundary and a small parking area at the end of Lovaca Drive.

This next trail segment is the best part of the entire hike, edging along the cliffed rim of the bluff escarpment and offering wide views of the prairie to the south, distant mountain ranges, and broad-shouldered Pikes Peak. The trail heads south and quickly reaches the bluff's rim. Scattered ponderosa pine rise above the grassy meadows, while a dense piney forest spills down the side of the bluff. Just after the trail reaches the rim, take a break and look southeast through a break in the trees toward Rattlesnake Butte, an unranked 7,410-foot flat-topped peak that lies within the park.

Continue southwest along the bluff edge to a great viewpoint atop a rocky cliff. Stop for a breather to enjoy the wide vista, with Pikes Peak anchoring the western horizon. Beyond on the distant edge of the limitless prairie are the landmark Spanish Peaks, the dark Wet Mountains, and the sawtooth Sangre de Cristo Range. The exposed rock here is Dawson arkose, a coarse sandstone that is also seen in Colorado Springs at Pulpit Rock and Palmer Park. It is a Tertiary-age formation that is some 50 million years old.

The trail continues twisting along the bluff edge, heading northwest in both grassland and pine forest. After 1.5 miles you return to the Y junction. Keep left and hike back on the connector trail past the windmill to a major trail junction at 2.1 miles. Keep right to start the west loop trail. If you don't want to do the west loop, go left and follow the trail back to the parking lot.

The west loop trail follows the edge between bluff and prairie. Right of the trail stretches a high grassland swept by wind, while to the left is the ponderosa pine woodland, which covers the bluff edge and the steep hillsides below. The trail follows the rim for about a half mile before making a sharp left bend to the south and descending the steep hillside.

Just before the trail begins its descent, look on the left side of the trail at a twisted ponderosa pine. This tall pine is a Ute prayer tree, deformed by Ute Indians who lived here centuries before Anglo-Americans settled. On pilgrimages to Pikes Peak, a sacred mountain to the Utes, a tree sapling was tied to the ground, with the bend pointing toward the sacred peak. This tree was tied where it bends sharply upward. After the tree was bound, the group of Utes circled the tree and prayed. The tree they believed would hold their prayers for 800 years and each gust of wind would give their prayers new breath and life.

The trail descends steeply across a rocky slope, making a couple switchbacks, before descending down a shallow draw and emerging on gentler slopes below. Continue hiking southeast through meadows along the forest edge before the trail tops a low rise and bends northeast. The last trail section runs across a slope above the fishing pond until it reaches a junction with the trail you initially used to climb the bluff face. Turn right at the junction and descend 0.2 mile back to the trailhead, restrooms, and the parking area. If your kids still have pent-up energy after the 5-mile hike, let them loose on the playground equipment and they're guaranteed to sleep on the drive home.

## MILES AND DIRECTIONS

**0.0** The trailhead is at the northwest corner of the road and parking areas (GPS: 39.074583, -104.523505). Hike up a doubletrack trail, staying on the main trail at a junction. A left turn takes you to the pond.

**0.2** Reach a major trail junction. Continue straight up the hill. The trail to the left is the return trail at the end of the hike.

**0.4** The trail, after gaining 195 feet, reaches the top of the bluff escarpment. After a few hundred feet, you will reach a three-way trail junction (GPS: 39.077482, -104.527214). Go right and hike northwest.

**0.55** The trail passes a windmill with a water tank for horses and a picnic table (GPS: 39.078474, -104.524595).

**0.6** Reach a three-way trail junction (GPS: 39.078248, -104.523625). Keep left and begin hiking the lollipop, which will bring you back to this junction.

**1.0** At a trail junction at the northwest corner of the park, go right (south) at a three-way junction (GPS: 39.078964, -104.517446). The left fork goes 100 yards to a trailhead near houses.

# Homestead Ranch Regional Park Trail

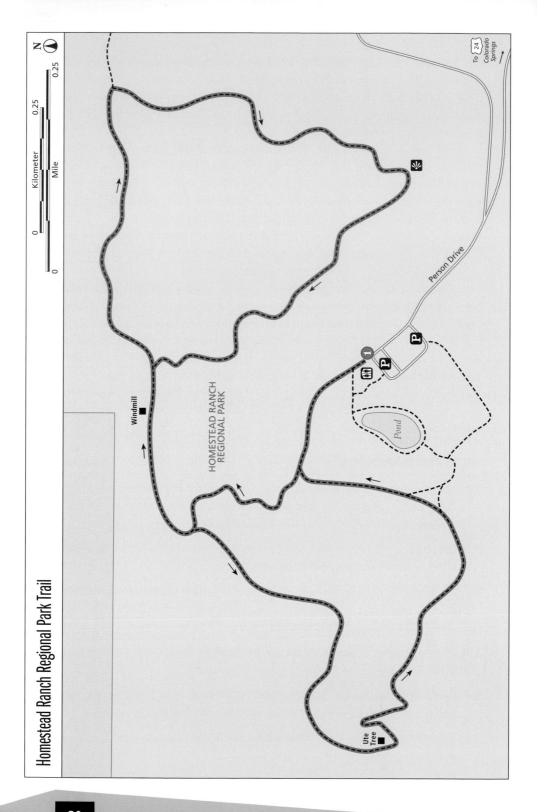

**1.3** The trail follows the eastern edge of the bluff, offering views across a valley to Rattlesnake Butte.

**1.4** Stop at a rim overlook for great views south toward the Spanish Peaks, Wet Mountains, Sangre de Cristo Range, and Pikes Peak (GPS: 39.073839, -104.519545).

**1.8** Reach a three-way junction where the loop started. Go straight toward the windmill.

**2.1** Reach the three-way junction where the uphill trail from the parking lot reaches the bluff top. Go right on the second leg of the hike.

**2.5** Begin descending a steep slope from the top of the escarpment. Pass a bent Ute medicine tree.

**2.9** Reach a trail junction (GPS: 39.073255, -104.526903). Go straight on the doubletrack trail. The right singletrack trail drops east to the pond below.

**3.1** End the second loop at a junction. Go right toward the trailhead, restrooms, and parking.

**3.3** End at the trailhead by the parking lots and restrooms.

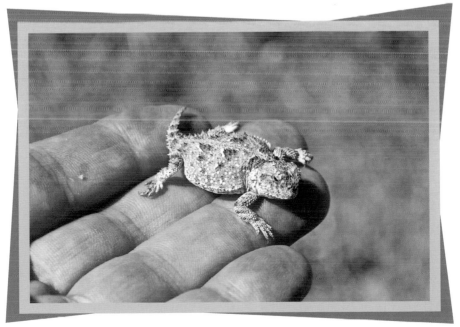

A small horned lizard perches on a hand along the trail.

# Calhan Paint Mines Trail

*The Paint Mines Trail is a spectacular loop hike that crosses open prairie grasslands to eroded badlands of colored sandstone used by ancient Native Americans for paint and pottery. The trail offers panoramic views of the surrounding prairie as well as distant Pikes Peak on the western horizon.*

**Start:** Paint Mines Interpretative Park Trailhead on the west side of the park

**Distance:** 3.7-mile loop

**Hiking time:** 1.5 to 3 hours

**Difficulty:** Easy

**Elevation gain:** 205 feet

**Trail surface:** Single- and double-track dirt path

**Seasons:** Year-round. Summers are hot. Winter days can be snowy and windy.

**Schedule:** Open daily, sunrise to sunset

**Other trail users:** None

**Canine compatibility:** Dogs not permitted

**Land status:** El Paso County Park

**Fees and permits:** None

**Maps:** USGS Calhan. Park map on El Paso County Parks website.

**Trail contact:** El Paso County Parks, 2002 Creek Crossing, Colorado Springs, CO 80906; (719) 520-7529; http://adm.elpasoco.com/CommunityServices/Park Operations/Pages/default.aspx

**Special considerations:** Use extreme caution in the badlands area. Stay on the trails to avoid damaging the fragile rock formations. Watch children around drop-offs. Watch for rattlesnakes in summer. Summer can be hot; no shade along the trail. Wear a hat and bring plenty of water as none can be found along the trail.

**Finding the trailhead:** Drive east from Colorado Springs on US 24 for 25 miles to Calhan. On the east side of Calhan, turn right (south) on Yoder Street, which becomes Calhan Highway. Drive south on the road for 0.5 mile to Paint Mine Road. Turn left (east) on Paint Mine Road and drive to a large parking area and the trailhead on the left (**GPS:** 39.020507, -104.274266). A restroom is at the parking area. Another parking lot is 0.6 mile farther along the road on the south side of the park.

## THE HIKE

The 3.7-mile-long Paint Mines Trail offers a wonderful hike that explores the high prairie and unusual badlands south of Calhan in eastern El Paso County. The single- and doubletrack trail has easy grades, several interpretative signs, and lots of history.

The Paint Mines, a small eroded badland south of Calhan and US 24, is one of those unknown off-the-beaten-track places that amazes when you first visit it. Eroded into the flank of a bluff, the mines are a wonderland of narrow sharp canyons, rounded alabaster-white boulders, and rainbow-dyed hoodoos. The colorful mines, however, are only one part of the 753-acre Paint Mines Interpretative Park, an El Paso County park, which spreads across a broad grassy valley and protects a swathe of short-grass prairie.

The Paint Mines form a miniature painted desert that was frequented by Native Americans, including Paleo-Indians for as long as 10,000 years and, in the past 700 or 800 years, the Cheyenne and Arapahoe. They mined the colored clay for ceramics and to paint pottery and used petrified wood to make projectile points and scrapers. Later settlers in the 1800s used the clay for bricks. The Calhan Paint Mines Archeological District is listed on the National Register of Historic Places for their prehistoric significance.

Hoodoos and shale cliffs line a shallow canyon in the heart of the Paint Mines.

Begin the hike at the trailhead on the east side of the parking lot off Paint Mine Road south of Calhan. A restroom is at the parking area, but there's no water. The hike goes clockwise, following two loop trails across the rolling prairie before finishing at the Paint Mines area. Hike east 0.1 mile to a three-way T intersection. Go straight (east). A right turn, however, travels 0.7 mile south to the Paint Mines if you want to go there first.

The first trail segment makes a 1.1-mile loop across prairie and up a dry drainage. Hike northeast on the wide trail and after 0.4 mile reach an interpretative sign that explains Colorado prairie ecology. Drop into a broad dry wash and turn southwest. The sandy singletrack trail twists up the willow-filled arroyo between clay banks until it reaches a four-way trail intersection. Go left (southeast).

The next 1.3-mile trail section makes a wide-open loop across the southeastern part of the park to a junction just north of the southern parking lot. The trail quickly leaves the wash and climbs to a bench that overlooks eroded white badlands, with dry eroded hummocks of soft sandstone. Bend left here and follow the trail as it contours northeast across a basin to an eroded badland and an old quarry where clay was excavated for bricks. The trail continues uphill left of the badlands to a bench, an interpretative sign detailing human habitation here, and a great view west across the park to distant Pikes Peak.

The trail turns southwest and gently climbs to a Y-fork trail junction at 2.4 miles. Go right (west) on the next 0.6-mile trail segment, which ends at the Paint

The trail bends north around the Paint Mines' badlands.

0    Kilometer    0.4

0    Mile    0.4

N

To Calhan
and 24

P

2

PAINT MINES
INTERPRETIVE
PARK

Paint Mine Road

Paint
Mines

P

Paint Mine Road

Paint Mine Road

Mines. The south parking lot is 0.1 mile to the southwest on Paint Mine Road from this junction. Back on the main trail, hike west and reach another Y junction after a few hundred feet. Keep left on the main trail, which descends onto north-facing slopes and contours west across a shallow ravine. At 2.8 miles is a marvelous overlook above the Paint Mines. Drop down to the eastern edge of the Paint Mines to a metal bench and enjoy a view of the white, gray, yellow, orange, and ocher badlands below. Continue down the trail to the bottom of a deep wash and a trail junction.

Go left (south) and hike 0.2 mile up the bottom of the deep arroyo into the heart of the Paint Mines. All around you are twisted gullies, standing blocks of sandstone, hoodoos carved into fanciful shapes by erosion, and tumbled boulders all tinted by every color of the rainbow. The exposed rock here is Dawson arkose, a coarse sandstone interspersed with clay layers that was deposited 55 million years ago when this region was covered with a tropical hardwood forest. Don't climb on the fragile formations—they're easily damaged by human activity. Also control your children since there are lots of drop-offs.

Return to the trail intersection with the main trail and head north. The last 0.7-mile trail section climbs away from the Paint Mines and returns to the trailhead. Walk north along the sandy floor of the dry arroyo for 0.2 mile to a four-way junction. Go left (west).

The last half-mile trail section begins with a gradual climb up a hill to a high metal bench and a good view south to the mines. Continue north on the trail as it gently descends an open grassland to a T junction. Go left (west) and walk another 0.1 mile to the hike's terminus at the trailhead and parking lot.

## MILES AND DIRECTIONS

**0.0** Trailhead at the parking lot on the east side of Paint Mine Road (GPS: 39.020451, -104.274082).

**0.1** Trail junction (GPS: 39.020863, -104.273012). Go straight for the loop hike. For a short hike, go right to the Paint Mines.

**0.4** Interpretative sign about ecology.

**1.1** Four-way trail intersection (GPS: 39.017359, -104.268546). Go left on the loop hike.

**1.2** Reach a ridge overlooking the Paint Mines.

**2.4** Reach a T-shaped trail junction on a high grassland (GPS: 39.014091, -104.261903). Go right. South parking area is 0.1 mile to the left.

**2.8** Reach the crest of the trail and a great view of the Paint Mines (GPS: 39.014107, -104.267976).

**3.0** Reach a trail junction in the bottom of a dry wash (GPS: 39.014879, -104.269186). Go left to the Paint Mines (or right to the trailhead). After exploring the mines return to this junction and go north down the wash.

**3.2** Leave the wash and go left up a slight grade to a trail junction (GPS: 39.017213, -104.269554). Go left (west) on the uphill trail.

**3.7** Arrive back at the trailhead and parking lot.

# Bluestem Prairie Open Space Trail

*This easy trail, crossing open grass prairie and through a prairie-dog town, makes a half-circle, out-and-back hike around Big Johnson Reservoir southeast of Colorado Springs.*

**Start:** South side of the open-space parking lot on the west side of Goldfield Drive
**Distance:** 4.4 miles out and back
**Hiking time:** 1.5 to 2 hours
**Difficulty:** Easy
**Elevation gain:** Minimal—17 feet
**Trail surface:** Doubletrack dirt and gravel trail
**Seasons:** Year-round
**Schedule:** Open daily, sunrise to sunset
**Other trail users:** None

**Canine compatibility:** Dogs not permitted
**Land status:** Public land. City of Colorado Springs Open Space
**Fees and permits:** None
**Maps:** USGS Ellsmere and Fountain quads
**Trail contact:** Colorado Springs Parks, Recreation and Cultural Services, 1401 Recreation Way, Colorado Springs, CO 80905-1975; (719) 385-5940; www.springs gov.com

**Finding the trailhead:** The Big Bluestem trailhead is easily accessed from I-25 by taking South Academy Boulevard, exit 135, on the south side of Colorado Springs. Go east on South Academy about a mile, exit south on US 85/87, and drive south to Fontaine Boulevard. Turn left (east) and drive to Goldfield Drive. Turn left (north) on Goldfield and drive a short distance to the open-space parking area and trailhead on the right (**GPS:** 38.743751, -104.694456).

0        Kilometer    0.5

0        Mile        0.5

N

*To*
*Colorado Springs*

BLUESTEM PRAIRIE
OPEN SPACE

Powers Boulevard

*Big Johnson*
*Reservoir*

Goldfield Drive

P

3

21

Fontaine Boulevard

**🍂 Green Tip:**
*Carry a reusable water container that you fill at the tap.*
*Bottled water is expensive; lots of petroleum is used to*
*make the plastic bottles; and they're a disposal nightmare.*

The open space is considered a mixed-grass prairie, with a variety of native grasses including big bluestem, little bluestem, blue grama, buffalo grass, side-oats grama, sleepy grass, and needlegrass. Other plants include thistle, silver sage, rabbitbrush, yucca, and flowers like Easter daisy, sand lily, scarlet gilia, and prickly poppy. The big bluestem species is a rare and endangered grass species, making this protected parkland a valuable haven for its continued survival.

The trail continues north and after 1.2 miles passes another sign, which details the area's colorful history. In the early nineteenth century, trappers, traders, and Indians traveled along the old Cherokee Trail. This overland route, also called the Trapper's Trail, began in Oklahoma and traversed part of Kansas into the Colorado Territory along the Santa Fe Trail before striking north from today's Pueblo along the Front Range to Wyoming. A historic site along the old pioneer trail is just north of the open space at Jimmy Camp Creek. A trading post operated by trader James (Jimmy) Daugherty, who was murdered by Indians, was located here. Later the area was part of the 30,000-acre Banning-Lewis Ranch, a huge cattle ranch founded in 1897.

Past the history sign the trail bends across a dry wash on the northeast corner of the lake and crosses a wide sloping plain with a mostly abandoned prairie-dog town. As the trail heads northwest, the vegetation increases dramatically with tall grass and low sagebrush. The trail sidles alongside a barbed fence until the hike ends after 2.2 miles at a wooden post directly north of the reservoir.

Past this point the trail continues almost directly west along the fence line until it ends at Goldfield Road. The trail does not circumnavigate the lake since the section south of the fence is private property and a hike back to the parking lot requires walking along the shoulder of the road.

From the turnaround point, retrace the trail back 2.2 miles to the trailhead and parking area.

## MILES AND DIRECTIONS

**0.0** Start from the parking lot and trailhead on the east side of Goldfield Drive (GPS: 38.74366, -104.694362).

**1.2** The trail reaches a sign about the history of the area, including the Cherokee Trail, on the northeast side of the reservoir.

**2.2** Reach the turnaround point on the trail at the north end of the reservoir at a wooden fence post (GPS: 38.757573, -104.696696). The trail continues through sagebrush but eventually ends. Turn around here to hike back to the trailhead.

**4.4** Arrive back at the trailhead and parking lot.

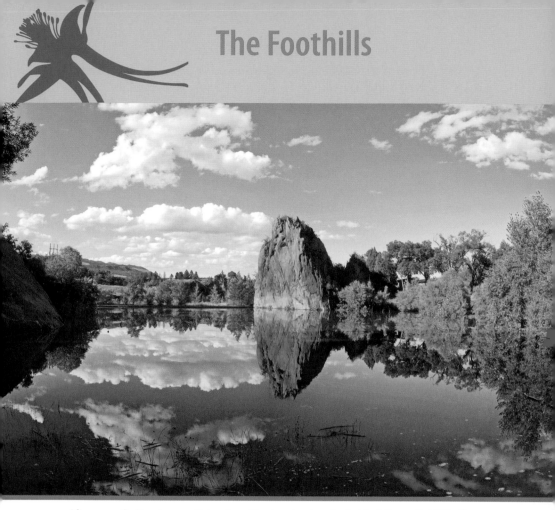

Afternoon reflections in a pond brimming with rainwater along the Red Rock Canyon Trail (hike 7).

Colorado Springs spreads across the foothills below Pikes Peak. These low hills, rising sharply from the plains as rocky hogbacks and broad mesas, form distinctive landscapes. Some of the most spectacular natural features in the Pikes Peak region, including the famed sandstone formations at the Garden of the Gods as well as Red Rock Canyon Open Space and Palmer Park, lie within the foothills zone against the towering mountain escarpment. Numerous trails, mostly easy and moderate in difficulty, thread through these natural parks, offering quick and easy hiking getaways from the bustle of Colorado Springs, the forty-first-largest city in the United States.

# Palmer Trail to Susan G. Bretag Trail Loop

*This excellent loop hike follows four different trails around the spectacular rock formations in Garden of the Gods Park—the Palmer Trail, Scotsman Trail, Perkins Central Garden Trail, and Susan G. Bretag Trail. The loop offers fun, easy hiking on a good surface as well as spectacular views of the cliffs and ramparts and Pikes Peak from rocky ridges and wooded valleys.*

**Start:** Main parking lot at north end of Juniper Way Loop road

**Distance:** 2.6-mile loop

**Hiking time:** 1 to 2 hours

**Difficulty:** Moderate

**Elevation gain:** 200 feet

**Trail surface:** Singletrack dirt path and doubletrack paved trail

**Seasons:** Year round

**Schedule:** Open daily; May 1 to Oct 31, 5 a.m. to 11 p.m.; Nov 1 to Apr 30, 5 a.m. to 9 p.m.

**Other trail users:** Equestrians on parts of the Scotsman Trail

**Canine compatibility:** Leashed dogs only. Pick up your dog's waste.

**Land status:** City of Colorado Springs park

**Fees and permits:** None; Colorado Springs city park rules apply

**Maps:** USGS Cascade. Trail map available at the visitor center.

**Trail contact:** Colorado Springs Parks, Recreation and Cultural Services, 1401 Recreation Way, Colorado Springs, CO 80905-1975; (719) 385-5940; www.springsgov.com

**Finding the trailhead:** From I-25, take exit 146 and drive west on Garden of the Gods Road until it dead-ends at 30th Street against the mountains. Turn left (south) on 30th Street and drive south to Gateway Road, opposite the Garden of the Gods Visitor and Nature Center. Turn right (west) on Gateway Road and follow it until it merges with Juniper Way Loop, a loop road that encircles the main Garden of the Gods zone. Turn right (north) on the one-way road and follow it to the large Main Parking Lot on the left (**GPS:** 38.881198, -104.880319). The trailhead is at the north side of the parking lot at a crosswalk (**GPS:** 38.88157, -104.880402).

Alternatively, approach from I-25 and downtown Colorado Springs by driving west on Cimarron Street/US 24 from I-25 to Ridge Road, a half mile past 31st Street. Exit right and follow Ridge Road north to a stop sign at Colorado Avenue. Cross Colorado Avenue (may be busy) and drive up a steep hill on Ridge Road to the Garden of the Gods. At the one-way Juniper Way Loop road, go right and drive to the Main Parking Lot on the north side of the park.

## THE HIKE

This 2.6-mile hike loops around the perimeter of the Garden of the Gods, following parts of four different Garden trails—Palmer Trail, Scotsman Trail, Perkins Central Garden Trail, and Susan G. Bretag Trail. This is an interesting hike that offers great views of the soaring sandstone formations. The first hike section, following Palmer Trail, climbs onto wooded ridges west of North and South Gateway Rocks before dipping down to Scotsman Picnic Area. The next segment follows Scotsman Trail back to the central Garden zone, where it picks up the paved Perkins Central Garden Trail. The last part follows the Susan G. Bretag Trail north up a broad valley east of the rock formations and back to the parking lot and trailhead.

The trails are all singletrack except for the wide concrete sidewalk section. Expect spectacular scenery and a close-up intimate experience with the different rock formations as well as the transitional ecosystems found at the Garden of the Gods. Most of the trail is quiet with few other hikers, although the paved section through the main Garden zone is usually busy, especially on summer days when tourists jam the pavement. The trail also crosses the park roads four times. Use the designated crosswalks for safety.

Start the hike at the trailhead on the north side of the Main Parking Lot off Juniper Way Loop. Walk north across the road at a crosswalk to a trail junction.

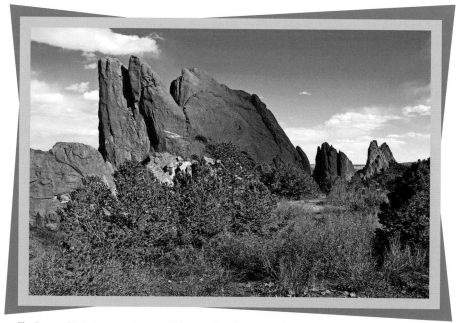

The Tower of Babel towers above the Palmer Trail on the north side of the Garden of the Gods.

Go left on the Palmer Trail. The trail coming in from the right, the Susan G. Bretag Trail, is the return trail. The first trail segment on the Palmer Trail, named for General William Jackson Palmer, an early settler and the founder of Colorado Springs, runs 1.2 miles from the junction to the Scotsman Picnic Area southwest of the central Garden zone.

The Palmer Trail, paralleling the road, heads northwest through copses of Gambel oak before bending south. It slowly gains elevation and after 0.3 mile reaches a scenic overlook. Walk 75 feet southeast off the trail for the best view and a superb photo opportunity. All the main rock formations—North Gateway Rock, South Gateway Rock, Gray Rock, Keyhole Rock, Montezuma Ruins, and the Three Graces—tower to the south, their ragged outlines etched against the sky.

Past the overlook the trail turns west and contours across a steep shallow canyon before climbing onto east-facing slopes opposite North Gateway Rock, the park's highest sandstone formation. The trail continues climbing through a piñon pine and juniper woodland until it reaches a high point and then descends to a shoulder. This is another great viewpoint. Note the Kissing Camels, a small arch perched atop North Gateway Rock on the left, and the Weeping Indian, the white-rock profile of an Indian face on South Gateway Rock. Hike south down the rocky trail and, after 0.8 mile from the trailhead, reach a trail junction. From here a short trail heads left to the central Garden zone. Stay straight on the main Palmer Trail. Ignore another side trail that jogs over to the road 100 feet farther down.

The Palmer Trail passes beneath the west face of the Giant Footprints, a couple of tilted slabs composed of 220-million-year-old Fountain Formation sandstone, then descends southwest parallel to the park road through scrub-oak groves for 0.4 mile. When the trail reaches the edge of the road at 1.2 miles, you're opposite the Scotsman Picnic Area. Cross the road to a parking lot and walk over a bridge. A restroom, open in summer only, is to your left. Go right on Scotsman Trail.

Follow the Scotsman Trail northeast for 0.35 mile. The sandy trail, often used by horse strings from nearby stables, slowly climbs toward the Garden's rock formations. At an obvious trail junction, keep left and hike up to Juniper Way Loop road. Cross the road just north of a small parking area and follow a wide trail into the central Garden zone.

The next half mile of trail follows parts of the paved Perkins Central Garden Trail, the most popular and most scenic trail at the Garden of the Gods. Hike north and then east on the paved path, passing north of the Three Graces and Montezuma Tower, both slender spires that are popular with rock climbers. At an obvious Y junction, go left (north) and hike to the Gateway, the huge gap between North and South Gateway Rocks. At the trail junction here below the dedication plaque, go right on a paved trail and walk 0.15 mile east to Juniper Way Loop.

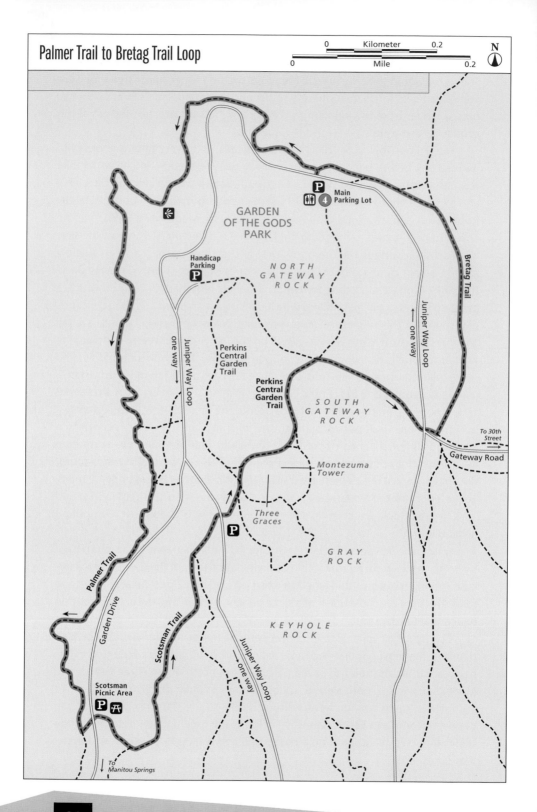

Kilometer
0       0.2

Mile
0       0.2

N

**P** Main
Parking Lot
**4**

GARDEN
OF THE GODS
PARK

Handicap
Parking
**P**

*N O R T H
G A T E W A Y
R O C K*

Perkins
Central
Garden
Trail

**Perkins
Central
Garden
Trail**

*S O U T H
G A T E W A Y
R O C K*

Bretag Trail

Juniper Way Loop

one way

one way

Juniper Way Loop

*Montezuma
Tower*

To 30th
Street

Gateway Road

*Three
Graces*

**P**

*G R A Y
R O C K*

Palmer Trail

Garden Drive

Scotsman Trail

*K E Y H O L E
R O C K*

Juniper Way Loop

one way

Scotsman
Picnic Area
**P** 🌲

To
Manitou Springs

The last trail segment follows the Susan G. Bretag Trail for 0.5 mile back to the trailhead and parking lot. Cross the road at a crosswalk and then turn north on the marked trail. Follow the wide trail north in a broad valley between white rock formations on the west and the Dakota Hogback to the east. The trail crosses an open meadow covered with grass and yucca.

After 0.3 mile it reaches a Y junction with the Dakota Trail. Keep left and follow the trail, which bends northwest. End at the start of the Palmer Trail. Cross the road back to the trailhead and parking lot. If you're thirsty or need the facilities, a water fountain and restrooms are located on the southeast side of the parking lot.

After doing this hike check out the other Garden of the Gods hikes detailed here—all are scenic and worth your footsteps.

## MILES AND DIRECTIONS

**0.0**  Start at trailhead on the north side of the Main Garden Parking Lot (GPS: 38.88157, -104.880402). Cross the road to a T junction. Go left (west) on Palmer Trail.

**0.3**  Scenic overlook on the left (GPS: 38.881298, -104.883461). Walk down from the trail for the best photos.

**0.8**  Trail junction with short trail to Garden zone on left (GPS: 38.877218, -104.884248). Go straight.

**1.2**  Reach road opposite Scotsman Picnic Area (GPS: 38.872343, -104.885498). Cross road to the left at a crosswalk, then cross bridge to Scotsman Trail and restrooms (GPS: 38.872161, -104.884861). Go right.

**1.6**  End Scotsman Trail at Juniper Way Loop (GPS: 38.87569, -104.88253). Cross road at a crosswalk to the central Garden zone. Go left and follow a trail straight to the paved Perkins Central Garden Trail.

**2.1**  End the Central Perkins Garden Trail section at Juniper Way Loop on the east side of the park (GPS: 38.877193, -104.878011). Cross the road to the Susan G. Bretag Trail. Go left (north) up a wide valley on the Bretag Trail.

**2.6**  End Susan G. Bretag Trail at junction with Palmer Trail. Go left across the road to the trailhead and parking lot.

# Ute Trail and Chambers Trail Loop

*This short, fun hike explores the southeast side of the Garden of the Gods Park on a couple of excellent footpaths—the Ute Trail and Chambers Trail. The hike crosses broad meadows with tall grass and summer wildflowers, plunges through groves of Gambel oak, and passes beneath shady cottonwoods. Most of the hike follows the old Ute Trail, a route once followed by Ute Indians.*

**Start:** South parking lot at the southeast part of Juniper Way Loop road
**Distance:** 1.2-mile loop
**Hiking time:** About 1 hour
**Difficulty:** Easy
**Elevation gain:** 200 feet
**Trail surface:** Single- and double-track dirt trail
**Seasons:** Year-round
**Schedule:** Open daily; May 1 to Oct 31, 5 a.m. to 11 p.m.; Nov 1 to Apr 30, 5 a.m. to 9 p.m.
**Other trail users:** Multiuse trail with horses and mountain bikers

**Canine compatibility:** Leashed dogs only. Pick up your dog's waste.
**Land status:** City of Colorado Springs park
**Fees and permits:** None. Colorado Springs city park rules apply.
**Map:** USGS Cascade
**Trail contact:** Colorado Springs Parks, Recreation and Cultural Services, 1401 Recreation Way, Colorado Springs, CO 80905-1975; (719) 385-5940; www.springs gov.com

**Finding the trailhead:** From I-25 take exit 146 and drive west on Garden of the Gods Road until it dead-ends at 30th Street against the mountains. Turn left (south) on 30th Street and drive south to Gateway Road opposite the Garden of the Gods Visitor and Nature Center. Turn right (west) on Gateway Road and follow it until it merges with Juniper Way Loop, a loop road that encircles the main Garden of the Gods zone. Turn right (north) on the one-way road and follow it past the Main Parking Lot on the left then down the west side of the park. Keep left at a junction and continue south past Keyhole Rock to a junction with Ridge Road. Keep left and bend around to the South Garden Parking Lot on the right (**GPS:** 38.869729, -104.878099). The trailhead is at the north side of the parking lot at an information kiosk (**GPS:** 38.870133, -104.878223).

Alternatively, approach from I-25 and downtown Colorado Springs by driving west on Cimarron Street / US 24 from I-25 to Ridge Road, a half mile past 31st Street. Exit right and follow Ridge Road north to a stop sign at Colorado Avenue. Cross Colorado Avenue (may be busy) and drive up a steep hill on Ridge Road to the Garden of the Gods. At the one-way Juniper Way Loop road, go right and drive to the South Garden Parking Lot on the right side of the road.

## THE HIKE

This short loop hike, following parts of the Ute Trail and Chambers Trail, is a marvelous and scenic excursion around the southeast corner of the Garden of the Gods Park. It offers spectacular views of the soaring rock formations, tallgrass meadows, a pond (sometimes filled with rainwater) lined with cottonwood trees, and an historical link to the Ute Indians, the park's first residents.

Start the hike at the South Garden Parking Lot on the east side of Juniper Way Loop, a one-way scenic road that loops around the central Garden of the Gods zone. The trailhead is located at a ramada on the north side of the parking lot. Before hiking, be sure to read four interpretative signs at the ramada, which provide information on the Ute Indians, Zebulon Pike's expedition in 1806, and the plants and animals that live here, and include a 1930s photo of the Garden filled with cars at an Easter sunrise service.

Hike north from the trailhead on a dirt trail. The trail parallels the park road and, after 100 yards, reaches a stone marker next to a small parking area. The granite stele, placed by the Daughters of the American Revolution in 1935, reads: "This Stone Marks the Indian Trail Used by the Plains Indians to Ute Pass." At this point where the Ute Trail descends north on a hillside, a famous photograph was taken of a string of Utes riding horses single-file up the trail.

From the marker descend the wide trail through a broad meadow covered with tall grass and studded with spiky yuccas, clumps of skunkbrush, and scattered groves of Gambel oak. After crossing a deep arroyo, which drains out of a rocky canyon, on a bridge, the trail passes beneath looming Gray Rock. This towering rock formation, also called Cathedral Rock and Kindergarten Rock, is composed of the upper layer of Lyons sandstone, a fine-grained sandstone with extensive cross-bedding, indicating that it was deposited in a sand dune environment during the Permian period between 225 million and 270 million years ago. Later during the Laramide orogeny, an intense mountain-building period about 70 million years ago, the horizontal sandstone was thrust upward as the Rocky Mountains slowly rose to the west. Erosion then attacked the rising layers, stripping off softer rock surrounding the Lyons and leaving today's bare-rock monuments.

The trail passes a couple large boulders, tumbled down from Gray Rock, on the left. These room-size blocks, called the Snake Pit by climbers, is a popular spot for bouldering, the art of climbing difficult problems on small rocks. The east face of Gray Rock also offers lots of excellent climbing routes up its vertical

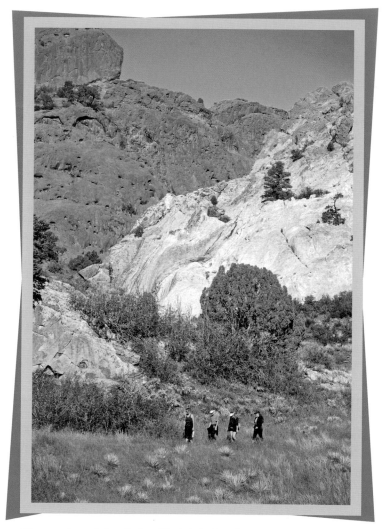

Hikers pass beneath Gray Rock and Keyhole Rock on the Ute Trail.

faces. Check out *Rock Climbing Colorado* (FalconGuides, 2010) for route descriptions and information on climbing at the Garden of the Gods.

Hike north along the edge of the grassy meadow, and after 0.25 mile reach a trail junction with the right-hand loop of the Ute Trail. Continue straight on the Ute Trail. The sandy trail heads through broad meadows filled with wavering grass and gray with clumps of sage. At an obvious Y fork, take the right trail. The left one heads up to the loop road. After passing through a dense copse of Gambel or scrub oak, the trail bends right, crosses a small wooden bridge, and, 0.45 mile from the trailhead, reaches a major three-way trail junction immediately south of the park entrance road. Take a sharp right turn here onto Chambers Trail. A post marks the junction with signs pointing out three trails.

Go southeast on Chambers Trail across the meadow, with great views of the red rock formations, including Gray Rock, South Gateway Rock, and North Gateway Rock, on the western skyline. The open trail eventually threads across a shale slope below the Dakota Hogback, a high elongated ridge to the left, before reaching the top of an old earthen dam above Rock Ledge Ranch on the east and a catchment basin on the right that fills with rainwater every ten years or so. On the north side of the dam is an obvious three-way trail junction. Continue straight across the dam on short Valley Reservoir Trail. A sharp left turn is the Galloway-Homestead Trail, while the Chambers Trail continues down left to Rock Ledge Ranch Historic Site.

The Rock Ledge Ranch is worth a short visit for the pioneer history of the Pikes Peak region if you have the time. Follow the Chambers Trail down to the ranch and meander around. It's best to visit on weekends when the place is buzzing with activity. The site was originally settled in 1867 by Scotsman Walt Galloway, who established a 160-acre homestead along Camp Creek. He built a rustic log cabin and planted a garden, irrigating it with water from the creek. Eventually he sold his property to the Chambers family, who built Rock Ledge Ranch. Elsie Chambers later called him ". . . a plain, plodding day laborer, but exemplified what persistence can do in securing a home in his own name, by staying in one place and cultivating the regulation patch of garden demanded by Uncle Sam."

Hike across the top of the dam and bend right, passing a junction with Niobrara Trail, which strikes up left onto the hogback. After 0.9 mile from the trailhead, you reach a junction with the Ute Trail loop, which comes in from the northwest. Go left at this Y junction on the Ute Trail and climb a slight hill for a couple hundred feet to the last junction. Go right (west) on Ute Trail Connection.

Follow this narrow track up and over a hogback, passing some low tilted sandstone cliffs. At the top of a hogback is a short spur that trots north a few hundred feet to an overlook. Follow the main trail down a gentle slope on the west side of the hogback and end at a trailhead at the southern end of the South Garden Parking Lot.

# The Historic Ute Trail

The Mountain Utes traveled along ancient trails down Ute Pass to the mineral springs and the Garden of the Gods. In his book *The Indians of the Pikes Peak Region*, early pioneer Irving Howbert wrote that the Indian trail through the Garden of the Gods was a branch of the Ute Trail. This trail came down Ute Pass northeast of Pikes Peak to the springs in Manitou, then headed down Fountain Creek's canyon to today's Becker's Lane, where the trail climbed toward Ridge Road and the Garden of the Gods. It swung around a low hill, following today's park loop road, and passed by the South Parking Lot before descending down a hill still followed by today's trail. The Ute Trail descended across today's Rock Ledge Ranch east of the Garden's rock formations, climbed over the Mesa, and headed northeast along today's Fillmore Street before exiting the valley through Templeton Gap.

Howbert also remembered that more than 300 Utes camped near Balanced Rock in the cold winter of 1866–67. He wrote: "They did not bother us in Colorado City, and we felt no great alarm. They were more inclined to be friendly than otherwise. But one day a party of them came into town and made a demand upon us for 20 sacks of flour. They told us that they were nearly out of provisions and were in danger of starving. They said that they had come to ask that we give them the flour, but that so pressing was the need that if we were to refuse they would take it anyhow.

"The matter was talked over by the people of the town and not a person was found who did not think it the right thing to give them that for which they asked. It was the general belief that they were facing starvation and much sympathy was felt for them. So the 20 sacks of flour were presented and the Indians went away with it, grateful for the food."

Nothing exists of the historic Ute Trail today except a short section at the Garden of the Gods, which can only be documented by historic photographs that show Ute Indians riding up the trail.

## MILES AND DIRECTIONS

**0.0**  Start at the trailhead at the north end of the South Garden Parking Lot (GPS: 38.870137, -104.878229).

**0.2**  Ute Trail stone marker beside park loop road and trail. Go north downhill.

**0.3**  Reach a trail junction with the loop formed by the Ute Trail (GPS: 38.872114, -104.877855). Go straight and pass another trail junction to the right. Continue straight (north).

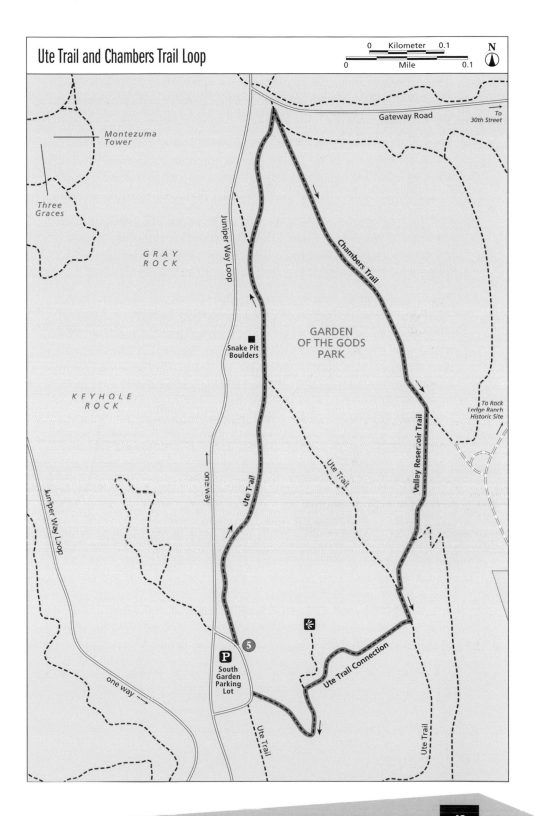

# Ute Trail and Chambers Trail Loop

0  Kilometer  0.1

0  Mile  0.1

N

Gateway Road

To 30th Street

Montezuma Tower

Three Graces

GRAY ROCK

Juniper Way Loop

Chambers Trail

GARDEN OF THE GODS PARK

Snake Pit Boulders

KEYHOLE ROCK

one way

Ute Trail

Ute Trail

Valley Reservoir Trail

To Rock Ledge Ranch Historic Site

Juniper Way Loop

one way

P

5

South Garden Parking Lot

Ute Trail Connection

Ute Trail

Ute Trail

one way

**0.5** After passing a social trail that goes left to the road, continue to a major three-trail junction just south of the park entrance road (GPS: 38.876764, -104.877576). Make a sharp right turn and head southeast on the Chambers Trail.

**0.8** Reach a junction with the Galloway-Homestead Trail and the Valley Reservoir Trail (GPS: 38.873036, -104.875063). Go right on Valley Reservoir Trail and hike across the top of an old dam. The Chambers Trail continues southeast, descending down to the southern end of Rock Ledge Ranch.

**0.9** Past the old dam, reach a junction with the Niobrara Trail, which goes left (GPS: 38.871356, -104.875326). Continue straight on the Valley Reservoir Trail. In a few hundred feet, you will reach a trail junction with the Ute Trail (GPS: 38.870713, -104.875519). Continue straight up a slight hill.

**1.0** At a trail junction go right (west) on Ute Trail Connection (GPS: 38.870353, -104.875354). Hike to the top of a hogback (GPS: 38.869678, -104.876867), where you can go right to an overlook. Keep left and go downhill to the trail's end at the south end of the South Garden Parking Lot. (*Option:* If you want a longer hike, instead of going west on the Ute Trail Connection cutoff, continue straight on the Ute Trail. This half-mile trail segment heads south, then bends around the southern end of the rounded hogback and climbs up to the trailhead at the southern end of the parking lot for a 2.7-mile hike.)

**1.2** End the hike at the trailhead at the south end of the parking area (GPS: 38.869377, -104.877859).

## Ancient Artifacts

Evidence, including hearths found in 1993, indicates that ancient people camped at the Garden of the Gods around 1330 BC, or 3,330 years ago, while radiocarbon dates from hearths and fire rings show that there were seasonal encampments at the Garden of the Gods beginning by 250 BC. Artifacts of early Native Americans here include broken pottery bits, stone tools, and projectile points or arrowheads.

# Perkins Central Garden Trail

*This short scenic loop hike follows a paved wheelchair-accessible trail that explores the heart of the Garden of the Gods Park, a spectacular natural wonder of uplifted sandstone rock formations on the west side of Colorado Springs. The trail is simply one of the best easy hikes in the Colorado Springs area and one that every visitor and resident should do.*

**Start:** Main parking lot at the north end of the Garden of the Gods loop drive
**Distance:** 1.2-mile lollipop
**Hiking time:** 30 minutes to 1 hour
**Difficulty:** Easy. Wheelchair- and stroller-accessible.
**Elevation gain:** Minimal
**Trail surface:** Concrete sidewalk
**Seasons:** Year-round
**Schedule:** Open daily, sunrise to sunset
**Other trail users:** None

**Canine compatibility:** Leashed dogs only
**Land status:** City of Colorado Springs park
**Fees and permits:** None
**Maps:** USGS Manitou Springs; Garden of the Gods park trail map
**Trail contact:** Colorado Springs Parks, Recreation and Cultural Services, 1401 Recreation Way, Colorado Springs, CO 80905-1975; (719) 385-5940; www.springs gov.com

**Finding the trailhead:** From I-25 take exit 146 and drive west on Garden of the Gods Road until it dead-ends at 30th Street against the mountain front. Turn left (south) on 30th Street and drive south to Gateway Road opposite the Garden of the Gods Visitor and Nature Center. Turn right (west) on Gateway Road and follow it until it merges with Juniper Way Loop, a loop road that encircles the main Garden of the Gods zone. Turn right (north) on the one-way road and follow it to the large Main Parking Lot on the left (south) side of the road. The trailhead is at the southeast corner of the lot.

Alternatively, approach from the south by driving west from I-25 on US 24 to 31st Street. Exit right and follow 31st Street north to a stop sign at Fillmore Street. Turn right on Fillmore, drive 1 block, and make a left turn on 30th Street. Follow 30th Street north to Gateway Road. Turn left on Gateway Road and follow the directions above to the trailhead (**GPS:** 38.880937, -104.88015).

## THE HIKE

The Perkins Central Garden Trail, a 1.2-mile hike that follows a paved path that loops around the major rock formations in the Garden of the Gods, a Colorado Springs city park, gets you up close and personal with the Garden's soaring sandstone rock formations. The wide trail, accessible to both wheelchairs and strollers, has gentle gradients and plenty of spectacular scenic views, some of the best in Colorado. This short hike is simply one that every resident of and visitor to Colorado Springs should enjoy. The trail is accessible year-round, with every time of day and every season offering new perspectives, views, and experiences.

The Garden of the Gods, nestled against the southern end of the Rampart Range on the west side of Colorado Springs, is a huge outdoor sculpture garden dominated by towering rock monuments. Here rise twisted, faulted, and uplifted layers of sandstone that tell the geologic story of the constantly changing earth—the uplift and erosion of ancient mountain ranges, periodic inundations by seas, and the comings and goings of different lives.

The story of the earth from a couple billion years ago until the present is seen at the Garden of the Gods. Few other places in the United States boast the variety and age of exposed rock like the Garden. Every different rock strata is a page from a great book, each showing its own story from its own world.

Hikers enjoy a brisk winter morning below South Gateway Rock.

Begin the paved trail at the southeast corner of the large Main Parking Lot on the north side of the Garden of the Gods off Juniper Way Loop, a one-way road that encircles the main Garden zone. A restroom, open year-round, and water fountain are left of the trailhead. To the right is a ramada with an interpretative display.

Hike south down the wide paved trail to a viewpoint surrounded by a circular stone wall. North Gateway Rock, also called Gate Rock, towers above the trail to the west. This huge salmon-colored formation is the highest in the Garden, looming over 300 feet above the footpath. Continue down the trail to the Gateway, a broad open gap between North Gateway on the right and South Gateway Rock on the left. A couple squat pinnacles, Red Twin Spire and White Twin Spire, sit on the west side of the Gateway. On the right side of the trail just before the Gateway is a boulder covered with inscriptions, some dating back to early park visitors in the nineteenth century.

A large plaque on the narrow south face of North Gateway Rock details the gift of the Garden of the Gods to the city of Colorado Springs and honors its benefactor, railroad magnate Charles Elliott Perkins. Perkins purchased most of the Garden in 1879 but allowed public visitation. Two years after Perkins death in 1907, his children donated the land to the city as a park that would "be kept forever open and free to the public." From Perkins's original 480 acres, the Garden of the Gods Park, now a designated National Natural Landmark, has grown to 3,300 acres.

The towering rock formations were long a sacred place to Native Americans, who first camped here as long as 3,300 years ago and undoubtedly scrambled to the lofty summits. The Garden was later sacred to many other Indian tribes, including the Apache, Arapaho, Cheyenne, Comanche, Kiowa, Pawnee, Shoshone, and Ute peoples. The Utes, a Colorado mountain tribe, particularly revered the Garden of the Gods and camped below the formations. Evidence of their passage includes petroglyphs pecked onto sandstone surfaces and historic photographs taken in the nineteenth century.

Park visitors always wonder how the Garden received its name. Early visitors first called the area Red Rock Corral. Later, in the summer of 1859, surveyors M. S. Beach and Rufus Cable visited the site while laying out what is now Old Colorado City. Inspired by the scenery, Beach told his friend, "Rufus, this is a capital place for a beer garden." Cable, however, fittingly replied, "A beer garden? No, this is a fit place for the gods to assemble. We should call it Garden of the Gods!" At the Gateway the trail splits. Take the left fork and hike beneath the sharp northern edge of South Gateway Rock and past Red and White Twin Spires on the right. A low stone wall here makes a good bench to have a drink of water and watch rock climbers clamber up the spires. The trail bends left into the central Garden, a broad valley with open grasslands, groves of Gambel oak, and scattered juniper trees.

Follow the trail past the vertical west face of South Gateway Rock on the left, passing below the east face of Montezuma Tower. If you want to add a short scenic 0.2-mile loop to the hike, take a left off the main trail and hike up a wide dirt trail, which climbs south to a rocky overlook north of Keyhole Rock. Expect great views here of the Garden's rock formations and Pikes Peak to the west. Don't scramble onto the ledges on Keyhole Rock south of the overlook: It's an area reserved for technical climbing and is dangerous, especially for children. From the overlook descend west through a grove of thousand-year-old junipers and down to the paved trail just west of Three Graces Plaza.

Three Graces Plaza is a small open area flanked by low stone walls at the southern end of the paved trail. Looming above the circular plaza is 135-foot-high Montezuma Tower, a tall, frail spire on the right, and the three narrow fins of the Three Graces directly above the plaza. This is a great spot to sit on a stone wall and marvel at the soaring sandstone formations. Helen Hunt Jackson, a nineteenth-century writer and author of *Ramona*, described the Garden of the Gods this way: "You wind among rocks of every conceivable and inconceivable shape and size . . . all bright red, all motionless and silent, with a strange look of having been just stopped and held back in the very climax of some supernatural catastrophe."

From the plaza, hike west on the paved trail down a gentle slope. A side trail goes left to the park road and some small roadside parking lots. Continue north on the main Perkins trail for 0.3 mile, paralleling the park loop road to the left. Benches along the way allow you to sit and marvel at the surrounding rock formations. From the earliest days the bizarre rocks have teased the imaginations of countless visitors who saw fanciful shapes, some reflected by names including Weeping Indian and Kissing Camels. Take a look across the grassy vale and see if you can spot these two shapes. Kissing Camels is a fragile skyline arch perched high atop North Gateway, while the Weeping Indian is the profile of a chief composed of white rock that faces north on the sheer west face of South Gateway Rock.

At the north end of the Garden zone, the trail bends east, passing through thickets of scrub oak and juniper trees before emerging below the abrupt west face of North Gateway Rock. Check out an interpretative exhibit below the face and take a moment to watch the darting flights of white-throated swifts and swallows, which nest on the rock walls. In spring and summer you may hear the shrieking cry of a prairie falcon looking for a meal of mouse, snake, or pigeon. The falcons generally nest on the upper east face of North Gateway Rock in spring and summer. Another rare inhabitant of the Garden of the Gods is the honey ant, which lives in a handful of colonies scattered through the park.

The trail turns southeast and passes beneath the abrupt west face of North Gateway Rock, before reentering the Gateway. From here, retrace your steps back on the paved trail for 0.2 mile to the trailhead, restrooms, water fountain, and parking area.

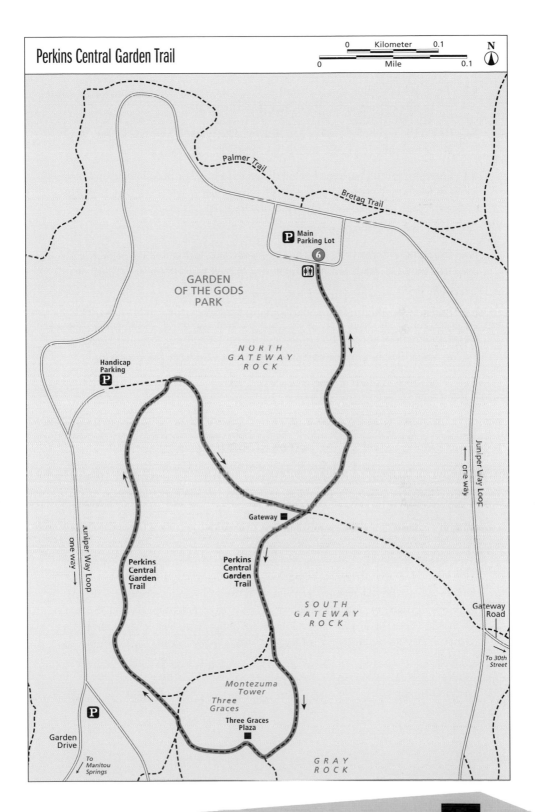

0    Kilometer    0.1

0    Mile    0.1

**N**

Palmer Trail

Bretag Trail

**P** Main
Parking Lot

6

GARDEN
OF THE GODS
PARK

*N O R T H
G A T E W A Y
R O C K*

Handicap
Parking
**P**

Juniper Way Loop

one way

Gateway ■

Juniper Way Loop

one way

**Perkins
Central
Garden
Trail**

**Perkins
Central
Garden
Trail**

*S O U T H
G A T E W A Y
R O C K*

Gateway
Road

To 30th
Street

*Montezuma
Tower*

*Three
Graces*

Three Graces
Plaza ■

**P**

Garden
Drive

To
Manitou
Springs

*G R A Y
R O C K*

## MILES AND DIRECTIONS

**0.0**  Begin at the trailhead at the southeast corner of the Main Parking Lot on the north side of the park (GPS: 38.880937, -104.88015).

**0.2**  Reach the Gateway, a wide gap between North and South Gateway Rocks, and a trail junction (GPS: 38.878426, -104.880322). Keep left.

**0.3**  Enter the central Garden zone on the west side of South Gateway Rock. Keep left at a junction. After about 500 feet you will reach a trail junction (GPS: 38.875929, -104.880857). Keep right to Three Graces Plaza. A left turn follows a dirt trail up a hill to an overlook.

**0.5**  Trail junction west of the Three Graces rock formation (GPS: 38.876376, -104.882078). Keep left and follow the paved trail on the west side of the open area.

**0.8**  Junction with trail to accessible parking area. Keep right.

**1.0**  Trail junction. Keep left on main trail through Gateway. Soon you will come to a trail junction on the east side of Gateway. Go left toward parking.

**1.2**  Arrive back at the trailhead and parking lot.

### Sacred Ground

The Garden of the Gods, with its soaring sandstone formations and strange aura of serenity, silence, and a touch of eternity, was undoubtedly a sacred place to Native Americans. The mythology of many tribes, including the Kiowa, Pawnee, Cheyenne, Arapaho, Comanche, Apache, Shoshone, and Ute groups, describes this as a special place.

   The Mountain Utes were particularly fond of the Garden of the Gods, often camping among the rocks, hunting for deer and elk, and soaking and drinking from the sacred bubbling waters in today's Manitou Springs. Several accounts by early settlers document that the Utes often camped at the Garden of the Gods, particularly in winter. Buckskin Charley, their famed chief after Ouray in the late nineteenth century, was auspiciously born at the Garden.

# Red Rock Canyon Trail

*This out-and-back classic hike is flanked by towering sandstone walls and travels up an old road in the heart of Red Rock Canyon, the centerpiece of Red Rock Canyon Open Space on the west side of Colorado Springs. An interesting side hike climbs up to a historic stone quarry, then returns back to the main trail.*

**Start:** Eastern end of the park road off Ridge Road
**Distance:** 2.2 miles out and back
**Hiking time:** 1 to 2 hours
**Difficulty:** Easy
**Elevation gain:** 150 feet
**Trail surface:** Doubletrack dirt trail up a closed road
**Seasons:** Year-round. Trail can be muddy or snowy in winter.
**Schedule:** Open daily, dawn to dusk
**Other trail users:** Runners, mountain bikers, equestrians
**Canine compatibility:** Leashed dogs only
**Land status:** City of Colorado Springs

**Fees and permits:** None
**Maps:** USGS Manitou Springs. Colorado Springs RRCOS map at www.springsgov.com.
**Trail contact:** Colorado Springs Parks, Recreation and Cultural Services, 1401 Recreation Way, Colorado Springs, CO 80905-1975; (719) 385-5940; www.springs gov.com
**Special considerations:** Don't leave valuables, including purses and cameras, visible in your vehicle at the parking areas. Break-ins do occur. Bring everything of value with you on your hike.

**Finding the trailhead:** Red Rock Canyon Open Space is south of the Garden of the Gods Park and US 24. To access the park from downtown Colorado Springs and I-25, take the Cimarron Street/US 24 exit (exit 141) and drive west 3.5 miles toward the mountains. Access the parking areas and trailheads by turning left (south) on South Ridge Road from US 24, which is the only left turn between 31st Street and the first Manitou Springs exit. Use extreme caution turning on the highway. Drive south on Ridge Road for 0.1 mile and turn left into the park. Drive through a roundabout and follow the park road to a large parking area on the right (**GPS:** 38.853612, -104.880523). Portable toilets and a trail map are available at a trailhead at the east end of the parking lot (**GPS:** 38.853326, -104.879251). You can also park in another lot at the end of the park road to the southeast.

## THE HIKE

The 1.1-mile-long Red Rock Canyon Trail explores Red Rock Canyon, the scenic centerpiece of 1,474-acre Red Rock Canyon Open Space. The city of Colorado Springs purchased the park's initial 787 acres in 2003, saving the area from trophy homes, a golf course, and resort development. Red Rock Canyon, splitting the center of the parkland from south to north, is a mile-long canyon lined with tall sandstone cliffs and floored with copses of scrub oak, cottonwood trees, and meadows blanketed with tall grass and wildflowers. Besides its natural beauty and dramatic geology, Red Rock Canyon also harbors both archaeological and historical sites including an old quarry that operated from 1886 until 1915.

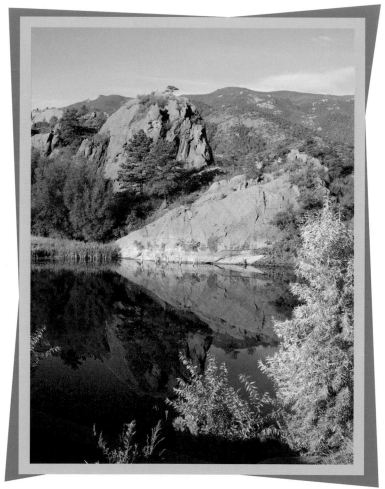

Sandstone hogbacks reflect in a pond at Red Rock Canyon.

Red Rock Canyon Trail is an easy hike up the canyon from the parking lot, following a closed dirt road. The trail has easy grades and great scenery and is popular, especially on weekends. While the described hike ends at the start of the Roundup Trail in the south part of the canyon, it can be combined with it as well as Red Rock Rim Trail to create a longer loop hike.

Begin the hike from the trailhead at the east side of the main parking lot, on the north side of the park opposite US 24. Portable toilets and a trail map are available at the trailhead. An alternative parking area is located past the first large parking area at the end of the park road below Red Rock Canyon itself. If you park there, knock 0.2 mile off your hike.

The first trail segment runs east and then south for 0.4 mile before joining an old road. Just east of the trailhead is a junction with the Mesa and Greenlee Trails, which head south up another closed road. Continue hiking straight and pass the left side of a freestyle-biking area. Here the wide gravel trail bends south. Follow the trail between the south parking area and a sandstone cliff that was quarried in the nineteenth century. The trail slowly climbs and then bends east to join the old Red Rock Canyon road. If you hike from the south parking area, it's 0.2 mile to this point.

Hike up the road for 0.1 mile, passing a locked gate, to the site of the old Bock house, now a picnic pavilion. The Red Rock Canyon property once belonged to John George Bock, who acquired it during the 1920s and 1930s. Bock started with a tourist camp and stables by Fountain Creek and then bought the other land from stone companies, paying only back taxes. After his death his two sons, John and Richard, wanted to build a World Trade Center here with two golf courses, luxury homes and condos, a shopping center, office buildings, a sports arena, and thirteen lakes. They were unable to get the area rezoned, so in the 1970s it was turned into a landfill and gravel pit. In the 1990s another large developer attempted to resurrect the Bock plan but was denied annexation by both Manitou Springs and Colorado Springs, leaving the door open for its purchase as a Colorado Springs park.

The next trail segment follows the old road up the east side of Red Rock Canyon for 0.4 mile to its junction with Quarry Pass Trail.

For an alternative hike, go right at the pavilion and descend down to a small lake. Follow the singletrack 0.5-mile Red Rock Canyon Path, a hiker-only trail, along the west side of the canyon to the Quarry Pass Trail Junction.

At the junction go right and follow Quarry Pass Trail for 0.1 mile up into Kenmuir Quarry, a nineteenth-century stone quarry and historic site. The Lyons sandstone blocks quarried here were loaded onto train cars on a railroad spur that ran into the canyon. The stone was then shipped to Colorado Springs as well as Denver, Kansas, and Texas for buildings and foundations. Many buildings in Denver were built with the striking red sandstone blocks from here. The stone, however, didn't weather well, and the canyon's quarries, operated by the Greenlee family in Denver, closed down by 1915. Much of the sandstone was quarried between 1888 and 1893. This side trail climbs up to the quarry. Make sure you climb the staircase chopped into bedrock to enter the quarry. After visiting it retrace your steps back to the main trail.

The last trail segment continues south for a quarter mile on the old road, steadily climbing a long hill to a major trail junction and the Red Rock Canyon Trail turnaround point at 6,400 feet. Take a minute to enjoy the view. Directly west across the wooded canyon is the Wiggins Wall and a deep defile called Black Bear Canyon. This and the other cliffs in Red Rock Canyon are popular with rock climbers, who enjoy more than one hundred established climbing routes in the canyon. From this high point, retrace the trail north to the parking lot.

## MILES AND DIRECTIONS

**0.0** Begin at the trailhead at the east end of the open-space park's main parking lot (GPS: 38.853326, -104.879251). Restrooms and a trail map are here. Hike southeast on a wide trail, passing a freestyle-biking area and another parking area.

**0.4** Climb up a gradual hill and reach a junction with a closed dirt road (GPS: 38.84971, -104.879644).

**0.5** Hike south past a gate to a stone pavilion (GPS: 38.848932, -104.880134) and a small lake on the right. Stay on the road and continue hiking south up the east side of the canyon. (*Option:* Red Rock Canyon Path, a singletrack trail, begins at the pavilion and follows the west side of the canyon to the Quarry Pass Trail junction.)

**0.9** After hiking below tall cliffs above the trail, arrive at the junction with Quarry Pass Trail (GPS: 38.843297, -104.882469). Go right on Quarry Pass Trail and hike 0.1 mile up to the historic quarry site. After viewing, return back 0.1 mile to the junction and continue straight on the main trail.

**1.1** End the first half of your hike at the top of a hill at a junction with Red Rock Rim Trail (GPS: 38.840008, -104.884362) which goes left (east). Turn around and hike back toward the trailhead. (*Option:* Continue south and follow the Roundup Trail and Contemplative Trail back to the parking area or hike the Red Rock Rim Trail back to the east parking area.)

**2.2** After hiking north down the main canyon trail, arrive back at the trailhead.

### Options
For extra credit you can continue hiking. Several excellent loop hikes fan out from the end of the Red Rock Canyon Trail. The best hike continues south up the

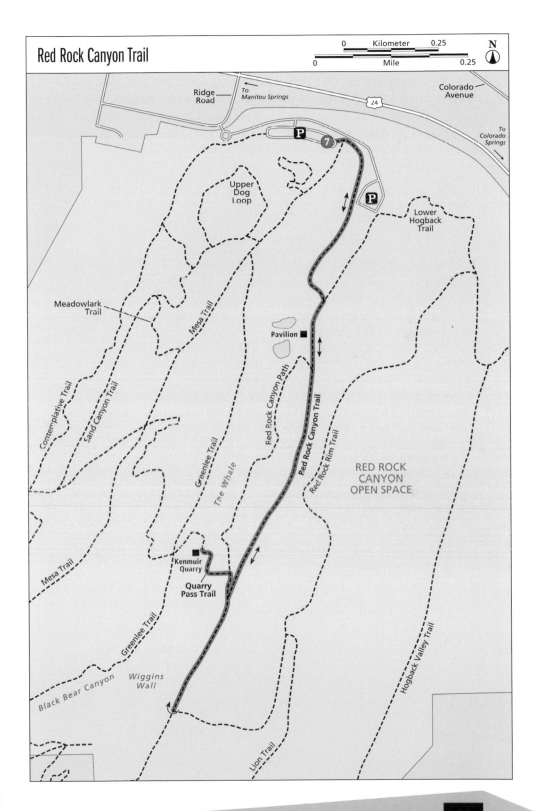

Red Rock Canyon Trail

canyon for 0.2 mile before turning west up a deep canyon. Follow the 1.3-mile Roundup Trail up and out of the canyon, then dip across the heads of a couple shallow canyons before descending north to the southern end of the Contemplative Trail. This creates an excellent 3.5-mile loop.

Another good option from the junction at the end of the trail is to go left and follow the Red Rock Rim Trail for 1.4 miles back to the upper parking lot.

## Red Rock Canyon's Historic Quarries

The ruddy Lyons sandstone, forming the west wall of Red Rock Canyon, became a popular stone for building in the 1880s and was used in buildings in Colorado Springs, Manitou Springs, and Denver, including the Redstone Castle in Manitou and the Molly Brown House in Denver. The rock, called Manitou sandstone, was popular for its color, easily carved, and sometimes used as an accent with other stone.

The canyon had two main quarries—the Kenmuir and Snider Quarries. The Kenmuir Quarry, the large quarry in the middle of the canyon, was operated by the Greenlee Company and employed hundreds of workers, who used steam equipment and drills to excavate stone. Many workers lived in the canyon. In 1886 the Colorado Midland Railroad built a spur line into the canyon; blocks were loaded by crane onto flatcars and transported around the state.

A decline in the use of stone around 1900 coupled with the growing use of concrete and steel for building forced the quarries to close, leaving their stair-stepped walls as a historic legacy of early Colorado Springs.

# Contemplative, Roundup, and Red Rock Canyon Trails Loop

*This excellent loop hike, combining parts of four trails, offers a grand walking tour that winds among soaring sandstone formations and threads through canyons in the western sector of Red Rock Canyon Open Space.*

**Start:** West side of large parking lot on north side of the park. Hike ends at east side of parking lot.

**Distance:** 3.3-mile loop following 4 different trails

**Hiking time:** 1.5 to 2 hours

**Difficulty:** Easy with gradual grades

**Elevation gain:** 450 feet

**Trail surface:** Singletrack dirt trail and closed dirt road

**Seasons:** Year-round. Trail can be icy in winter; bring spikes.

**Schedule:** Open daily, dawn to dusk

**Other trail users:** Hikers-only on the Contemplative Trail. Mountain bikes and horses allowed on other trail segments.

**Canine compatibility:** Leashed dogs only

**Land status:** Public land in a Colorado Springs open space

**Fees and permits:** None

**Maps:** USGS Manitou Springs; Colorado Springs RRCOS map

**Trail contact:** Colorado Springs Parks, Recreation and Cultural Services, 1401 Recreation Way, Colorado Springs, CO 80905-1975; (719) 385-5940; www.springs gov.com

**Special considerations:** Don't leave valuables, including purses and cameras, visible in your vehicle at the parking areas. Break-ins do occur. Bring everything of value with you on your hike.

**Finding the trailhead:** Red Rock Canyon Open Space is south of Garden of the Gods and US 24. To access the area from downtown Colorado Springs and I-25, take the Cimarron Street/US 24 exit (exit 141) and drive west 3.5 miles toward the mountains. Access the parking lot and trailhead by turning left (south) on Ridge Road from US 24, which is the only left turn between 31st Street and the first Manitou Springs exit. Use extreme caution turning since the highway is busy. Drive south on Ridge Road for 0.1 mile and turn left into the park. Drive through a roundabout and go left. Park at the first lot near its western end. The trailhead is at the west end of the lot (**GPS:** 38.853554, -104.881362). The end of the hike is at the trailhead on the east side of the lot, which is a quarter mile east of the hike start.

## THE HIKE

This fantastic 3.3-mile hike, combining 0.2 mile of the Sand Canyon Trail, the 0.6-mile Contemplative Trail, the 1.1-mile Roundup Trail, and the 1.3-mile Red Rock Canyon Trail, forms a loop hike on the west side of Red Rock Canyon Open Space, which is west of Colorado Springs. The easy hike wanders through soaring fins of sandstone, dense thickets of scrub oak, open ponderosa pine woods, and, in summer, flower-strewn meadows.

The Contemplative Trail section is serene and peaceful since it is open to hikers only, although occasional renegade mountain bikers do use the trail. Several benches are scattered along the winding trail, allowing lots of opportunities for

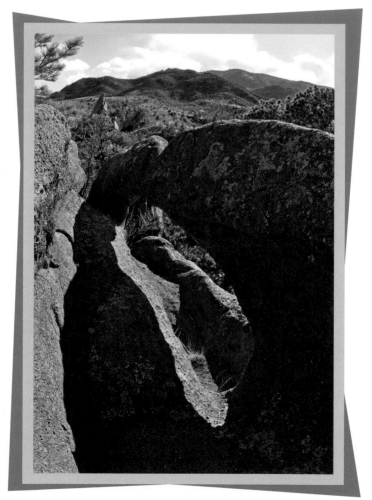

A hidden arch tops a sandstone fin above the Contemplative Trail.

contemplation and nature study. Keep an eye out for wildlife, including mule deer and black bears, in the broad valley below the trail.

Interpretive signs and a map are available at the trailhead, located on the western side of the large parking area on the north side of the park and opposite a roundabout on the park entrance road. At the east end of the parking area, 0.2 mile from the west end, is the trailhead where the hike ends. Portable toilets and a park trail map are available at the east end of the lot.

Hike west from the parking lot, passing a roundabout on the road at the park entrance off Ridge Road, and bend south on the first part of the Sand Canyon Trail. Bock Fin, a towering rock hogback composed of coarse 300-million-year-old Fountain Formation sandstone, looms above the trail. After 0.2 mile you reach a trail junction. Continue straight on the Contemplative Trail. The Sand Canyon Trail jogs left at the junction and climbs east.

The 0.6-mile Contemplative Trail segment twists south beneath tall rock formations, dipping across shallow valleys and climbing short hills. One spectacular trail section squeezes through a rock-walled passageway. Tall ponderosa pines, groves of Gambel oaks, and pocket meadows of tall grass and wildflowers fill shady vales below the rocks. Occasional cliff viewpoints offer great views across wide Sand Canyon and north to the Garden of the Gods and the Rampart Range. Keep an eye out for grazing mule deer or an occasional black bear rambling down the valley. At its southern terminus the trail ascends timber steps and ends at Sand Canyon Trail, here an old roadbed.

Go straight (south) from this trail junction on the Roundup Trail. This 1.35-mile segment heads steadily uphill through pines and oaks, slowly climbing and switchbacking for 0.5 mile onto a wide ridge and a junction with Mesa Trail. Continue south on the Roundup Trail for 0.2 mile, dipping across the head of a shallow valley and reaching a junction with Greenlee Trail.

Continue straight on the Roundup Trail and traverse across the head of Black Bear Canyon, which drains east into Red Rock Canyon. After a quarter mile the trail again reaches Mesa Trail, which goes left to end atop a stone hogback. From the junction descend down a steep slope on a couple of wide switchbacks and follow the trail down the bottom of a dry, narrow canyon, passing through a gateway of soaring sandstone cliffs and, 0.4 mile from the last junction, reach the head of Red Rock Canyon and a trail map.

The last hike segment follows wide Red Rock Canyon Trail down the canyon for 1.3 miles to the trailhead at the eastern end of the main parking lot. The trail, the most beautiful one in the park, follows an old road. Sandstone cliffs tower above the trail in a wide valley filled with broad meadows that are broken by copses of Gambel oak and tall cottonwood trees. Red Rock Canyon is a popular place for local rock climbers, who find adventures on its slabs and faces, as well as a great spot for wildlife watching on quiet days.

The trail descends along the east side of the canyon and after 0.8 mile reaches a pavilion built on the site of the old Bock house. Red Rock Canyon, after its quarry days were over, was acquired bit by bit by John G. Bock, who moved to Colorado from Philadelphia in 1923 to recuperate from tuberculosis, over a 20-year period. Bock built roads and trails and opened Roundup Stables, where he rented out horses.

The original Bock house sat on the pavilion site. After the site became Colorado Springs parkland, the house was too run-down to restore so it was razed and the pavilion was built using original walls and building stone. Near the pavilion is a pond, which reflects mountains, sky, and red rock when it's filled with runoff, and seven interpretative signs about park history, natural history, and geology.

Continue down the trail and around a gate to a junction. The closed road continues straight to a parking area. Go left on the trail and hike down the west side of the valley past the remains of an old quarry and the parking lot. Bend left and continue hiking to the end of the trail at the east trailhead at the long main parking lot. Portable toilets are at the trailhead.

## MILES AND DIRECTIONS

**0.0** Start from the railhead at the far west end of the main parking lot (GPS: 38.853554, -104.881362) and follow the Sand Canyon Trail southwest.

**0.2** Reach the junction of Sand Canyon and Contemplative Trails on the south side of Bock Fin (GPS: 38.851352, -104.884387). Go right on the Contemplative Trail and hike south below sandstone hogbacks.

**0.8** Climb timber stairs to the south junction of the Contemplative Trail, which ends here, and Sand Canyon Trail (GPS: 38.845263, -104.88856). Go south on the Roundup Trail.

**1.3** Hike south for 0.5 mile to the junction of the Roundup Trail and the Mesa Trail (GPS: 38.840697, -104.890837). Go straight on the Roundup Trail.

**1.5** Hike across a shallow canyon for 0.2 mile to the junction of the Roundup and Greenlee Trails (GPS: 38.840044, -104.889396). Continue straight on the Roundup Trail.

**1.7** Hike 0.25 mile across the head of Black Bear Canyon to another junction of the Roundup and Mesa Trails (GPS: 38.839255, -104.887475). Go straight on the Roundup Trail and descend into a canyon.

**2.1** Reach the end of the Roundup Trail and the start of the Red Rock Canyon Trail below a gap between sandstone hogbacks (GPS: 38.83832, -104.885426).

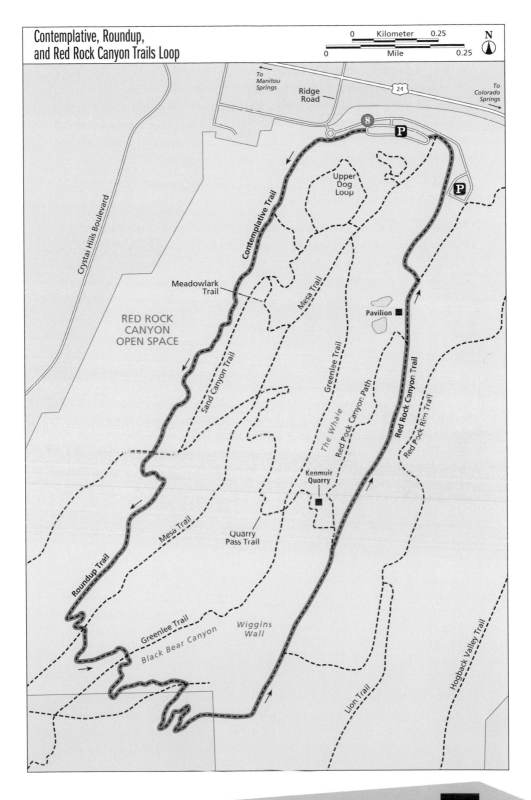

Contemplative, Roundup,
and Red Rock Canyon Trails Loop

0    Kilometer    0.25

0    Mile    0.25

N

To Manitou Springs

Ridge Road

24

To Colorado Springs

8

P

P

Upper Dog Loop

Crystal Hills Boulevard

Contemplative Trail

Meadowlark Trail

Mesa Trail

Pavilion

RED ROCK CANYON OPEN SPACE

Sand Canyon Trail

Greenlee Trail

The Whale

Red Rock Canyon Path

Red Rock Canyon Trail

Red Rock Rim Trail

Kenmuir Quarry

Mesa Trail

Quarry Pass Trail

Roundup Trail

Greenlee Trail

Black Bear Canyon

Wiggins Wall

Lion Trail

Hogback Valley Trail

**2.2** Hike north on the closed-road trail to the junction of the Red Rock Canyon Trail and the Red Rock Rim Trail, which comes in from the right (GPS: 38.840008, -104.884358). Continue straight and down a long hill, then along the east side of Red Rock Canyon. After a quarter mile reach the junction with Quarry Pass Trail (GPS: 38.843289, -104.882461). (*Option:* Go left if you want to scramble up to the historic Kenmuir Quarry.) Continue straight down Red Rock Canyon another 0.4 mile to a pavilion.

**3.0** Reach a junction past the pavilion and a gate (GPS: 38.849727, -104.879643). Go left on the main trail and descend down the west side of the canyon.

**3.3** End the hike at the east trailhead on the far eastern end of the main parking area (GPS: 38.853318, -104.879159).

## Pikes Peak Region Geology

The Pikes Peak region, including the Garden of the Gods and Red Rock Canyon, is renowned among geologists for its unique geological value. Colorado Springs itself has more exposed geological history within its city limits than any other American city, with every geologic period represented except the Silurian. The exposed rock formations form the pages of a book that tells the story of the earth's history with stone evidence of a constantly changing planet—the uplift and erosion of great mountain ranges; an inundation of seas; great fields of sand dunes; and the evolution of life from fish to dinosaur to mammal. The age of the rocks range from Pikes Peak granite formed in a batholith 1.08 billion years ago to almost recent Quaternary gravel deposits left by streams swollen with glacial snowmelt within the last 30,000 years.

# Coyote Run Trail

*This short, fun, lollipop-loop hike in Cheyenne Mountain State Park, perfect for families with small kids, explores the foothills above the park visitor center, crossing open meadows, scrub oak forests, and scattered ponderosa pines on open slopes.*

**Start:** West side of parking lot at park visitor center

**Distance:** 1.4-mile lollipop

**Hiking time:** 1 to 2 hours

**Difficulty:** Easy

**Elevation gain:** 130 feet

**Trail surface:** Singletrack dirt path

**Seasons:** Year-round

**Schedule:** Open daily for day-use only, 6 a.m. to 10 p.m.; recommended use is sunrise to sunset

**Other trail users:** Mountain bikers

**Canine compatibility:** Dogs not permitted

**Land status:** Colorado state park land

**Fees and permits:** Daily fee to enter the park

**Maps:** USGS Cheyenne Mountain. Cheyenne Mountain State Park trail map at website.

**Trail contacts:** Cheyenne Mountain State Park, 410 JL Ranch Heights, Colorado Springs, CO 80926; (719) 576-2016; www .parks.state.co.us/parks/cheyenne mountain

**Finding the trailhead:** From I-25 on the south side of Colorado Springs, take the South Academy Boulevard exit (exit #135) and drive west on South Academy past Pikes Peak Community College. Continue west to CO 115 and turn south on CO 115. Drive south on the divided four-lane highway to a stop light. The park entrance is to your right, opposite Fort Carson Gate 1. Drive west on JL Ranch Heights Road to the park visitor center. Park in the visitor center lot and pay an entrance fee in the center. The trailhead is on the west side of the parking lot (**GPS: 38.734981, -104.819768**).

## THE HIKE

The 1.4-mile-long Coyote Run Trail makes a great loop hike for kids and families in the scrubby hills above the Cheyenne Mountain State Park visitor center. Before doing the hike, the visitor center makes a good stop, with lots of informative displays as well as books about the area's natural history. The easy-to-follow, singletrack trail has minimal elevation gain, gradual grades, plenty of rest stops, and great views. It's well marked with signposts at regular intervals as well as posts with GPS coordinates if you need to contact a ranger for help.

Start the hike on the west side of the parking lot at the visitor center, at 6,055 feet. The trailhead is between two benches right of a ramada with an interpretative display about trail etiquette. Hike west for 100 feet to a sign on the left that explains the park's web of life. Continue to a registration box on the right and sign in.

The trail heads west alongside a dry wash and through scrub oak thickets for 0.12 mile to a Y junction with a trail sign in a garden of granite boulders. This point is the start of the Coyote Run loop trail. Go left (south) to begin the loop hike.

The next 0.8-mile trail segment runs south, crossing the park road, to a junction with the Boulder Run Trail. The trail twists through a shallow wooded draw studded with boulders and shaded by oaks and pines. Several interpretative signs

Coyote Run Trail twists across hillsides covered with grass, scrub oak, and pines below Cheyenne Mountain.

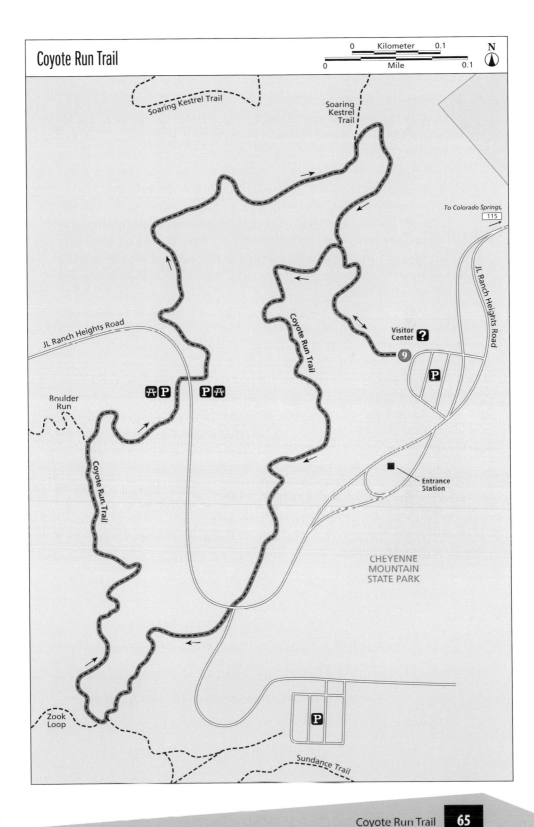

Coyote Run Trail

0 Kilometer 0.1
0 Mile 0.1

N

Soaring Kestrel Trail

Soaring Kestrel Trail

To Colorado Springs, 115

JL Ranch Heights Road

JL Ranch Heights Road

Coyote Run Trail

Visitor Center

9

P

Boulder Run

Coyote Run Trail

Entrance Station

CHEYENNE MOUNTAIN STATE PARK

Zook Loop

P

Sundance Trail

about park wildlife, including black bears, prairie dogs, and mountain lions, are scattered along the way. The trail reaches the park road at its turnoff to Limekiln Grove Trailhead. Cross the road and pick up the trail again on the road's west side.

Past some big granite boulders, swing across meadows on the northern edge of broad Limekiln Valley to a trail fork with a granite block in the fork. The left fork is 1.0-mile-long Zook Loop Trail, another pleasant hike. Take the right fork and stay on Coyote Run Trail. The trail bends north and gradually climbs, passing a sign about lizards, to a Y junction with the Boulder Run Trail, which heads left.

Go right on Coyote Run Trail and hike past some picnic tables to a building with restrooms and a road. Follow small signs with arrows pointing which way the trail goes, and walk along the right (east) side of the building on a sidewalk. Cross the road at a crosswalk to the east side of the road and another building and small parking area for the picnic area. Cross the road to the left (north) and pick up Coyote Run Trail.

Hike north on the trail, dipping in and out of shallow rocky drainages, and after 1.1 miles reach a junction with Soaring Kestrel Trail just past a bench beneath a tall ponderosa pine. Keep right on the marked Coyote Run Trail.

The next trail section descends about 0.1 mile from the junction to the lower trail fork near the visitor center. The trail bends sharply right (south) and descends open stony terrain, passing a sign about rattlesnakes. Prairie rattlers do live at the park but are rarely seen. These warm rocky slopes, however, form an ideal habitat for rattlesnakes. It's more likely, however, that you will see a bull snake, which resembles a rattlesnake and often mimics a rattler's behavior by coiling up and making a rattling noise in its throat.

To finish the hike, continue descending past small ponderosa pines to the first trail junction at a shaded rock garden. Go left (east) and hike a tenth of a mile back to the trailhead, parking lot, and visitor center.

## MILES AND DIRECTIONS

**0.0**  Begin at the trailhead on the west side of the visitor center parking lot (GPS: 38.734981, -104.819768).

**0.1**  Trail junction (GPS: 38.736009, -104.820484). Start of the loop trail. Go left.

**0.9**  Junction with Boulder Run Trail (GPS: 38.734155, -104.823598). Keep right.

**1.0**  Reach a picnic area and JL Ranch Heights Road (GPS: 38.73476, -104.822347).

**1.1**  Junction with Soaring Kestrel Trail. Keep right (GPS: 38.737017, -104.82027).

**1.3**  Trail junction (GPS: 38.736009, -104.820484). End of the loop trail. Go left.

**1.4**  Arrive back at the trailhead and parking area at the visitor center.

# Blackmer Loop Trail

*This secluded loop hike threads for almost 5 miles through an ecosystem of tallgrass meadows, thickets of scrub oak, and a shady ponderosa pine forest on the high western part of Cheyenne Mountain State Park.*

**Start:** Raccoon Ridge Trailhead on north side of parking lot at camper services building
**Distance:** 4.7-mile lollipop
**Hiking time:** 2 to 3 hours
**Difficulty:** Moderate
**Elevation gain:** 250 feet
**Trail surface:** Singletrack dirt path
**Seasons:** Year-round. The trail can be icy in winter.
**Other trail users:** Mountain bikers
**Canine compatibility:** Dogs not permitted
**Land status:** State park land

**Fees and permits:** Daily fee to enter the park
**Schedule:** Open daily; 6 a.m. to 10 p.m. for day use; recommended use is sunrise to sunset
**Maps:** USGS Cheyenne Mountain. Cheyenne Mountain State Park trail map at website.
**Trail contact:** Cheyenne Mountain State Park, 410 JL Ranch Heights, Colorado Springs, CO 80926; (719) 576-2016; www .parks.state.co.us/parks/cheyenne mountain

**Finding the trailhead:** From I-25 on the south side of Colorado Springs, take the South Academy Boulevard exit (exit #135) and drive west on South Academy past Pikes Peak Community College. Continue west to CO 115 and turn south on CO 115. Continue on the divided highway to a stop light opposite the main entrance to Fort Carson. The park entrance is to your right (west), opposite Fort Carson Gate 1. Drive west on JL Ranch Heights Road to the park visitor center and entrance station. After paying the entrance fee, drive up the park road to the campground. Park on the right in a large lot at the camper services building. The trailhead for the first hike leg—Raccoon Ridge Trail—begins at the north side of the parking lot (**GPS:** 38.73769, -104.828351).

## THE HIKE

The Blackmer Loop Trail, threading through shallow shady ravines and contouring across gentle hillsides covered with open meadows and scrub oak thickets, is one of the best day hikes in 2,701-acre Cheyenne Mountain State Park just south of Colorado Springs. The singletrack dirt trail, shared with mountain bikers, offers interesting hiking with solitude, diverse plant communities, lots of wildlife including mule deer, and great views of craggy Cheyenne Mountain looming to the west.

The trail is marked with seventeen round trail markers, making it easy to follow. Other markers that are evenly spaced along the trail give GPS coordinates in case you get lost or want to track the trail. Hiking Blackmer Loop Trail requires that you first park at the camper services building in the park's campground and follow the Raccoon Ridge Trail and then part of Boulder Run Trail to reach the start of Blackmer Loop, making the entire hike 4.7 miles long.

Cheyenne Mountain State Park offers 20 miles of hiking on sixteen trails on wooded foothills below the sharp escarpment of rugged Cheyenne Mountain. The well-maintained trails, ranging in difficulty from easy to hard, can be easily combined to create longer hikes. The trails are open to hikers and mountain bikers, but no horses or pets are allowed on the trails to protect both fragile ecosystems as well as the park's abundant wildlife. Smoking is not permitted on any of

The Blackmer Loop Trail winds through meadows and oak groves below Cheyenne Mountain.

the trails. After doing these two hikes, consult the comprehensive park trail map, available at the visitor center or park website, to plan other hikes.

To begin the hike, drive up the park road from the visitor center and park at a large lot on the right side of the road at the campground visitor services area. From here you have two choices to reach the Blackmer Trailhead. The best and most scenic alternative is to follow the 0.6-mile Raccoon Ridge Trail, which begins at the north side of the parking lot and spirals southwest past some tent campsites to the park road and its junction with Boulder Run Trail. Hiking this trail adds another mile to your hike.

Alternatively, park at the lot and hike 0.3 mile down the road to the same trail junction on the right. Look for the Boulder Run Trail and a marker on the right (west) side of the road and right of a concrete drain and locked gate. This adds 0.6 mile to the hike.

After hiking from the parking lot to the start of Boulder Run Trail on the park road, follow the first trail segment on Boulder Run Trail for 0.1 mile to the start of the Blackmer Loop Trail. Hike west through groves of scrub oak and broad meadows to a Y-shaped junction at 6,408 feet on a south-facing hill. Both forks at the junction are for Blackmer Loop. Take the right trail fork. A park trail map is available on the right side of the junction.

Hike west on the good trail for 0.4 mile to a junction with Cougar's Shadow Trail. The trail slowly climbs as it swings through meadows flanked by scrub oak. Stop at a bench with a view to the east and read an interpretative sign that details the area's earliest inhabitants, including the Ute Indians. Past the bench the trail works southwest across open meadows. Keep an eye out for bull snakes in the tall grass by the trail's edge.

Past some large boulders the trail turns south and reaches a junction with Cougar's Shadow Trail below shady ponderosa pines. Go straight or left on the main trail. Cougar's Shadow Trail, a 0.9-mile path, is an alternative to Blackmer here. This trail climbs southwest, then contours south and drops down to meet Blackmer farther south.

From the junction, the next Blackmer Trail section runs southwest for 0.9 mile to the southern Cougar's Shadow Trail junction. This segment offers great hiking, with the trail threading through boulder gardens, passing beneath stately ponderosa pines, and edging grassy glades rimmed with scrub oak as the trail slowly climbs to its high point. To the west towers the bulk of 9,565-foot Cheyenne Mountain above the forest. Several interpretative signs about bats, climate, and ponderosa pines are found along the way. At the ponderosa sign is a bench. Take a seat here to admire a ponderosa pine splitting a crack in a 10-foot-high granite boulder.

Past the high point, the trail dips down and meets Cougar's Shadow Trail in a wooded ravine. Go left (east) at this three-way junction. The next Blackmer

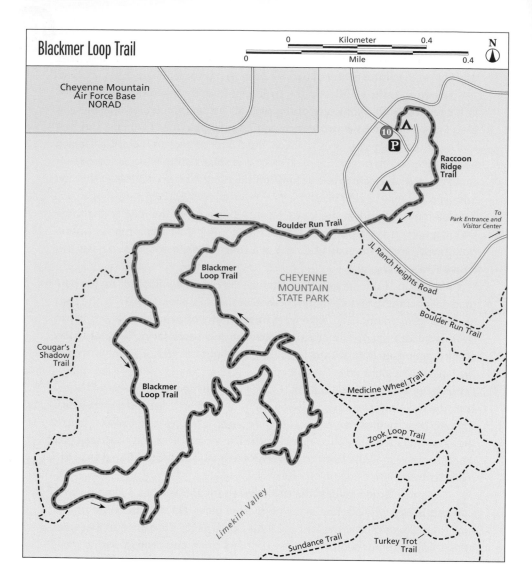

## Blackmer Loop Trail

Kilometer
0            0.4
Mile
0            0.4

N

Cheyenne Mountain
Air Force Base
NORAD

10

P

Raccoon
Ridge
Trail

Boulder Run Trail

To
Park Entrance and
Visitor Center

Blackmer
Loop Trail

CHEYENNE
MOUNTAIN
STATE PARK

JL Ranch Heights Road

Boulder Run Trail

Cougar's
Shadow
Trail

Blackmer
Loop Trail

Medicine Wheel Trail

Zook Loop Trail

Limekiln Valley

Sundance Trail

Turkey Trot
Trail

🌰 **Green Tip:**
*Stay on established trails to avoid damaging vegetation and creating new social trails. Try to stay on durable surfaces that will be least affected by your passage, like rock, gravel, dry grasses, or snow.*

Loop Trail segment runs northeast for 1.4 miles, twisting down wooded slopes and following shallow draws filled with boulders. Occasional breaks in the trees allow views eastward to Fort Carson and the tawny prairie beyond. As the trail descends, the forest thins with scrub oak and meadows becoming prevalent. At the edge of a shallow valley, Blackmer reaches a three-way junction. A side trail heads right to join Zook and Medicine Wheel Trails. Stay left on the main trail. A trail map is at the junction.

The final section of the Blackmer Loop climbs 0.8 mile from the junction back to the beginning of the loop and the end of Boulder Run Trail. The trail steadily climbs uphill, passing through jumbles of granite boulders in the valley before reaching open meadows on a south-facing slope. An interpretative sign details the transition life zone that you're passing through, a species-rich ecosystem where the foothills scrubland meets the montane forest. Past the sign the trail edges across the hillside and meets the three-way junction that marks the start of the Blackmer Loop.

Go straight (east) on the main trail, which now becomes Boulder Run Trail. Hike 0.1 mile back to the park road, then cross the road and follow Raccoon Ridge Trail for 0.6 mile back to the parking lot.

## MILES AND DIRECTIONS

**0.0** Begin at the parking area at the camper services building. Start from the north side of the lot on Raccoon Ridge Trail (GPS: 38.737679, -104.828354).

**0.5** Junction with Raccoon Ridge Trail and park road. Cross road to Boulder Run Trail (GPS: 38.734753, -104.830736).

**0.6** Y junction Boulder Run Trail and start of Blackmer Loop Trail (GPS: 38.735111, -104.832847). Go right.

**0.9** Three-way junction with north end of Cougar's Shadow Trail. Go left.

**1.8** Three-way junction with south end of Cougar's Shadow Trail. Go left.

**3.2** Three-way junction with side trail to Zook and Medicine Wheel Trails (GPS: 38.731573, -104.831489). Keep straight or left.

**4.0** Return to the Y junction with Boulder Run Trail and the start of the Blackmer Loop. Go straight.

**4.1** Reach a parking area and the park road. Cross the road to start the final segment on Raccoon Ridge Trail. Go straight.

**4.7** Arrive back at the trailhead, parking lot, and camper services building.

# Aiken Canyon Trail

*The Aiken Canyon Trail explores a pristine foothills ecosystem with grasslands, piñon-juniper woodlands, and ponderosa pine forests along the edge of the Front Range south of Colorado Springs.*

**Start:** Turkey Creek Ranch Road trailhead just west of CO 115
**Distance:** 3.8-mile lollipop
**Hiking time:** 3 to 5 hours
**Difficulty:** Moderate
**Elevation gain:** 400 feet
**Trail surface:** Singletrack dirt path
**Seasons:** Year-round
**Schedule:** Open only Sat, Sun, Mon; dawn to dusk
**Other trail users:** None
**Canine compatibility:** Dogs not permitted

**Land status:** Area owned by Colorado State Land Board and leased by the Nature Conservancy
**Fees and permits:** None
**Map:** USGS Mt. Big Chief quad
**Trail contact:** The Nature Conservancy in Colorado, 2424 Spruce St., Boulder, CO 80302; (303) 444-2950; www.nature.org/our initiatives/regions/northamerica/unitedstates/colorado/places weprotect/aiken-canyon -preserve.xml

**Finding the trailhead:** From Colorado Springs drive south on I-25 and take exit 135 for Academy Boulevard. Go west on Academy to CO 115. Turn south on CO 115 and drive 11.5 miles. At 0.1 mile past mile marker 32, turn right (west) onto Turkey Creek Ranch Road. Drive a couple hundred yards to the marked preserve parking area and trailhead on the right (**GPS: 38.619792, -104.888352**).

## THE HIKE

The Aiken Canyon Trail explores the 1,621-acre Aiken Canyon Nature Preserve, a unique and pristine foothills ecosystem along the mountain edge southwest of Colorado Springs. The main Aiken Canyon Trail covers 3.4 miles with a short (0.2-mile) out-and-back trail that climbs to a lookout point atop a hill. An option includes a mile-long out-and-back spur trail that goes up the canyon until it peters out. Hike all three trails for a 5.8-mile-long loop. The hike described here includes the main trail and the short spur to the lookout for a total of 3.8 miles.

Ponderosa pines line an intermittent creek and the Aiken Canyon Trail.

Aiken Canyon, a section of state land leased by the Nature Conservancy, lies along the southern edge of the Front Range below Pikes Peak. An unspoiled foothills ecosystem with a variety of habitats and plant communities, including tallgrass meadows, piñon-juniper woodlands, mixed coniferous woodlands with ponderosa pine, Douglas fir, and spruce, and shrublands composed of Gambel oak and mountain mahogany, blankets the canyon and surrounding hills. The preserve is also rich in wildlife, including mammals like black bears, mountain lions, mule deer, elk, squirrels, and foxes. Occasional reptiles like rattlesnakes and bull snakes are also sometimes spotted.

With its diversity of habitats and plant communities, the canyon is well known as one of the best bird-watching spots along the Front Range, with more than one hundred bird species sighted here, including many migratory species. Many of the birds fly south to Central America in winter, then migrate north to breed and nest here in spring, the best birding season. These species include western tanagers, black-headed grosbeaks, and other migratory birds. The canyon itself is named for famed nineteenth-century ornithologist Charles Aiken, who surveyed the area in the 1870s.

The Aiken Canyon area is considered one of the best remaining examples of the southern Front Range foothills ecosystem, which has been built up along the edge of the mountains north of here to Colorado Springs and Denver. The Nature Conservancy signed a ninety-nine-year conservation lease with the State of Colorado in 1991 to manage and protect this unique area as well as educate the public. A straw-bale visitor center at the trailhead offers educational programs for students and visitors.

Begin the hike at a gravel parking lot on the right side of Turkey Creek Ranch Road just west of CO 115. Follow a wide, flat trail a few hundred feet to an information kiosk with four panels that explain and interpret the nature preserve. The left panel details what the Nature Conservancy is all about; the second panel talks about the partnership between the Conservancy and the Army at Fort Carson east of the preserve; the third panel is about the trail and exploring the area; and the fourth panel, on the right, is about saving Colorado's grasslands.

Go left from the kiosk to the El Pomar Foundation Field Station, a visitor center that is usually open on weekends, and restrooms. The trail, however, goes right from behind the kiosk and heads east through tall grass, sage, and clumps of scrub oak. After a short distance you reach a trail sign that details the hike and warns you to stay on the trail to avoid damaging vegetation, disturbing wildlife, and affecting scientific research. The sign also lists the preserve rules: no pets, hunting, camping, or vehicles; no smoking or alcohol; and collecting plants, rocks, and animals is prohibited.

The trail goes left from the sign and reaches the first of several wooden interpretative plaques that explain the area's natural history, plant life, and animal inhabitants. After 0.2 mile the trail reaches a dry creek bed and follows it northwest toward the mountains, dipping in and out of the rocky bed and passing beneath scattered ponderosa pines, junipers, and piñon pines. Look for occasional cairns or stacks of rocks to stay on the trail, especially in spots where it might be washed out.

Eventually the trail leaves the wash and heads west up a gently sloping plain covered with tall grass, wildflowers, and a shrubland of Gambel or scrub oak and mountain mahogany. This shrubland is important habitat for wildlife, including mule deer, elk, coyotes, and lots of bird species. Look overhead for soaring raptors including Cooper's and sharp-shinned hawks, prairie falcons, and golden eagles, while turkeys forage in the underbrush. Keep an eye out on warm days for the occasional rattlesnake that might be sunning in the middle of the narrow trail.

As the trail slowly climbs, the shrubland gives way to a pygmy woodland of juniper and piñon pine, which again provides important habitat for wildlife. This pristine area has been virtually undamaged and ungrazed since the early 1900s. The trail continues following the creek bed, which is occasionally a shallow braided stream after heavy thunderstorms. One trail section passes beneath towering ponderosa pines that line the wash. Finally, after 0.7 mile you reach a trail junction and the start of the hike's loop segment.

The trail heads northwest across a broad meadow and then dips across the creek bed, where water, forced aboveground by bedrock, riffles over a rock bench. Continue hiking west above the south bank of the wash beneath a forest of tall ponderosa pines.

Red sandstone buttresses and cliffs rise above the trail on the sides of the narrowing canyon. The rock here is Fountain Formation sandstone, a rough conglomerate deposited some 200 million years ago on an outwash plain below an ancient mountain range. Farther west the trail passes through thin layers of limestone and dolomite before reaching the bedrock formation called Silver Plume quartz monzonite, a type of granite that forms the steep slopes and mountain peaks on the west side of the preserve.

The trail winds along the creek past the sandstone ramparts and then bends north and crosses a wide meadow. Continue north on the narrow trail, climbing up a steep ravine to a saddle, a large rounded boulder, and a signed junction with the Overlook Trail at 1.5 miles. Go right on the Overlook Trail and climb 0.2 mile to a scenic viewpoint atop a small, sharp peak with great views southeast across scrubby hills on Fort Carson. Retrace the trail back to the junction for a 0.4-mile detour.

From the junction, go right on the main trail and descend north 0.1 mile to another trail junction on the south side of a broad grassy meadow. If you want a longer adventure hike, take the 0.8-mile spur Canyon Trail, which heads west up a narrowing canyon, crossing tree-fringed meadows and then following an intermittent creek. The narrow part of this canyon is cool and moist with tall Douglas

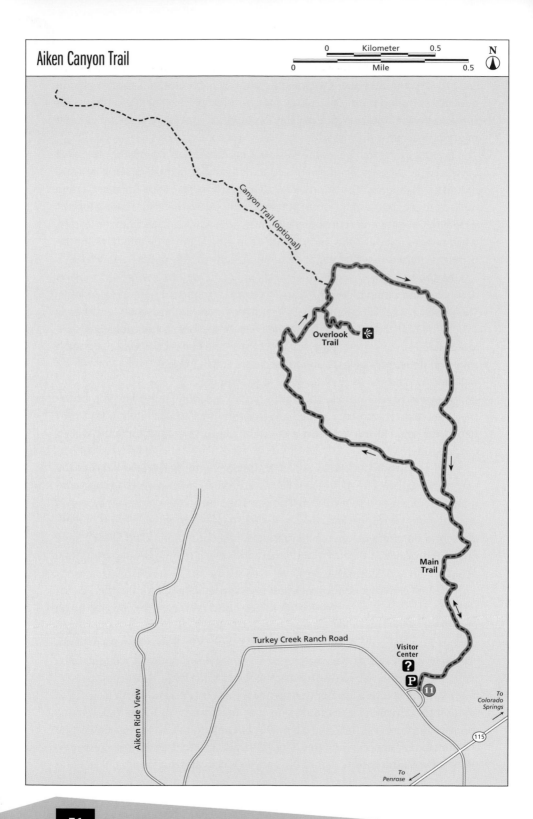

Aiken Canyon Trail

Canyon Trail (optional)

Overlook
Trail

Main
Trail

Turkey Creek Ranch Road

Aiken Ride View

Visitor
Center

To
Colorado
Springs

To
Penrose

firs shading the trail. At the end of the spur, you reach the remains of an old stone cabin and the turnaround point. Retrace your steps back to the main trail for an extra 1.6 miles of hiking.

At the main trail go left and hike northeast. The trail crosses a big meadow before bending east and following a creek, which often flows during wetter months. Tall ponderosa pines line the trail, providing welcome shade in summer. The trail crosses the creek four times, with the last crossing across a smooth bench of worn sandstone. At some rocky bluffs the trail bends south and leaves the creek, ascending on to a lush sloping plain covered with tall grass, yuccas, copses of scrub oak, and scattered junipers and piñon pine. The trail skirts along the western edge of a big meadow against a rocky mountain before crossing a small creek and at 3.1 miles reaching the Y junction and the end of the loop trail.

From the major trail junction, follow the trail for 0.7 mile back to the kiosk, trailhead, and parking area.

## MILES AND DIRECTIONS

**0.0** Parking lot and trailhead on the north side of Turkey Creek Ranch Road (GPS: 38.61982, -104.888339). After 200 feet you come to an information kiosk (GPS: 38.620467, -104.888119). Go left to the preserve visitor center. The hike goes right behind the kiosk on the trail.

**0.2** Trail reaches a dry creek bed (GPS: 38.621049, -104.886381) and follows it northwest toward the mountains.

**0.7** Trail junction and start of the hike's loop segment (GPS: 38.626692, -104.886868). Go left at the fork.

**1.5** Junction with Overlook Trail at a saddle (GPS: 38.634267, -104.893014). Go right to hike 0.2 mile to the overlook at the top of a small peak, then return to this junction. Go north and downhill on the main trail.

**2.0** Junction with canyon spur trail. (*Option:* Take the left spur trail for an optional 2-mile out-and-back hike up a wild and scenic canyon. Go left when you return to the main trail and hike northeast to a creek.)

**3.1** Return to the Y junction with the main trail. Go left.

**3.8** Reach the trailhead and parking area.

> 🍂 **Green Tip:**
> *Be courteous of other hikers. Many people visit natural areas for quiet, peace, and solitude, so avoid making loud noises, playing music, and intruding on others' privacy.*

# Ute Valley Park Loop

*This easy loop hike with minimal elevation gain explores the forest and rocky bluffs at Ute Valley Park, a Colorado Springs city park on the northwest edge of the city below the Rampart Range.*

**Start:** Trailhead at parking lot on south side of Vindicator Drive

**Distance:** 2.7-mile lollipop

**Hiking time:** 1 to 2 hours

**Difficulty:** Easy

**Elevation gain:** 120 feet

**Trail surface:** Single- and double-track dirt trail

**Seasons:** Year-round

**Schedule:** Open daily; May 1 to Oct 31, 5 a.m. to 11 p.m.; Nov 1 to Apr 30, 5 a.m. to 9 p.m.

**Other trail users:** Multiuse trail with runners and mountain bikers

**Canine compatibility:** Leashed dogs only. Pick up your dog's waste.

**Land status:** City of Colorado Springs City Park

**Fees and permits:** None. Colorado Springs city park rules apply.

**Map:** USGS Pikeview

**Trail contact:** Colorado Springs Parks, Recreation and Cultural Services, 1401 Recreation Way, Colorado Springs, CO 80905-1975; (719) 385-5940; www.springs gov.com

**Finding the trailhead:** To reach Ute Valley Park from I-25, take the Woodmen Road exit (exit 149) and turn west. Drive west on Woodmen Road, which turns into Rockrimmon Boulevard for 1.8 miles to Vindicator Drive. Turn right (west) on Vindicator and drive 0.8 mile. Turn left (south) into the parking lot (**GPS:** 38.925021, -104.85702). The trailhead is at the southeast corner of the lot.

## THE HIKE

Ute Valley Park is a wonderful city park with craggy bluffs and a 7.6-mile trail network that explores its ridges, bluffs, and valleys among the suburbs of northwest Colorado Springs below the towering Rampart Range. This 338-acre Colorado Springs city park offers a quick hiking getaway with easy grades, wide trails, and plenty of privacy. Even if the parking lot is full on Vindicator Drive, Ute Valley Park has plenty of room to roam and hike among its high rocky ridges and wooded valleys.

A foothills ecosystem, with a mixed woodland of ponderosa pine, scrub oak, juniper, and piñon pine interspersed with wildflower-strewn meadows, covers Ute Valley Park. The park's bare-bones landscape is composed of sandstone, with the main formation being a long hogback on the west side of the park.

When hiking, especially in summer, keep an eye out for rattlesnakes. They're common here in the park. Keep an eye on dogs and children, especially if they're scrambling around on the rocks where rattlers are usually found. Other wildlife spotted here includes black bears, mountain lions, coyotes, and red foxes.

To start your Ute Valley hike, begin at the main trailhead at the southeast corner of the parking lot off Vindicator Drive. Hike southeast on a wide trail for 120 feet past a couple benches to a trail junction. Go right on the right trail and cross a boardwalk. Hike past a small pond lined with fuzzy cattails, then descend

Pikes Peak rises beyond hikers on the Scrub Oak Path in Ute Valley Park.

southwest on a doubletrack trail across a broad meadow in a valley. Alternatively, go south from the parking area on a wide trail and join the above trail after 0.1 mile.

At 0.2 mile there is a major Y-shaped trail junction at a ponderosa pine. Go left on singletrack Beaver Trail, marked with a "Hiking Only" sign. No mountain bikes are allowed on this next trail section. The right turn at the Y is Pine Ridge Trail, the return trail for this open hiking loop.

The next hike section, running on a good trail for 0.6 mile to the next trail junction, heads southeast across a broad sandstone bench through a sparse ponderosa pine and scrub oak woodland that is interrupted by short-grass meadows and spiky yucca. The trail gently rises up a hill and then begins a long, winding descent. A cliff-rimmed canyon parallels the trail to the right.

As the trail descends, look for a narrow trail on the left just before the main trail drops into the wide main valley at 0.7 mile. Go left (east) on this side trail for 150 feet to a small sandstone arch that spans a trail. The unique window is 5 feet high and 6 feet wide. Follow the trail through the arch. Avoid climbing on top of the arch; it's fragile and already has a deep crack on one side and one in the middle of the span. After viewing the arch return back to the main trail and descend south into a broad open valley.

The wide trail bends southeast along the valley floor beside a deep arroyo carved by heavy runoff from summer thunderstorms. Follow the trail eastward until it divides at a Y junction marked with a trail sign. Go either right or left to avoid a dense thicket of scrub oak. The shorter right trail (0.2 mile) dips across the edge of the arroyo and climbs back out, while the left trail (0.2 mile) passes the oaks and reaches another trail. Go either way to the next trail junction.

Go right at this junction on a doubletrack trail and cross the arroyo on a dirt-covered steel culvert. Continue straight ahead for 0.2 mile to a T-shaped trail junction at the forest edge on the south side of the valley. Go left (east) at this junction on the main trail and hike 100 feet to a Y-shaped trail junction. Angle right on sandy Bear Trail at 1.1 miles.

The next quarter-mile segment heads south on Bear Trail, gently climbing up a sandy double- to singletrack trail through an open ponderosa pine forest. Stop and sniff the pines and decide if they smell like butterscotch or vanilla. Watch for mountain bikers on this segment. It's popular with pedal heads that sometimes fly down the trail without warning.

Partway up the hill an old road veers left. Stay on the narrow trail to the right. At 0.2 mile from the last junction (this is the halfway point, 1.1 miles from the trailhead), a side path heads west, but you'll continue straight on the main trail for another hundred feet to a major junction at 1.2 miles. Go right (west) here on Scrub Oak Path. Look for a trail marker at the junction.

The next 0.4-mile trail segment on Scrub Oak Path climbs west through a ponderosa pine and scrub oak forest, twisting through the trees and occasionally crossing bedrock. This singletrack trail segment is popular with mountain bikers. The trail emerges from the forest to an old road and a major trail junction at 1.7 miles. Stop, catch your breath, and enjoy a great view of Pikes Peak here.

An alternate trailhead for this hike is found down the closed road at the end of Piñon Park Drive to the west of the junction. Along this old road are several large boulders, which are a popular workout spot for local rock climbers.

Go right (north) at the trail junction for the last major segment on Pine Ridge Trail, which runs 0.6 mile north along the east side of a high hogback. The wide, rocky trail slowly climbs uphill. At a high point at 1.9 miles, scramble right across some sandstone slabs and balanced boulders to a flat, rocky outcrop for good views east across Ute Valley Park. This is a perfect place to stop for a snack and drink of water before heading back to the main trail. Hummingbird Trail heads east from this junction.

Continue hiking north and slightly downhill on the straight, rocky trail, passing a couple more viewpoints of Pope's Valley to the east. Then descend down to a willow-lined ravine and an intermittent creek. Cross a small footbridge over the creek and ascend back to the first major trail junction with Beaver Trail at 2.4 miles. Keep right and follow the Bobcat Cutoff Trail 0.2 mile back to the parking lot and trailhead.

A natural arch hides along the Beaver Trail in Ute Valley Park.

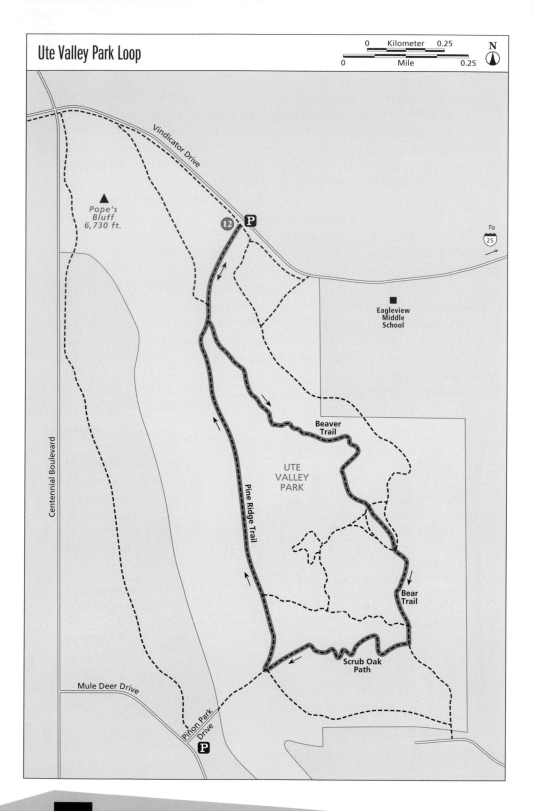

Ute Valley Park Loop

0 Kilometer 0.25
0 Mile 0.25

N

Vindicator Drive

Pope's Bluff
6,730 ft.

12 P

To 25

Eagleview Middle School

Centennial Boulevard

UTE VALLEY PARK

Beaver Trail

Pine Ridge Trail

Bear Trail

Scrub Oak Path

Mule Deer Drive

Piñon Park Drive

P

You can combine this loop hike with other Ute Valley Park trails to create either longer or shorter loops. Consult the map for details. For extra credit you can also climb 6,730-foot Pope's Bluff, the park's high point on the northwest side of the park and almost directly west of the trailhead and parking lot. To climb the bluff, hike to the first trail junction, then head west across the valley on a trail to a steep social trail that climbs onto the hogback. Scramble north to the rocky summit and a great view across Piñon Valley to the mountain escarpment.

## MILES AND DIRECTIONS

**0.0** Trailhead is at the southeast side of the parking lot (GPS: 38.924955, -104.857107) on the south side of Vindicator Drive. Hike south on the Bobcat Cutoff Trail.

**0.2** Reach the first trail junction (GPS: 38.922449, -104.858196). Go left on Beaver Trail.

**0.7** A small natural arch is 150 feet to the left of the trail. Soon the trail splits in the bottom of the valley. Go either right or left around a scrub oak thicket.

**0.8** Reach a trail junction (GPS: GPS: 38.916362, -104.851371). Go right across a culvert in the bottom of the valley. After about 500 feet come to another trail junction. Go left (east) down the valley. Do not go south on the narrow trail.

**0.9** Reach a major trail junction (GPS: 38.915807, -104.850926). Go right (south) on Bear Trail.

**1.1** Trail junction. Go straight, not right on the narrow trail.

**1.2** Reach a trail junction in a group of pines (GPS: 38.913158, -104.850829). Go right on Scrub Oak Path, a trail marked by a sign.

**1.7** Reach a major trail junction (GPS: 38.912607, -104.856038). Go right (north) on Pine Ridge Trail, a wide doubletrack trail. Look west for a great view of Pikes Peak.

**1.9** Hike north on the east side of a long rocky hogback or ridge to a high point. Hummingbird Trail heads east here.

**2.4** Descend slightly downhill on the rocky trail and reach a junction past a small bridge (GPS: 38.922438, -104.858209). This is the junction with Beaver Trail at the beginning of the loop hike. Go straight toward the parking lot.

**2.7** Arrive back at the trailhead and parking lot.

*This loop trail offers an excellent tour through the colorful sandstone bluffs of Palmer Park in northeast Colorado Springs.*

**Start:** Southeast corner of the Yucca and Mesa Trails parking area off Paseo Road. Ending trailhead is at north side of lot.

**Distance:** 4.0-mile loop

**Hiking time:** 2 to 3 hours

**Difficulty:** Easy

**Elevation gain:** Minimal

**Trail surface:** Singletrack dirt surface

**Seasons:** Year-round

**Schedule:** Open daily, dawn to dusk

**Other trail users:** Runners, mountain bikers

**Canine compatibility:** Leashed dogs only. Pick up your dog's waste.

**Land status:** City of Colorado Springs park

**Fees and permits:** None. All city park rules must be obeyed.

**Maps:** USGS Pikeview; downloadable park trail map from Colorado Springs Parks website

**Trail contact:** Colorado Springs Parks, Recreation and Cultural Services, 1401 Recreation Way, Colorado Springs, CO 80905-1975; (719) 385-5940; www.springs gov.com

**Finding the trailhead:** From I-25 take the Fillmore Street exit (exit 145). Drive east on Fillmore Street, which becomes North Circle Drive beyond the Union Boulevard intersection, for 2.5 miles to Paseo Road. Take a left onto Paseo Road and drive 0.8 mile northwest past the Colorado Springs Country Club golf course. Drive through the gated park entrance on Paseo Road, drive to the top of a hill, and make a left turn toward Lazy Land and Ute Crest Picnic Area. Drive a short distance to a Y junction and go left to a parking area at the end of the road (**GPS:** 38.879944, -104.7724). The trailhead is at the southeast corner of the parking area. Palmer Park also has an entry road from Academy Boulevard on the east. To reach the trailhead from the east, turn west on Maizeland Road from Academy Boulevard and drive 2 blocks. Turn right on Paseo Road and enter Palmer Park. Follow Paseo to a right turn to the trailhead.

## THE HIKE

Seventy-three-acre Palmer Park lies smack in the middle of Colorado Springs. This rock-rimmed natural area surrounded by city sprawl is an enclave of forest and grassland with grand vistas of Pikes Peak and the Front Range escarpment and offers over 25 miles of trails for a quick hiking getaway.

The park has a great variety of trails, including closed roads, constructed and maintained trails, and social trails. All the main trails are signed with posts at junctions with arrows indicating which way to go. The Yucca and Mesa Trails on top of the north bluff are very popular with walkers and dogs, while the better-maintained trails are used by mountain bikers and equestrians from Mark Reyner Stables on Paseo Road.

A hiker passes below sandstone hoodoos on the Templeton Trail.

Palmer Park is composed of two flat-topped bluffs lined with rim-rock cliffs, crumbling sandstone buttresses, fanciful hoodoos, and toadstool-shaped rocks tucked among the pines like primitive sculptures. The feldspar-rich sandstone and conglomerate, called Dawson arkose by geologists, has a rough granular texture and a hardness that ranges from crumbling rock with the consistency of brown sugar to hard compact stone that forms cliff bands as high as 80 feet.

The high headlands at Palmer Park, locally part of a range of hills called Austin Bluffs, are an isolated remnant of a large rock formation deposited by ancient streams and rivers flowing from the Pikes Peak massif during the late Cretaceous period some 60 million years ago. Nearby Pulpit Rock is composed of the same sandstone.

The 4-mile Templeton Trail is a great hike that circumnavigates the north bluff in the park, threading across flat sandstone benches above canyons, passing through stands of sturdy ponderosa pine and dense thickets of Gambel oak, and providing great views across downtown Colorado Springs to the abrupt mountain front.

Beginning at the Yucca Flats/Templeton Trailhead, Templeton Trail is easy to hike, with minimal elevation gain and loss. The trail roughly follows the 6,500-foot contour around the bluff. While it can be hiked in either direction, it is described here for hiking clockwise since the views are better and the trail is easier to follow. The first mile of the trail is the busiest as it's used by both hikers and mountain bikers. After rounding the southwest end of the bluff, the trail narrows and is usually deserted and quiet except for the din of traffic on Union Boulevard and Austin Bluffs Parkway in the valley below. Remember to bring water in summer since none is available; nor are there restrooms. Both are, however, found at the Edna Mae Bennett Trailhead on Paseo Road.

The trailhead is located at the southeast corner of the cul-de-sac parking lot. It might be hard to spot, but head down the first trail left of some scrub oaks. The trail descends through yucca and stunted oaks and reaches a junction with a spur of the Yucca Trail. Go right at the signed post and follow the trail west, contouring across a hillside high above Paseo Road and a shallow canyon.

After 0.4 mile you reach an overlook on a broad sandstone bench and a great view west across the bluffs toward the mountains. The trail bends north here, swings around a rocky draw, and at 0.5 mile reaches a junction with the Edna Mae Bennett Nature Trail, which it follows north for another 0.4 mile. The Bennett Trail goes south from the junction to its trailhead on Paseo Road.

After hiking through pines and along the rim rock, the trail passes a junction with the Yucca Trail at 0.7 mile and then another junction with the Bennett Trail, which descends to the left, at 0.9 mile. Keep right on the marked Templeton Trail and clamber up a boulder staircase. The trail, passing through ponderosa pines, dips across the top of a draw and contours west to a compact rock outcropping with a couple of pinnacles and a small arch at 1 mile. This is a good spot to scramble up for rock photos.

The trail heads southwest, following the rim edge and passing two spur trails that go right to the bluff-top Mesa Trail. At 1.4 miles there is a flat rock ledge that offers great views south across the city, and at 1.5 miles is the junction with the southern terminus of Mesa Trail. From here the hike becomes wilder and less popular.

Follow the Templeton Trail to the southern edge of the bluff and a fine view of 14,115-foot Pikes Peak. Now the trail descends rocky slopes on the southern bluff slope, passing beneath tawny cliff bands and scrambling over rounded boulders. At 1.9 miles the trail reaches the southwestern corner of the bluff and boulder pile.

The hike turns north here and for the next half mile winds through a forest of ponderosa pine and scrub oak. Cliffs, some as high as 80 feet, loom above the trail. The cliff tops are studded with stubby pinnacles and magical hoodoos. A housing development and busy Union Boulevard are west below the trail.

At 2.5 miles is an unmarked trail junction at the northwest corner of the bluff. Go either right or left since they meet up 0.1 mile ahead. The left trail is more scenic, edging across steep north-facing slopes then scrambling up boulders to the next junction.

After 2.9 miles the trail bends slightly southeast above Lazy Land valley to the east and crosses bedrock to a viewpoint above a perfect 20-foot-high toadstool with a balanced rock summit. The trail goes west here, contouring above a wide draw. At 3.1 miles is the junction with the Lazy Land Trail, which descends east to a group picnic area. Continue straight and contour southeast around the draw, passing a couple junctions with spur trails that go right onto the mesa top to the Mesa and Yucca Trails.

The marked junction with Palmer Point Trail is reached at 3.5 miles. Go right, uphill, and in 0.4 mile you reach the Mesa Trail, an old closed road on the bluff top. Turn left here and hike another 0.1 mile to the trailhead on the north side of the parking area and the end of our Templeton foot adventure.

## Austin Bluffs

The bluffs and prairie northeast of Colorado Springs, whose downtown was a huddled cluster of buildings back in 1870, was originally part of a ranch owned by Matt France, who sold the property to sheep rancher Henry Austin in 1873. The area became known as Austin Bluffs. General William Jackson Palmer (1836–1909), founder of Colorado Springs, later purchased the property and donated it to the city as a public park in 1907.

## MILES AND DIRECTIONS

**0.0** Trailhead on the southeast side of the parking area (GPS: 38.879841, -104.772265). Go south to a junction.

**0.1** Junction of Templeton Trail and Yucca Trail. Go right at signed post.

**0.4** Reach an overlook (GPS: 38.87848, -104.77572).

**0.5** Junction with the Bennett Trail. Keep straight.

**0.7** Junction with Yucca Trail spur. Keep straight.

**0.8** Junction with Bennett Trail. Go right up stony trail (GPS: 38.88185, -104.77613).

**0.9** Trail junction. Go left.

**1.0** Arch and hoodoos (GPS: 38.88282, -104.77698).

**1.2** Junction with the Mesa Trail.

**1.4** Canyon Overlook (GPS: 38.88188, -104.77927).

**1.5** Junction with Mesa Trail. Keep left.

**1.7** Reach the south end of the bluff. Good views of Pikes Peak. Trail descends west below cliffs.

**1.9** Trail reaches the southwest corner of the bluff and turns north along the western edge of the escarpment (GPS: 38.88110, -104.78448).

**2.5** Trail junction (GPS: 38.88735, -104.77987). Go either left or right since the trails meet up 0.1 mile northeast.

**2.6** Reach the northwest corner of the bluff. The trail bends east here and goes through pine woods above Austin Bluffs Parkway.

**2.9** Trail bends south above the shallow Lazy Land valley to the east. After a few hundred feet, stop on the rim rock and admire a perfect 20-foot-high toadstool with a balanced rock summit (GPS: 38.88682, -104.77470).

**3.1** Junction with the Lazy Land Trail. Continue west and contour around the head of a draw.

**3.2** Junction with Mesa Trail. Keep straight on main trail.

**3.4** Junction with Yucca Trail, which goes up left. Continue straight.

0     Kilometer     0.4

0     Mile     0.4

N

**3.5**    Junction with Palmer Point Trail (GPS: 38.88457, -104.77168). Go up right.

**3.9**    Reach the Yucca Trail, a wide closed road, and go left (south) toward the parking area.

**4.0**    End the hike at the north side of the parking lot (GPS: 38.8800, -104.77233).

# Edna Mae Bennett Nature Trail

*This loop trail explores ponderosa pine woods and sandstone bluffs, including a unique shelter cave, at Palmer Park.*

**Start:** North Cañon Trailhead on north side of Paseo Road just past the west park entrance

**Distance:** 2.6-mile lollipop

**Hiking time:** 1 to 2 hours

**Difficulty:** Moderate

**Elevation gain:** 130 feet

**Trail surface:** Single- and double-track dirt path

**Seasons:** Year-round

**Schedule:** Open daily; dawn to dusk

**Other trail users:** Runners, cyclists, equestrians

**Canine compatibility:** Leashed dogs only. Pick up your dog's waste.

**Land status:** City of Colorado Springs park

**Fees and permits:** None. All city park rules must be obeyed.

**Maps:** USGS Pikeview; downloadable park trail map from Colorado Springs Parks website

**Trail contact:** Colorado Springs Parks, Recreation and Cultural Services, 1401 Recreation Way, Colorado Springs, CO 80905-1975; (719) 385-5940; www.springs gov.com

**Finding the trailhead:** From I-25 take the Fillmore Street exit (exit 145). Drive east on Fillmore Street, which becomes North Circle Drive beyond the Union Boulevard intersection, for 2.5 miles to Paseo Road. Take a left onto Paseo Road and drive 0.8 mile northwest past the Colorado Springs Country Club golf course. Turn left immediately after passing the gated park entrance and park in the lot at the North Cañon Trailhead just past Reyner Stables (**GPS:** 38.877803, -104.777684). Palmer Park also has entry roads from Academy Boulevard to the east, Austin Bluffs Parkway to the north, and Maizeland Road to the south. To reach the trailhead from the east, it's best to take the Maizeland Road entrance.

## THE HIKE

The Edna Mae Bennett Nature Trail, a 2.6-mile loop trail, is a wonderful and easy scenic hike through wooded ravines and rocky sandstone bluffs of 730-acre Palmer Park in the heart of Colorado Springs. The rustic trail climbs high above the surrounding neighborhood, offering excellent views of Pikes Peak and the mountains and exploring shallow canyons. Numerous rock buttresses and fanciful hoodoos shaped like primitive sculptures or giant mushrooms line the rough trail. While most Palmer Park trails are multiuse, you won't compete with mountain bikers on most of the Bennett Trail—it's just too rocky for biking fun. The trail is relatively easy to follow with plenty of trail markers as well as metal posts with arrows pointing the way.

Palmer Park, one of Colorado Springs first city parklands, is a scruffy bit of urban wildness surrounded by houses and roads. This park, a wooded enclave of ponderosa pine and scrub oak, offers grand vistas of the city and the Front Range mountain escarpment.

Begin the hike at the North Cañon parking lot on the left just past the park entrance. A trail map is on the left side of the parking area. Begin from the trailhead on the right side of the parking lot. Cross a wooden bridge and walk left past restrooms to a trail junction. Go right (north) on a narrow trail marked with a

A shelter cave frames Pikes Peak and Colorado Springs.

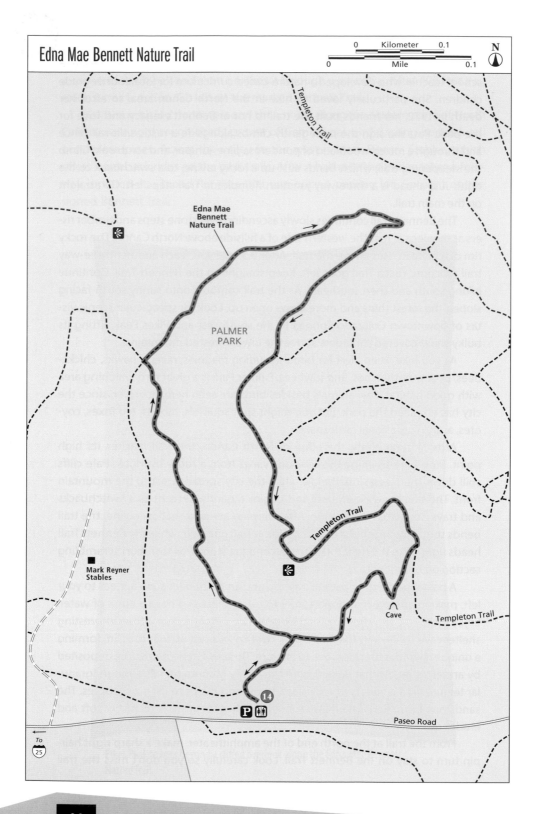

# Edna Mae Bennett Nature Trail

0    Kilometer    0.1

0    Mile    0.1

N

Edna Mae
Bennett
Nature Trail

Templeton Trail

PALMER
PARK

Templeton Trail

Mark Reyner
Stables

Cave

Templeton Trail

14

P

Paseo Road

To
25

and end up in the brush below. The trail rapidly descends stone stairs and steep grades in a ravine, before leveling out at the base of a craggy white bluff at a three-way trail junction. Do you recognize the junction? You should, as this is where the Edna Mae Bennett Trail splits. Take the left fork and easily walk 400 feet back to the trailhead, restrooms, and parking lot.

For extra credit, take more hikes in the park. Palmer Park boasts an extensive system of trails (check out the detailed map at the parking area) as well as other recreational opportunities, including mountain biking and nature study, to round out a full day outside. The park, donated to Colorado Springs by its founder, General William Jackson Palmer, in 1902, offers over 25 miles of multiuse trails. The Civilian Conservation Corps built 14 miles of the trails in the mid-1930s.

## MILES AND DIRECTIONS

**0.0** Start at the trailhead at the North Cañon parking lot (GPS: 38.877803, -104.777684).

**0.1** Reach the Bennett Trail loop junction (GPS: 38.878215, -104.777156). Go left. You will return on the right-hand trail.

**0.6** Reach a four-way junction at an old parking area (GPS: 38.880792, -104.778793). Go right at the northeast corner of the lot past an interpretative sign about Edna Mae Bennett.

**1.2** Reach a trail junction with the Templeton Trail (GPS: 38.88185, -104.77613). Go straight on the marked trail.

**1.7** Reach the high point above North Cañon and a viewpoint to the west.

**2.1** Reach a trail junction. Keep right.

**2.2** A rocky amphitheater and cave are to the left of the trail.

**2.5** Reach the first trail junction and the start of the Bennett Trail loop. Go left downhill to the trailhead.

**2.6** Arrive back at the trailhead and parking lot.

# Pulpit Rock Trail

*This short out-and-back hike leads to the summit of Pulpit Rock, a white-cliffed rampart in the Austin Bluffs Open Space that overlooks northern Colorado Springs and offers spacious views of the city and the mountain escarpment to the west.*

**Start:** Pulpit Rock Trailhead on east side of North Nevada Avenue
**Distance:** 2.1 miles out and back
**Hiking time:** 1 to 2 hours
**Difficulty:** Easy
**Elevation gain:** 490 feet
**Trail surface:** Single- and double-track dirt trail
**Seasons:** Year-round
**Schedule:** Open daily; May 1 to Nov 1, 5 a.m. to 11 p.m.; Nov 2 to Apr 30, 5 a.m. to 9 p.m.
**Other trail users:** Runners, mountain bikers
**Canine compatibility:** Leashed dogs only
**Land status:** City of Colorado Springs Austin Bluffs Open Space

**Fees and permits:** None
**Map:** USGS Pikeview
**Trail contact:** Colorado Springs Parks, Recreation and Cultural Services, 1401 Recreation Way, Colorado Springs, CO 80905-1975; (719) 385-5940; www.springs gov.com
**Special considerations:** Carry water. No restrooms at trailhead. Watch for rattlesnakes in summer. Use caution on summit because of abrupt drop-offs and lightning danger during summer thunderstorms.

**Finding the trailhead:** From I-25 in northern Colorado Springs, take exit 148 from either the north or south. Drive southeast from the interstate on North Nevada Avenue and make the first left turn onto North Nevada Avenue (confusing, but North Nevada ends at I-25 while the continuation is a frontage road on the east side of the interstate). Drive north beside I-25 on North Nevada Avenue for 0.6 mile and turn right (east) into a large parking area where the trailhead (**GPS:** 38.91863, -104.813926) is located. The parking lot is just south of a utilities substation.

## THE HIKE

Pulpit Rock, a gleaming castle lined with white sandstone ramparts, dominates the northern part of Colorado Springs and rises directly above I-25, the main north–south thoroughfare through the city. The rocky 6,610-foot summit, reached by a 1-mile hike, offers spectacular views of upper Monument Creek Valley as well as the steep mountain front and 14,115-foot Pikes Peak to the west. The hike, following the main trail and then a couple of social trails, is mostly easy with a final steep scramble up a loose-rock trail to the summit block.

Pulpit Rock lies in 585-acre Austin Bluffs Open Space, a Colorado Springs parkland that also includes University Park and Austin Bluffs to the southeast. This area protects a wide swath of bluffs, mesas, and valleys east of North Nevada Avenue, forming important wildlife habitat within the city, a valuable scenic and natural area, and a buffer from encroaching development.

The area is dominated by native plant communities, including grasslands, mixed shrubs, and scattered ponderosa pine on the cooler north-facing slopes. The tall-grass community on the lower slopes, with big bluestem and prairie sand-reed grasses, is considered significant by the Colorado Natural Heritage Program since it is relatively uncommon. The native shrublands are covered with copses of Gambel oak and skunkbrush, while the deep drainage that the trail initially crosses is filled with shady cottonwoods and Siberian elms, an intrusive species.

The rocky summit of Pulpit Rock towers above Colorado Springs.

The open space also provides a refuge for both large and small mammals as well as birds commonly found in the foothills of the Front Range a few miles to the west. Mule deer graze in meadows while raccoons and skunks live in the wooded valleys. Nomadic big mammals like black bears, mountain lions, and bobcats sometimes roam through the area, but it is too small for them to inhabit. Keep an eye out for rattlesnakes, which live among the rocky outcrops.

Begin the hike at the Pulpit Rock Trailhead on North Nevada Avenue next to a utilities substation on the north side of the parking lot. Pass through a metal portal and follow a wide dirt trail southeast for a couple hundred feet to the first trail junction at a tall metal tower. Go right on the main trail and descend into a

The upper cliffs of Pulpit Rock, composed of Dawson arkose, rise above I-25 and Monument Valley.

wide valley. Tall cottonwoods shade the east side of the trail while a fence on the west separates the open-space park from commercial development.

Cross a low concrete bridge over a dry wash and follow the trail up the south side of the valley to the second trail junction at a wide switchback. Go right on the main trail. Another trail heads left up the valley. Continue south into another shallow valley. Pulpit Rock rises directly to the south. After 0.6 mile the trail emerges onto a broad bench northwest of Pulpit Rock. Look for an obvious social trail that splits east here.

Hike east up the trail through grass and sage toward Pulpit Rock. After a few hundred feet it intersects another social trail. Go left on this singletrack trail and hike northeast and east, passing above a low cliff band, to the last trail junction. Go right on a good singletrack trail and hike uphill toward Pulpit Rock.

This last trail segment slowly steepens and becomes loose and rocky as it crosses clay slopes. The final trail section ends at a 40-foot-high cliff band. Scramble up left to the final obstacle, fractured bedrock that forms Pulpit Rock's summit. Look for the easiest passage up through the cliffs, making a few climbing moves onto the small, airy summit. Be extremely careful up here since there is a 90-foot vertical drop on the south and west sides of the summit. This is not a good place to bring small children or klutzy adults.

The summit views are simply spectacular, with much of Colorado Springs spreading below you and the high mountains rising beyond. The vista is breathtaking at both sunrise, when rosy light spreads across the mountains and valley below, and at sunset as the sun dips behind Pikes Peak.

Pulpit Rock, besides being an enclave for wildlife and a local landmark, also offers a fascinating geological story. The rocky outcrops, hoodoos, and tall cliffs at the summit area are part of the Dawson Formation, deposited by energetic streams flowing off the rising Rocky Mountains, including the Rampart Range to the west, during the late Cretaceous period some 65 million years ago. This upper rock unit, usually called Dawson arkose, is a coarse white-and-gray sandstone laced with pebbled conglomerate.

The lower exposure of the Dawson Formation is a gray pebbly sandstone interbedded with claystone and siltstone deposited in swamps and along sluggish rivers. The trail up Pulpit Rock mostly traverses this soft, easily eroded facies, which forms the vegetated slopes below the caprock. While fossilized dinosaur bones have been found in the Dawson Formation at other Colorado locales, none have been discovered around Pulpit Rock. A keen eye, however, can find ancient leaf imprints, plant material, petrified wood, and an occasional shark's tooth on the slopes below the rampart.

After enjoying the scenic views and meditating on Pulpit Rock's ancient history, head back to the parking lot by reversing your steps. Be careful descending down the rock steps below the summit and the loose upper trail. If you want to

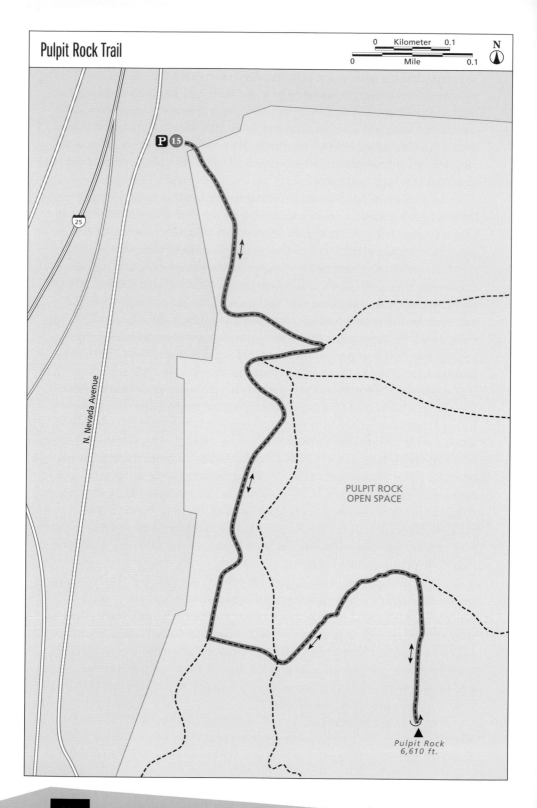

Pulpit Rock Trail

0 Kilometer 0.1
0 Mile 0.1

N

N. Nevada Avenue

25

P 15

PULPIT ROCK
OPEN SPACE

Pulpit Rock
6,610 ft.

shorten the hike, go straight at the first trail junction you reach instead of left, the way you came up. This other trail descends directly down to the main trail at a shallow valley.

## MILES AND DIRECTIONS

**0.0**  Begin the hike at the parking lot and trailhead (GPS: 38.918585, -104.813865). After a couple hundred feet, you come to the first trail junction at a large power pole. Go right and downhill on the main trail.

**0.3**  Second trail junction on the south side of a wide valley. Go right on main trail (GPS: 38.918209, -104.813398).

**0.6**  Third trail junction on the east side of the main trail. Go left (east) up a social trail toward Pulpit Rock (GPS: 38.912944, -104.813432).

**0.7**  Fourth trail junction. Go left on a good singletrack social trail and hike northeast (GPS: 38.912699, -104.812432).

**1.0**  Fifth trail junction at the intersection of two social trails. Go right on a good trail and hike uphill toward Pulpit Rock (GPS: 38.913641, -104.810348).

**1.1**  Scramble onto the summit of Pulpit Rock (GPS: 38.912254, -104.810339).

**2.1**  Arrive back at the trailhead and parking lot.

> **Green Tip:**
> *Pack out what you pack in, even food scraps because they can attract wild animals.*

# Spruce Mountain Trail

*This wonderful hike climbs to the eastern end of Spruce Mountain's long summit and follows a loop trail through an open pine woodland to Windy Point, the high point, at the mountain's west end. It is part of Douglas County Open Space.*

**Start:** Spruce Mountain Trailhead on Spruce Mountain Road / Douglas County Road 53 north of Palmer Lake
**Distance:** 5.3-mile double loop
**Difficulty:** Moderate
**Elevation gain:** 505 feet
**Trail surface:** Singletrack dirt
**Seasons:** Year-round. Winter is icy.
**Schedule:** Open daily, sunrise to sunset
**Other trail users:** Mountain bikers, runners, horses
**Canine compatibility:** Leashed dogs only
**Land status:** Douglas County public land
**Fees and permits:** None

**Maps:** USGS Larkspur. Douglas County Open Space map.
**Trail contact:** Douglas County Division of Open Space and Natural Resources, 100 Third St., Castle Rock, CO 80104; (303) 660-7400; www.douglas.co.us/openspace
**Special considerations:** Bring water; none found along trail. Watch for rattlesnakes. Steep cliffs are found at the end of the trail and below the summit—keep an eye on children and watch your step. No horse trailers at the trailhead; park those at Spruce Meadows Trailhead on Noe Road to the northeast.

**Finding the trailhead:** From Colorado Springs drive north on I-25 past Monument. At the top of Monument Hill, take exit 163, turn left (west) on County Line Road, and drive a couple miles to the north side of Palmer Lake. After crossing railroad tracks, the road dead-ends against Spruce Mountain Road / Douglas County Road 53. Turn right, drive 3.5 miles north, and make a left turn into the marked Spruce Mountain Open Space parking lot. The trailhead is at the west end of the parking lot (**GPS:** 39.167841, -104.874408).

## THE HIKE

The 5.3-mile-long Spruce Mountain Trail is a wonderful hike north of Palmer Lake and east of the Rampart Range, a low mountain range that runs from Ute Pass and the Garden of the Gods in Colorado Springs to the South Platte River at Waterton Canyon southwest of Denver. The singletrack trail climbs to the eastern end of Spruce Mountain's long mesa summit and then makes a long loop, first following the mountain's southern rim to its rocky 7,605-foot summit at the southwest end of the mesa before returning along its northern rim.

The trail offers easy hiking on a good single- and doubletrack dirt trail with gradual grades, open ponderosa pine and scrub oak woodlands, and spacious scenic views that stretch from Pikes Peak in the south to Longs Peak in the north. The trail and mountain are on Spruce Mountain Open Space land, a parkland that was purchased by Douglas County between 2000 and 2009 to protect it from development as a resort. A developer had proposed building a hotel on top of the mountain, a golf course on the rolling grassland below, and 180 luxury homes scattered across the property.

The hike begins from a trailhead at the west end of a parking area on the west side of Spruce Mountain Road north of Palmer Lake. The only amenities at the trailhead are a bear-proof trash container and a portable toilet. Park cars and trucks only in the lot; no trailers or horse trailers. Remember to pack out your

A hiker crosses broad meadows below Eagle Mountain near Spruce Mountain.

trash, keep your dog leashed, pick up your dog's waste, and stay on the trails—no shortcutting! Keep an eye out for mountain bikers and horseback riders on this multiuse trail.

At the trailhead, pass through a gate and walk 350 feet to the first trail junction. Go straight on the Spruce Mountain Trail and pass through a dense thicket of scrub oak. Continue hiking west up the slowly rising trail across open grassy meadows on the northern slope of Spruce Mountain. Eagle Mountain rises to the northwest, ringed by high sandstone cliffs like an ancient battlement. After 0.4 mile go left at a trail junction signed Mountain Top Loop, on Spruce Mountain Trail. Eagle Pass Trail goes straight.

The singletrack trail bends left and contours up the steep north flank of Spruce Mountain. The damp north-facing slope is blanketed in a mixed forest of scrub or Gambel oak, ponderosa pine, Douglas fir, and spruce trees. After 0.3 mile of climbing, the trail reaches a junction with Oak Shortcut Trail on a slight knoll. Go right on the main trail.

The next half mile of trail is the toughest section of the hike. The trail switchbacks up the wooded east side of the mountain, passing beneath a jutting outcrop of Dawson arkose, a coarse sandstone, before crossing onto the cooler northern slope. After climbing 0.6 mile from the last junction or 1.2 miles from the trailhead, you reach Greenland Overlook, a lofty viewpoint that overlooks the rolling grasslands of Greenland Open Space. More good views are southwest toward 14,115-foot Pikes Peak, which rises beyond humpbacked Mount Herman.

The trail slowly climbs and passes onto the north side of Spruce Mountain's long cliff-rimmed summit and reaches Paddock's Point, a rocky viewpoint that looks north at 7,515-foot Eagle Mountain. Continue up the trail through dry pine woods to the Y junction for the 2.3-mile-long Mountain Top Loop, which follows the south rim out to Windy Point and then continues back along the north rim to this junction. Go left on the doubletrack trail. This junction is 1.6 miles from the trailhead.

Follow the wide trail for the next 0.8 mile along the airy south rim of Spruce Mountain. Some strategically placed benches and picnic tables make for good snack stops. The trail dips across broad ravines, climbs gentle slopes, and passes lots of rock-rimmed overlooks. None of these are fenced and all are dangerous, with vertical drops of 60 feet. Keep a close watch on small children. The cliff rim is soft and loose.

After hiking 2.8 miles from the trailhead, you reach Windy Point, the 7,605-foot high point of Spruce Mountain, on the far western edge of the summit plateau. This exposed overlook makes for a good water break and some marvelous scenic views. Look southwest toward the town of Palmer Lake cradled in a broad valley below and snowcapped Pikes Peak rising beyond. *Warning:* This overlook is very dangerous. Keep away from the cliff edge.

After resting begin your return hike on the next trail segment, which runs 0.4 mile northeast from Windy Point to a junction with the Service Road. Go right on the doubletrack loop trail for the described hike. Alternatively, a left turn on the Service Road descends 0.5 mile to Eagle Pass Trail, which you can follow back east for 1.8 miles along the base of the mountain to the trailhead.

To complete the upper loop trail, keep right at the junction, and hike 0.7 mile along the wooded north rim of Spruce Mountain to the end of the loop at the Y

Pikes Peak and Mount Herman rise beyond Windy Point at the western rim of Spruce Mountain.

# Spruce Mountain Trail

junction. Go straight on the main trail. It is 1.6 miles from here to the trailhead and parking area. Retrace your steps back to Greenland Overlook, then down the switchbacks to Pine Junction.

Instead of going left on Spruce Mountain Trail, the way you came up, take a right on the Oak Shortcut Trail. Descend this short, steep trail for just over 0.1 mile to a junction with Spruce Meadows Trail. Go left (north) and follow the trail downhill for 0.2 mile to a cross junction with Spruce Mountain Trail. Turn right and hike a few hundred feet to the trailhead and the end of another great Pikes Peak Country hike.

## MILES AND DIRECTIONS

**0.0** Start at the trailhead on the west side of Spruce Mountain Road / Douglas County Road 53 (GPS: 39.167896, -104.874792). After 350 feet you cross a junction with Spruce Meadows Trail. Go straight on Spruce Mountain Trail.

**0.4** Junction with Eagle Pass Trail (GPS: 39.167804, -104.881156). Go left, following Spruce Mountain Trail.

**0.6** Junction with Oak Shortcut. Go right.

**1.2** Greenland Overlook.

**1.6** Junction with Mountain Top Loop Trail (GPS 39.163626, -104.883723). Go left on doubletrack trail and follow the trail along the south rim of Spruce Mountain.

**2.8** Reach Windy Point and the farthest west point on the hike (GPS: 39.15516, -104.898723). A short spur trail goes from the main trail to the point. Return to the trail and go left (north).

**3.9** Return to the Y junction. Go straight.

**5.3** After following the Oak Shortcut Trail northeast, you'll arrive back at the trailhead and parking area.

# Inner Canyon–Lake Gulch Loop Trail

*Two trails—Inner Canyon–Lake Gulch Loop Trail and Canyon View Nature Trail—explore the rim and inner canyon of Castlewood Canyon, an unusual state park on the high prairie north of Colorado Springs. The Inner Canyon–Lake Gulch Trail loops through the canyon, following Cherry Creek and winding among 25-million-year-old boulders.*

**Start:** Trailhead at Bridge Canyon Overlook parking area past the visitor center on the right

**Distance:** 2.0-mile loop

**Hiking time:** 1 to 3 hours

**Difficulty:** Easy

**Elevation gain:** 200 feet

**Trail surface:** Dirt and paved

**Seasons:** Year-round. Summers can be hot but shade is found. Winters can be cold and icy. In winter, snow may prohibit travel on the Inner Canyon Trail.

**Schedule:** Open daily. Gate at the east entrance opens at 8 a.m. Park closes at sunset.

**Other trail users:** Hikers only

**Canine compatibility:** Leashed dogs only

**Land status:** Colorado State Park

**Fees and permits:** Entrance fee charged to enter the park. No permits required.

**Map:** USGS Castlewood Canyon trail map available at visitor center and park website

**Trail contact:** Castlewood Canyon State Park, 2989 S. Highway 83, Franktown, CO 80116; (303) 688-5242; www.parks.state.co.us/parks/castlewoodcanyon

**Other:** Stay on designated trails. Mountain bikes are only allowed on park roads. Pets must be on a leash. Ground fires are prohibited. Gathering of artifacts, vegetation, and timber is prohibited. Drinking water, restrooms, books, and information are available at the park visitor center.

**Special considerations:** Carry water. Watch for rattlesnakes along the trail in summer.

## THE HIKE

Cherry Creek springs from the rolling hills of the Palmer Divide, a forested ridge that separates the Platte and Arkansas watersheds between Denver and Colorado Springs. The creek twists northward through grasslands and cattle ranches for 15 miles before slicing through cliff-lined Castlewood Canyon. Most of the 10-mile-long canyon, which lies southeast of Denver, is located within 2,303-acre Castlewood Canyon State Park.

The park preserves an environment more similar to that found in the Rocky Mountains 30 miles to the west than the surrounding prairie. With 19 inches of rainfall annually, the park harbors groves of ponderosa pine and Douglas fir on moist north-facing slopes. Quaking aspens, growing far below their normal 8,000- to 10,000-foot range, flourish in moist canyon draws. Grassy meadows, splotched with summer wildflowers, border the forest in the inner canyon, while twisted juniper and dense copses of scrub oak grow along the stony canyon rim.

Numerous hiking trails and walking paths lace this getaway of dense woodlands, tumbling water, and rough-hewn cliffs, offering hikers an opportunity to discover and explore Castlewood Canyon State Park's ecological diversity and unique scenery. Other visitor activities include picnicking beneath pines, climbing vertical cliffs, and observing the park's wildlife.

This book describes two of Castlewood's best walks. The Inner Canyon–Lake Gulch Loop Trail is a moderately rough trail that explores the canyon north of the park's visitor center. (Canyon View Nature Trail is a paved, wheelchair-accessible path that follows the west rim of the canyon.)

Hikers here should stay on the trails to avoid problems. Loose rock is found on the cliff bands and climbing the rocks should be left to experienced rock climbers with proper equipment. Beehives and wasp nests are found in cavities and cracks on the cliffs. Mosquitoes can be a problem in summer; carry bug juice to ward them off. Rattlesnakes abound in the canyon and are sometimes found on the trails. To avoid rattler encounters during the warmer months, do not bushwhack off the trail.

To hike the Inner Canyon–Lake Gulch Loop Trail, begin at the large parking area for Canyon Point at the end of the park road by picnic pavilions. Restrooms and drinking fountains (not open in winter) are here. Find the trailhead for the Inner Canyon Trail on the north side of the lot. Also find a large sign for Canyon View Nature Trail with a map of the lower canyon and park facilities.

Walk north on the paved trail, dropping slightly downhill toward the canyon rim. Scattered ponderosa pines and junipers dot the rim along with groves of scrub oak and open meadows. Picnic tables are found near the rim.

At the canyon rim, the paved path intersects the marked Inner Canyon Trailhead. Follow this trail straight ahead.

The narrow, gravel Inner Canyon Trail drops steeply downhill, winding through cliff bands and tall scrub oaks. Watch your footing on the steep sections, particularly if any ice or snow is present.

The trail emerges onto the boulder-strewn floor of Castlewood Canyon and crosses gurgling Cherry Creek on a wooden plank bridge to the creek's north bank.

Head northwest above the creek for about three-quarters of a mile, passing many large, lichen-covered boulders and plunging through a dense scrub oak

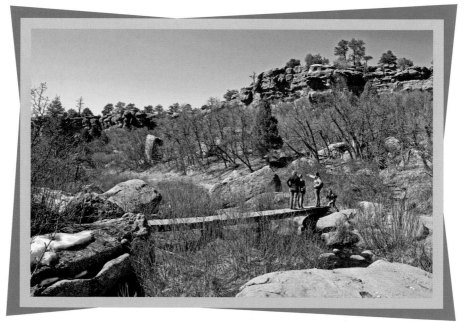

Hikers cross a plank bridge over Cherry Creek on the Inner Canyon Trail.

forest. The moist north-facing slopes on the opposite side of the canyon are thick with tall spruces, Douglas firs, and ponderosa pines.

Stop along the way and look at one of the immense boulders beside the trail that tumbled from the cliff rim above. The canyon's 25-million-year-old rock, called Castle Rock conglomerate, stretches along the east and west rims. The concrete-hard rock, deposited in an ancient river, is coarsely studded with volcanic pebbles and cobbles that jut out at odd angles.

The trail heads northwest and the canyon slowly deepens. At the mouth of the Inner Canyon, the trail intersects Lake Gulch Trail. This 0.9-mile trail heads south and southeast back to the walk's start.

The Inner Canyon Trail continues 0.2 mile northwest to the old dam ruins where it joins the Creek Bottom and Rim Rock Trails. Pick up a park map at the visitor center for information on these trails.

Take a left on Lake Gulch Trail, drop down to the creek, and cross via a wooden plank bridge. Follow the trail on the gravelly bank above the creek to a gravel bench, then along a bench that trends left around a forested headland to the western side of the hill.

The trail gradually ascends uphill, passing scrub oak copses and scattered pines. To the west, a broad grassy valley is dotted with grazing cattle and a couple of ranch houses and barns. Snowcapped mountains in the Front Range tower beyond the valley's western rim.

This valley was once part of a large lake formed by a downstream dam to the northwest where the canyon constricts. The earthen and stone dam, built in 1890, was used for flood control, irrigation, and recreation. The year after it was built, a panel of state engineers examined leakage in the dam and determined that "The dam has been built by irresponsible contractors under inadequate supervision." The dam's foundation, erected on a natural spring, was slowly weakened until the night of August 3, 1933, when a heavy rainstorm burst the dam, sending a 30-foot cascade of water surging downstream toward Denver. The flood caused two deaths, caused over $1 million in damage, and excavated a deep channel through Castlewood's lower canyon. The ruins of the dam still straddle the canyon narrows below the Inner Canyon Trail.

Once the trail reaches the rimrock, it enters a ponderosa pine forest. Stop and sniff the rough bark. The pine has a distinctive smell similar to butterscotch or vanilla. Also note the trees where the bark has been gnawed or girdled by porcupines in search of the sweet inner bark during cold winters when other food is buried by snow.

Follow the trail southeast along flat ground to the picnic pavilions, parking area, and the hike's end point. Restrooms and a drinking fountain, which operate only in warmer months, are found here.

Inner Canyon–Lake Gulch Loop Trail

Canyon View Nature Trail

To Visitor Center

Cherry Creek

Inner Canyon Trail

CASTLEWOOD CANYON STATE PARK

Canyon Point

Lake Gulch Trail

N

Kilometer
0        0.25        0.25

Mile
0        0.25

## MILES AND DIRECTIONS

**0.0**  Begin at the Inner Canyon Trailhead on the north side of the parking area at the end of the park access road (GPS: 39.333588, -104.744206). Walk north on the paved path toward the canyon.

**0.2**  Reach a junction with the Inner Canyon Trail and Canyon View Nature Trail (GPS: 39.335296, -104.743589). Go straight on Inner Canyon Trail and descend into the canyon. Cross the creek on a plank bridge and go west on the trail.

**1.0**  Reach a junction in the lower Inner Canyon with the Lake Gulch Trail (GPS: 39.339861, -104.752681). Go left on Lake Gulch Trail, crossing the creek and climbing the western slope of a cliff-rimmed mesa.

**1.7**  At a junction with the Amphitheatre Trail (GPS: 39.334287, -104.747319), continue straight on the main trail.

**2.0**  End at the trailhead on the west side of the parking lot and just east of restrooms and picnic pavilions (GPS: 39.333371, -104.74479).

A jumble of worn boulders line Cherry Creek in Castlewood Canyon.

# Canyon View Nature Trail

*The Canyon View Nature Trail is an out-and-back, wheelchair-accessible paved trail that explores the rim of Castlewood Canyon, an unusual state park on the high prairie north of Colorado Springs.*

**Start:** Trailhead at Bridge Canyon Overlook parking area past the visitor center on the right

**Distance:** 2.1 miles out and back

**Hiking time:** About 1 hour

**Difficulty:** Easy

**Elevation gain:** About 70 feet

**Trail surface:** Paved

**Seasons:** Year-round. Summers can be hot, but shade is found. Winters can be cold and icy.

**Schedule:** Open daily. Gate at the east entrance opens at 8 a.m. Park closes at sunset.

**Other trail users:** Hikers only

**Canine compatibility:** Leashed dogs only

**Land status:** Colorado state park

**Fees and permits:** Entrance fee charged to enter the park. No permits required.

**Map:** USGS Castlewood Canyon trail map available at visitor center and park website

**Trail contact:** Castlewood Canyon State Park, 2989 S. Highway 83, Franktown, CO 80116; (303) 688-5242; www.parks.state.co.us/parks/castlewoodcanyon

**Other:** Stay on designated trails. Mountain bikes are only allowed on park roads. Pets must be on a leash. Ground fires are prohibited. Gathering of artifacts, vegetation, and timber is prohibited.

**Special considerations:** Carry water. Watch for rattlesnakes along the trail in summer. Drinking water, restrooms, books, and information are available at the park visitor center.

**Finding the trailhead:** The easiest access from Colorado Springs and Denver to the canyon is by driving on I-25 to exit 182 in Castle Rock. Drive east for 6 miles on CO 86 to Franktown. Turn south at the crossroads onto CO 83 and drive 5 miles to the marked park visitor-center turn-off. Turn right (west) and drive along the rim 0.5 mile to the visitor center. The Canyon View Nature Trail walk begins at the Bridge Canyon Overlook parking area just past the visitor center on the right (**GPS:** 39.331129, -104.738895).

## THE HIKE

Visitors with physical challenges or those with small children and strollers will enjoy walking on Canyon View Nature Trail, a paved 0.7 (one-way) trail that traverses the west rim of Castlewood Canyon. The round-trip hike described here totals 2.1 miles if you hike to all the overlooks once (but be aware not all are wheelchair accessible). The trail offers marvelous views into the canyon from a series of rim-edge viewpoints.

Start the hike from either the parking lot for Bridge Canyon Overlook just east of the visitor center or at a large parking area at the end of the park road where the Inner Canyon Trail begins. This description begins from the parking area by the visitor center.

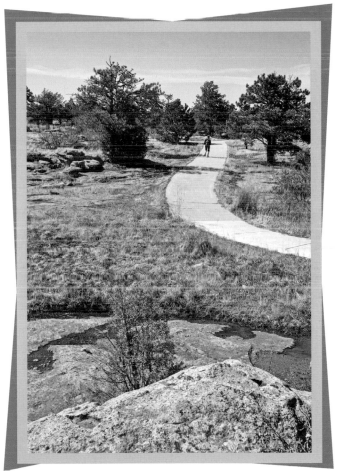

A hiker follows the paved Canyon View Nature Trail along the rim of Castlewood Canyon.

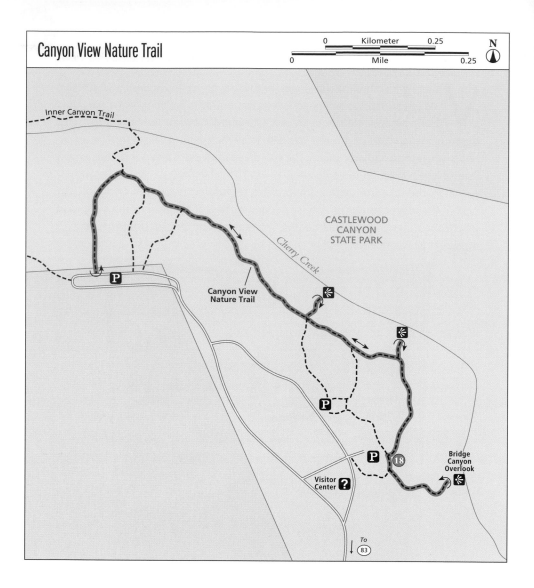

**Green Tip:**
*Stay on the trail. Cutting through from one part of a switch-back to another destroys fragile plant life and creates channels for damaging erosion.*

First hike 0.1 mile down a paved trail to Bridge Canyon Overlook. This view-point, which is not entirely wheelchair accessible, offers a great view into the lush canyon below and of the nearby concrete highway bridge. Retrace your steps 0.1 mile back to the parking area and follow the marked trail northwest along the canyon rim past two more viewpoints to the start of the Inner Canyon Trail after 1.2 miles.

From here hike south on the paved trail up a slight uphill grade to the park-ing area and restrooms at the northwest terminus of the park road and the end of the nature trail. To return to your vehicle at the parking lot by the visitor cen-ter, either follow a bike path alongside the road back for 0.4 mile to your car or retrace your steps back to the lot by following the paved nature trail for 0.7 mile. The scenery looks better the second time on the trail anyway!

## MILES AND DIRECTIONS

**0.0** Begin at the parking lot on the east side of the park visitor center. Locate the trailhead on the far right side of the parking lot (GPS: 39.329949, -104.737364).

**0.1** Hike east on the paved trail to Bridge Canyon Overlook (GPS: 39.329751, -104.735921).

**0.2** After retracing your steps, return to the first trailhead and parking lot.

**0.4** From the parking lot, walk to the middle trailhead for Canyon View Nature Trail (GPS: 39.330228, -104.737426) and hike northwest on the paved trail. Hike to a trail junction (GPS: 39.332238, -104.737104). Go right for a couple hundred feet to an overlook. Return to the main trail and go right.

**0.6** Reach a four-way trail junction (GPS: 39.332691, -104.73931). Go right for a couple hundred feet to an overlook, then return back to the junction and go right.

**1.0** Reach trail junction, keep straight.

**1.1** Reach trail junction, keep straight.

**1.2** Reach junction with Inner Canyon Trail (GPS: 39.335296, -104.743588); go left toward parking lot and restrooms.

**1.4** End of the trail at the north side of the parking lot at the end of the park road (GPS: 39.333588, -104.744206). Return to the trailhead via the paved path.

**2.1** Arrive back at the trailhead.

# The Mountains

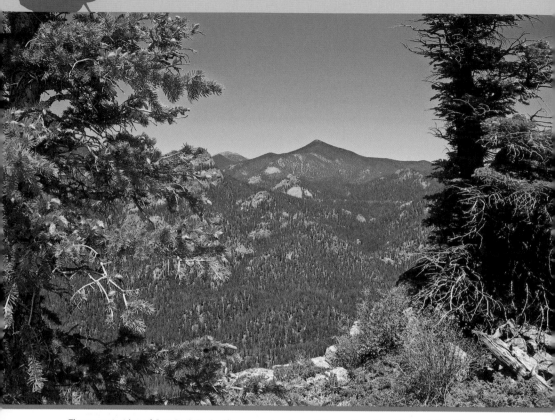

The summit ridge of Gray Back Peak offers expansive views of the southern Front Range (hike 22).

Pikes Peak, a 14,115-foot-high sentinel of granite and snow, dominates Colorado Springs as well as the surrounding area, dictating not only its fickle climate but also its diverse natural history. The Pikes Peak massif as well as lower mountain ranges, including the Rampart Range and the Tarryall Range, are laced with numerous excellent trails that offer four seasons of high-mountain adventure. Intrepid hikers can tackle strenuous hikes up the Mount Manitou Incline Trail and Blodgett Peak as well as the Devils Playground Trail to the airy summit of Pikes Peak, while easier hikes scale lower peaks, explore wooded valleys, discover waterfalls and clear cascading streams, recall the area's colorful gold-mining history, and follow hidden canyons filled with wildlife and birdsong.

# Mount Cutler Trail

*The easy Mount Cutler Trail gently climbs through a ponderosa pine and Douglas fir forest in North Cheyenne Cañon Park to the rounded summit of 7,220-foot Mount Cutler. The well-maintained and popular trail offers a leisurely hike with panoramic views of Colorado Springs, the Broadmoor Hotel, and the distant prairie.*

**Start:** Mount Cutler Trailhead on North Cheyenne Cañon Road

**Distance:** 1.8 miles out and back

**Hiking time:** 1 to 2 hours

**Difficulty:** Easy. Trail is mostly uphill but features gentle grades.

**Elevation gain:** 367 feet

**Trail surface:** Wide, singletrack dirt trail

**Seasons:** Year-round. Apr through Nov is best. Lower section of trail is icy in winter.

**Schedule:** Open daily; May 1 to Oct 31, 5 a.m. to 11 p.m.; Nov 1 to Apr 30, 5 a.m. to 9 p.m.

**Other trail users:** Runners. No mountain biking.

**Canine compatibility:** Leashed dogs only

**Land status:** North Cheyenne Cañon Park, a Colorado Springs city park

**Fees and permits:** None

**Map:** USGS Manitou Springs

**Trail contact:** Colorado Springs Parks, Recreation and Cultural Services, 1401 Recreation Way, Colorado Springs, CO 80905-1975; (719) 385-5940; www.springs gov.com

**Special considerations:** Stay on designated trail. Don't shortcut and cause erosion on steep slopes below the trail. Cliffs and drop-offs are on the upper trail; watch children along cliff edges. Trail can be icy in winter; use caution and wear micro-spikes as needed. Bring water in summer; none is available along the trail or at the trailhead.

**Finding the trailhead:** From I-25 take the Nevada Avenue/CO 115 exit (exit 140 B). Drive south on South Nevada Avenue/CO 115 for about a mile and turn right (west) onto Cheyenne Road. Follow Cheyenne Road for 2.6 miles to its end at Cheyenne Boulevard. If you approach via Cheyenne Boulevard, stay right on Cheyenne Boulevard at this intersection. Go left (west) on Cheyenne Boulevard for 0.1 mile to a Y intersection. Go right, through an open gate into North Cheyenne Cañon Park. Drive 1.4 miles up the park road to the Mount Cutler Trailhead on the left (**GPS:** 38.791822, -104.886974).

## THE HIKE

Serene, peaceful, and seemingly remote, North Cheyenne Cañon is one of Colorado Springs' best gems. The city park, tucked into the southwest side of the city, is a spectacular canyon with soaring granite cliffs and steep slopes wooded with ponderosa pine and Douglas fir. Just beyond charming residential districts, a winding access road climbs west into the canyon, which is also one of the city's oldest parks.

The 1.8-mile round-trip hike up Mount Cutler is the easiest and most accessible summit climb in the Pikes Peak region. It makes a great introduction to local peak-bagging for kids as well as for visitors. Expect great views across North and South Cheyenne Cañons; an easy grade with an elevation gain of 367 feet; peaceful pine and fir woods; and airy exposure on the last section.

Be careful and watch children as you hike along the exposed trail above South Cheyenne Cañon below the main summit and if you make the short hike out to the east summit, which perches high above dangerous, vertical cliffs. Some of the footing is on loose, slippery gravel scattered atop the granite bedrock.

Mount Cutler offers stunning panoramic views from its rounded summit of the dark forests spilling down steep mountainsides, the North and South Cheyenne Creek drainages, towering granite formations, and tumbling Seven Falls, as well as vistas of Colorado Springs and the high plains to the east. The wide trail climbs steadily but is an easy climb, with a thrilling touch of exposure as you traverse across the west- and south-facing shoulders of the mountain.

From the parking lot and trailhead on the south side of the park road at 6,797 feet in North Cheyenne Cañon, hike up a broad, well-used path through a dense evergreen forest that provides welcome shade in summer. The trail gently climbs and after 0.26 mile reaches an overlook with views of distant downtown Colorado Springs. The trail continues climbing, crossing steep slopes littered with fallen trees. The trail flattens out briefly beneath a squat rock tower, then bends through a gully and climbs again, reaching an overlook at 0.4 mile. An excellent view opens across the cliff-lined canyon to the urban sprawl of Colorado Springs.

At 0.5 mile is a saddle that separates North and South Cheyenne Cañons. The Mount Muscoco Trail heads right here. Keep straight ahead on the well-trod path for Mount Cutler. The trail traverses onto the dry southwest side of the mountain. Below are sparse pines clinging to rocky soil. The narrow trail edges across an exposed slope, with steep cliffs and drop-offs to your right. Keep your children in check here. As you hike, look down right from the trail and you'll glimpse Seven Falls cascading over granite benches far below.

The trail continues spiraling upward onto the south slope, passing a trail marker at a switchback at 0.8 mile. Keep left and scramble up the final steep trail section to 7,220-foot Mount Cutler's broad rounded summit at 1 mile. The summit offers 360-degree views, with the city and vast plains spreading east to the distant horizon, and the monumental peaks of the Front Range looming to the west.

For extra credit on your way down, go left (east) from the main trail just south of the summit on one of two trails. A short distance east of the main path, these two join together. Follow the trail another quarter mile east to Cutler's lower summit. This lofty perch, surrounded by airy cliffs, offers superb views of Colorado Springs and the Broadmoor Hotel below.

To return to the trailhead from Mount Cutler's summit, follow the trail back down. It's all downhill and the views are just as good as when you're hiking up.

## North Cheyenne Cañon

North Cheyenne Cañon has long been a coveted and revered Colorado Springs city park. In the 1870s the canyon was a popular excursion, with visitors following a rough wagon road up the canyon to view several spectacular waterfalls, picnic by the tumbling creek, and admire summer wildflowers. The area, owned by the Colorado College Land Company, was, however, closed on Sundays in 1882, leading to public outcry. The entrance gate was torn down by zealous citizens, speeches were made, and words were written by local notables like writer Helen Hunt Jackson to keep the canyon open, so the City of Colorado Springs purchased 640 acres in 1885 and made it into a park.

General William Jackson Palmer, Civil War veteran and founder of Colorado Springs, donated another 480 acres in 1907 and paid for the construction of a carriage road up the canyon and over High Drive, picnic areas and a pavilion, and several trails including the Mount Cutler Trail. Automobiles were first allowed into the park in 1917, although strict guidelines for driving up and down the canyon were enforced because the road was a single lane for most of its distance.

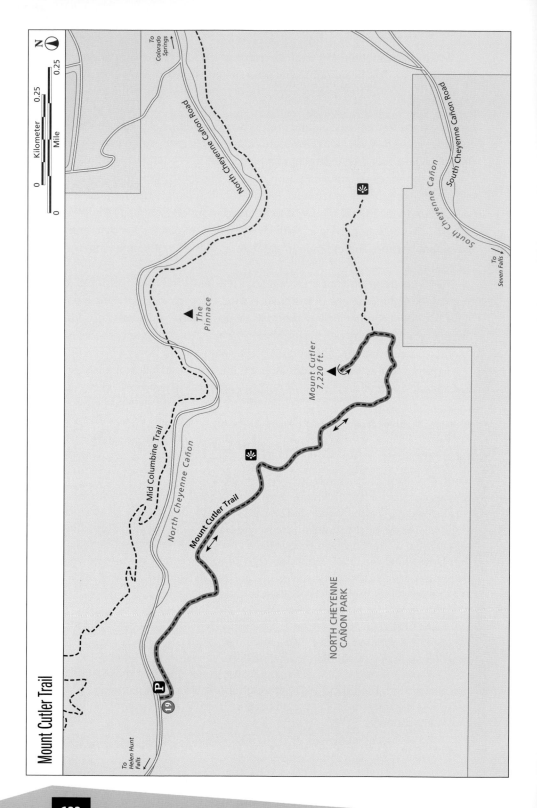

# Mount Cutler Trail

**N**

Kilometer
0    0.25

Mile
0    0.25    0.25

To
Colorado
Springs

North Cheyenne Cañon Road

South Cheyenne Cañon Road

South Cheyenne Cañon

To
Seven Falls

The
Pinnace

Mount Cutler
7,220 ft.

Mid Columbine Trail

North Cheyenne Cañon

**Mount Cutler Trail**

NORTH CHEYENNE
CAÑON PARK

To
Helen Hunt
Falls

19

P

## MILES AND DIRECTIONS

**0.0** Start at the trailhead on the north side of the park road (GPS: 38.791763, -104.8871).

**0.4** Reach an overlook with good views across the canyon toward downtown Colorado Springs.

**0.5** Trail reaches a saddle west of Mount Cutler's summit. Continue southeast across the southern flank of the mountain above South Cheyenne Canyon.

**0.9** Keep left at any junctions to reach the summit of Mount Cutler (GPS: 38.78780, -104.8774). Turn around to retrace your steps.

**1.8** Arrive back at the trailhead.

The Colorado Springs skyline lies beyond towering granite cliffs in North Cheyenne Cañon.

# 20

## Columbine Trail

*Columbine Trail is a 4.3-mile out-and-back route from the Starsmore Discovery Center at its eastern entrance to Helen Hunt Falls in North Cheyenne Cañon Park. The trail, accessed by three different trailheads, makes a great day hike with spectacular scenery, soaring rock formations, and one of the area's best waterfalls.*

**Start:** Starsmore Discovery Center on North Cheyenne Cañon Road at canyon entrance

**Distance:** 8.6 miles out and back

**Hiking time:** 2 to 5 hours

**Difficulty:** Moderate. Trail is gentle for the first mile then slowly climbs uphill with gentle grades.

**Elevation gain:** 1,005 feet total

**Trail surface:** Singletrack dirt trail

**Seasons:** Year-round. Apr through Nov is best. Parts of the trail may be icy in winter.

**Schedule:** Open daily, May 1 to Oct 31, 5 a.m. to 11 p.m.; Nov 1 to Apr 30, 5 a.m. to 9 p.m.

**Other trail users:** Trail runners. Mountain bikers often use it for a descent from the upper canyon. Open to horses, which are rarely seen.

**Canine compatibility:** Leashed dogs only

**Land status:** Public land owned by the City of Colorado Springs

**Fees and permits:** None

**Map:** USGS Manitou Springs

**Trail contact:** Colorado Springs Parks, Recreation and Cultural Services, 1401 Recreation Way, Colorado Springs, CO 80905-1975; (719) 385-5940; www.springs gov.com

**Special considerations:** Stay on the designated trail. Don't short-cut and cause erosion on steep gravel slopes below the trail. Trail can be icy in winter; use caution and wear spikes as needed. Bring water in summer; none is available along the trail.

**Finding the trailhead:** From I-25 take the Nevada Avenue/CO 115 exit (exit 140B). Drive south on South Nevada Avenue/CO 115 for about a mile and turn right (west) onto Cheyenne Road. Follow Cheyenne Road for 2.6 miles to its end at Cheyenne Boulevard. If you approach via Cheyenne Boulevard, stay right on Cheyenne Boulevard at this intersection. Go left (west) on Cheyenne Boulevard for 0.1 mile to a Y intersection. Go left toward Seven Falls and park immediately to the left in a large parking lot. The trail begins across the road at the Starsmore Discovery Center (**GPS:** 38.790961, -104.865120).

## THE HIKE

Columbine Trail is an out-and-back hike that ascends North Cheyenne Cañon for 4.3 miles from the Starsmore Discovery Center at its eastern entrance to its terminus on the road just before Helen Hunt Falls. The trail, accessed by three different trailheads, makes a great day hike with spectacular mountain scenery, soaring rock formations, trickling North Cheyenne Creek, moist wooded vales, and one of the best waterfalls in the Pikes Peak region. The hike, with its gentle grades and well-maintained gravel surface, is ideal for families as well as anyone wanting a casual hiking getaway.

North Cheyenne Creek, beginning at Stratton Reservoir just below the rounded summit of 12,367-foot Mount Almagre, drains east down a steep canyon before emptying through the southwest part of Colorado Springs and joining Fountain Creek. Columbine Trail, entirely within 1,277-acre North Cheyenne Cañon Park, a Colorado Springs city park, threads up the lower part of the canyon from its mouth below Mount Cutler to Helen Hunt Falls.

Lower North Cheyenne Cañon is a narrow gorge carved out of pink Pikes Peak granite by the rushing creek. Near the canyon mouth, North Cheyenne Creek makes three wide, looping meanders. Above soar rocky precipices, split by seams, ledges, and sheltered alcoves. In winter, snow and rivulets of ice cling to the cliffs, while summer exposes carpets of moss and yellow lichen-covered walls.

Mount Muscoco towers above a viewpoint along the Columbine Trail.

North Cheyenne Cañon was a popular tourist destination in the early days of Colorado Springs in the 1880s and 1890s. Locals brought eastern visitors to the canyon by carriage to marvel at the granite skyscrapers and the tumbling creek of clear water. One writer praised the canyon in an 1893 travel brochure: "This canyon abounds in beautiful waterfalls and cascades. . . . Beautiful, picturesque, grand, and in places awe-inspiring, are these stupendous gorges, awakening deepest emotions in all beholders." Columbine Trail was built in 1934 by a crew of unemployed men; a blacksmith sharpened as many as one hundred picks a day to hew the trail out of the granite hillsides.

Columbine Trail has three trailheads. The Lower Columbine Trailhead is at Starsmore Discovery Center at the entrance to the canyon. This is where most hikers start and is where the hike described here begins. The Middle Columbine Trailhead is at the north side of the road about 1.2 miles west of Starsmore. This is a good spot to begin the upper trail for a shorter hike. The Upper Columbine Trailhead is a two-car pullout on the switchback just before Helen Hunt Falls. It's better to park at the large parking area at the falls and walk 100 yards on the road's shoulder to the trailhead.

Columbine Trail starts behind the Starsmore Discovery Center, where a sign marks the trailhead. Walk past it on the wide trail, pass through an open gate, and turn left. The trail gently climbs uphill on slopes above North Cheyenne Creek

Looking down North Cheyenne Cañon to the Broadmoor Hotel and Colorado Springs from Columbine Trail.

through an open forest of ponderosa pine, Douglas fir, and Gambel or scrub oak before dropping down alongside the trickling creek. Hike west on the trail, which widens to an old closed road, passing beneath towering granite cliffs that hem in the lower canyon below Mount Cutler. Rappel Rock, a vertical 100-foot-high cliff, looms directly over the trail.

After a half mile the trail passes some picnic tables by the creek and reaches an old stone bridge, closed with a chain, and a parking area on the opposite side of the bridge. The trail takes a sharp left here and follows a series of tight switchbacks uphill before it levels out. The Pinnacle, a popular granite formation for rock climbers, towers above the trail here. Hike beneath Pinnacle Slab, a low-angle cliff that rises directly above the trail, and continue up the canyon past a boulder that overhangs the trail to Graduation Boulder. This roadside block of granite sits by the road below the trail. It is also a popular spot for local climbers to do boulder problems.

Columbine Trail spirals around the Pinnacle, which lifts tall dark cliffs over head. The sound of the creek filters up through a shady spruce-and-fir forest. After a mile of hiking, the trail reaches another stone bridge and crosses it to the road. Cross at a designated crosswalk and then follow the trail on the opposite side of the creek, with great views of the West Face of the Pinnacle and a high row of cliffs lining Mount Cutler's north flank. Reach the Middle Columbine Trailhead and a large gravel parking area after 1.2 miles.

Columbine Trail continues west from the middle trailhead, which is at a sign on the west side of the parking lot. Many hikers drive to this trailhead to only hike the upper trail section. The 3.1-mile-long upper trail gains lots of elevation along the north side of the canyon and offers great views into the canyon and east toward the Broadmoor Hotel complex.

Begin the Upper Columbine Trail from the middle trailhead, which is at a sign on the west side of the parking lot below Longfellow Pinnacle. The trail gently climbs up switchbacks across gravel slopes shaded by scattered pines, gaining elevation and leaving the road and creek far below. After passing below the Nose, a craggy cliff perched directly above the trail, continue to a switchback above for a great view down canyon to The Pinnacle and its slabby west face.

The gravel trail continues climbing and then leaves the main canyon and enters a shallow side canyon filled with wildflowers in summer and shaded by tall spruce and fir trees and a leafy understory of Gambel oak, skunkbrush, and Rocky Mountain maple trees. Look for columbines, the Colorado state flower, blooming in this moist vale in June and July. After a quarter mile of level hiking, the trail bends sharply left after crossing a trickling creek (only in springtime) fed by Columbine Spring and its junction with Spring Creek Trail. Go right on Spring Creek Trail for 0.2 mile to the Gold Camp Road if you desire. Columbine Trail goes left; follow a trail sign.

After leaving Spring Creek Canyon, the trail begins steadily climbing across steep south-facing slopes high above the narrow canyon floor. A couple of good overlooks offer views down into the canyon. Look for a couple of hidden waterfalls—Bridal Veil and Phantom Falls—alongside the twisting road far below. The trail continues west, threading over gravel slopes about 150 feet below the Gold Camp Road.

The dirt Gold Camp Road follows the old rail bed of the Cripple Creek District Railroad, affectionately called "The Short Line," a narrow-gauge railroad that twisted over 30 miles from a mill at Old Colorado City to the twin towns of Cripple Creek and Victor from 1901 to 1920. The railroad, hauling both passengers and gold ore to and from the "world's richest gold camp," passed through nine tunnels and climbed on an average 3.8 percent grade, making it one of the steepest railroads in the world at that time. After its last train in May, 1920, a Colorado Springs businessman bought the railroad, tore up the tracks, and turned it into the toll Gold Camp Road. You can still drive most of the narrow road except for a closed 7-mile-long section from the top of North Cheyenne Cañon Road to St. Peters Dome. It offers gorgeous views that are still the same as those seen by President Teddy Roosevelt, who called it, in typical theatrical fashion, a trip that "bankrupts the English language."

Columbine Trail levels out and contours across gravelly slopes with great vistas of Mount Muscoco, Stove Mountain, and Mount Rosa. Eventually the trail reaches a high ridgeline and a trail junction. A short spur trail runs 100 yards north to the Gold Camp Road. Jog left on Columbine Trail from the marked junction and walk another 100 feet. The trail descends right onto steep slopes. Before dropping down, however, go left on another short spur and hike out to a couple marvelous rocky points that yield spectacular views down the canyon.

Descend downhill on a series of switchbacks and then follow the trail as it contours east before climbing over another ridgeline. The trail descends into a deep canyon filled with tall fir and spruce trees, offering welcome shade on sunny days. Past the bottom of the canyon and a rocky talus slope, Columbine Trail climbs steadily out of the canyon on its western side, eventually swinging out on a broad gravel ridge. Then the trail gently descends down to the western trailhead on a switchback of the paved road just before Helen Hunt Falls and the Cub Visitor Center, at 4.3 miles from the trailhead.

If you've shuttled a car to the falls parking area, carefully walk down the narrow shoulder of the paved road to your vehicle as well as restrooms. If you haven't seen Helen Hunt Falls before, take a short walk up a trail to a bridge above it. The falls are usually alive and kicking with whitewater in May and June. If you didn't shuttle a car and are hiking out and back, turn around at the trailhead and follow Columbine Trail back to one of the lower trailheads. It's usually a fast and easy hike since it's mostly downhill.

Columbine Trail

## Helen Hunt Jackson

Helen Hunt, called the "greatest poet in America" by Ralph Waldo Emerson, emigrated from New England to Colorado Springs in 1873 for the dry salubrious air. Two years later she married local banker William Sharpless Jackson, but instead of socializing, Helen explored the Pikes Peak region. Over the next few years, she wrote seven books as well as many articles and poems, many about the area as well as Colorado Springs, which she described as "a town lying due east of the great mountains and west of the sun."

In 1879 Helen Hunt Jackson left the Springs for the East with the mission of improving the government's treatment of Native Americans. She wrote *A Century of Dishonor* in 1881 and then her famed novel *Ramona*, a tragic story about a native girl living in California that has been reprinted more than 300 times. She died on August 12, 1885, and was buried at Inspiration Point above Seven Falls in South Cheyenne Cañon, a site she dearly loved. Her family later had her reinterred at Evergreen Cemetery in Colorado Springs.

### MILES AND DIRECTIONS

**0.0** Start at the trailhead behind Starsmore Discovery Center at the mouth of North Cheyenne Cañon (GPS: 38.790972, -104.865602). Hike west on the good trail south of the creek.

**1.2** Reach the Middle Trailhead for Columbine Trail (GPS: 38.791668, -104.879321).

**1.9** Reach Spring Creek Canyon (GPS: 38.794977, -104.886334).

**2.6** Overlook down the canyon to the south of the trail (GPS: 38.791936, -104.893852).

**4.3** End of the trail at a switchback just before Helen Hunt Falls (GPS: 38.788813, -104.901598).

**8.6** Arrive back at the trailhead at Starsmore Discovery Center.

*Option*
A shorter easy hike begins at the Lower Columbine Trailhead at Starsmore Discovery Center and heads west for 1.1 miles to the Middle Columbine Trailhead, where you turn around and return for a pleasant 2.2-mile hike through the rugged lower canyon.

# St. Mary's Falls Trail

*The St. Mary's Falls Trail is a great out-and-back hike that follows the old Gold Camp Road trail before cutting up scenic Buffalo Canyon to a cascading waterfall perched on Stove Mountain above North Cheyenne Cañon. It's a fine half-day hike with great views, moderate grades, and one of the area's best falls.*

**Start:** Top of North Cheyenne Cañon Road above Helen Hunt Falls
**Distance:** 6.4 miles out and back
**Hiking time:** 3 to 5 hours
**Difficulty:** Moderate
**Elevation gain:** 1,490 feet
**Trail surface:** Closed gravel road and singletrack dirt trail
**Seasons:** Year-round. Apr through June are the best months to see the waterfall. Watch for snow and ice in winter.
**Schedule:** Open daily
**Other trail users:** Mountain bikers

**Canine compatibility:** Dogs allowed
**Land status:** USDA Forest Service public land
**Fees and permits:** None
**Map:** USGS Manitou Springs
**Trail contact:** Pike National Forest, Pikes Peak Ranger District, 601 S. Weber St., Colorado Springs, CO 80903; (719) 636-1602; www.fs.usda.gov/psicc
**Special considerations:** Camping is allowed along the trail but you must be 300 feet from any water.

**Finding the trailhead:** From I-25 take exit 140 A or B for South Nevada Avenue. Drive south on South Nevada Avenue for 0.4 mile, turn right (west) on West Cheyenne Road, and drive 2.8 miles to the junction of North Cheyenne Cañon Road (right) and South Cheyenne Cañon Road (left). Go right on North Cheyenne Cañon Road and drive 3.2 miles up the winding paved road, passing Helen Hunt Falls at 2.6 miles. Continue up to a large dirt parking area at the junction of North Cheyenne Cañon Road, Gold Camp Road, and High Drive, and park. The trailhead is on the west side of the parking lot at a metal gate across the closed Gold Camp Road (**GPS:** 38.790707, -104.904071).

# 21

## THE HIKE

The 6.4-mile round-trip hike to St. Mary's Falls follows two trails and is a popular and excellent excursion. It follows the closed section of the Gold Camp Road in North Cheyenne Cañon before heading up Buffalo Canyon to a lovely waterfall that tumbles down a steep granite slab. The hike is best done in spring when snowmelt swells the waterfall.

Begin the hike at a large parking area and trailhead at the top of North Cheyenne Cañon Road where it intersects the Gold Camp Road and High Drive. The lower Gold Camp Road ends at this parking area and the hike follows the closed section of the road west. The trailhead is a large metal gate on the west side of the parking lot.

Hike west for 1.2 miles on the closed Gold Camp Road. This first easy hike section follows a doubletrack gravel road bed, formerly the rail bed of the old Short Line Railroad in the early twentieth century, which gradually gains elevation as it heads west on the north side of the deep canyon. After 0.7 mile the trail makes a wide 180-degree bend to the left and crosses North Cheyenne Creek and the junction with Seven Bridges Trail (#622), which goes west up the floor of the canyon.

The St. Mary's Falls Trail climbs through a pine forest in Buffalo Canyon to the 60-foot-high waterfall.

Continue east on the old Gold Camp Road trail after the bend. The wide trail continues to gain elevation on the south side of the canyon and eventually reaches closed railroad Tunnel #3. The trail leaves the Gold Camp Road here, climbs over the top of the tunnel, and then descends its east side, passing above Silver Cascade Slab, a granite cliff laced with climbing routes.

This point can also be reached from Helen Hunt Falls below by following a short trail up to Silver Cascade Falls and then scrambling up steep rocky slopes to the Gold Camp Road. Because this last section has no trail and is prone to erosion, it is not included in this book as a viable hiking route to access the St. Mary's Falls Trail.

Just past the east side of the closed tunnel and after 1.2 miles, the trail reaches Buffalo Creek and the trailhead for the St. Mary's Falls Trail (#370) at 7,700 feet. This major trail junction can be easily missed if you aren't paying close attention. After passing the tunnel look for tumbling Buffalo Creek on your right and a metal trail sign, which can be hard to spot. This is where the 1.6-mile-long trail to St. Mary's Falls begins (GPS: 38.785765, -104.906579).

Go south on the singletrack St. Mary's Falls Trail up wide Buffalo Canyon. The trail follows Buffalo Creek, passing through a shady forest of pine, spruce, fir, and quaking aspen. The trail and canyon make a gradual bend to the left and begin gaining elevation. Just north of a low saddle, the trail reaches a junction with a short path that passes over the saddle and drops down a short distance to the Gold Camp Road below.

Keep right at this obscure junction and continue up the trail, gradually gaining elevation in Buffalo Canyon. The creek left of the trail riffles over boulders and plunges over numerous short waterfalls. When the trail reaches the first major switchback, take a left on a short path that leads to a pleasant cascading falls. Here the creek slides down a bedrock slab.

Back on the main trail, go right after the switchback and cross a steep hillside to the next switchback, which takes the trail left. After a short distance there is a major trail junction with a metal sign. Go left on the trail for 500 feet to the base of St. Mary's Falls at 8,880 feet. The water sweeps down a wide trough of slabby granite, splashing and dashing for over 60 feet. At the base are some halved logs for crossing boulders when the creek is running high with snowmelt. There is also a metal plaque on a dead tree commemorating Eamon Murphy, who died in 2008 scrambling up 9,782-foot Stove Mountain, the rock-rimmed peak that towers south of the falls. The best time to view the falls is in May when plenty of water feeds it from melting snow on Mount Rosa to the west. Usually it's a mere trickle by midsummer.

**Option:** A right turn at the trail junction leads up a series of switchbacks on the steep mountainside for 0.2 mile to the top of St. Mary's Falls. Here are more great views down the canyon to sprawling Colorado Springs. Be careful at the

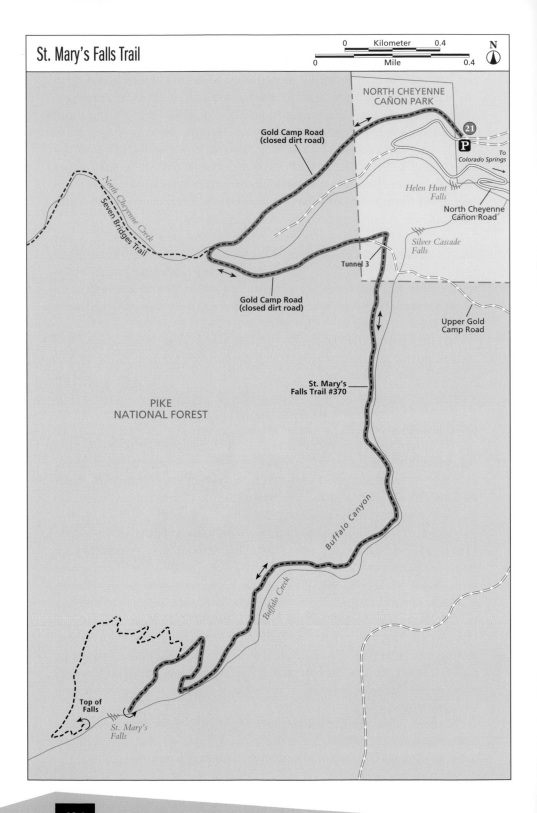

0        Kilometer        0.4

0        Mile        0.4

**N**

NORTH CHEYENNE
CAÑON PARK

Gold Camp Road
(closed dirt road)

21

**P**

To
Colorado Springs

*North Cheyenne Creek*

*Seven Bridges Trail*

*Helen Hunt
Falls*

North Cheyenne
Cañon Road

Tunnel 3

*Silver Cascade
Falls*

Gold Camp Road
(closed dirt road)

Upper Gold
Camp Road

St. Mary's
Falls Trail #370

PIKE
NATIONAL FOREST

*Buffalo Canyon*

*Buffalo Creek*

Top of
Falls

*St. Mary's
Falls*

top because of slick water-polished granite as well as loose rock. The trail continues west from the top of St. Mary's Falls, continuing up Buffalo Canyon and then climbing to the summit of 11,499-foot Mount Rosa, another 3 miles from the top of the falls.

Your hike, however, ends at the falls. Turn around and hike back down the trail to the road and then back along the old Gold Camp Road to the trailhead and your car.

## MILES AND DIRECTIONS

**0.0**  Trailhead at end of North Cheyenne Cañon Road and its junction with Gold Camp Road and High Drive (GPS: 38.790674, -104.90404). Hike west from the parking lot on the closed section of Gold Camp Road.

**0.7**  Reach Seven Bridges Trail, which goes right up the canyon (GPS: 38.786593, 104.914598). Stay on the closed road trail and hike east on the south side of the canyon.

**1.2**  After hiking over closed Tunnel #3, the trail reaches Buffalo Creek and the signed trailhead for St. Mary's Falls Trail (GPS: 38.785734, -104.906613). Go right (south) on the singletrack trail. Pay attention at this junction so that you don't continue hiking east on the road; it's easy to miss the right turn.

**1.5**  Reach a trail junction. The left fork goes over a low saddle and drops down to Gold Camp Road. Keep right on the main trail up Buffalo Canyon.

**3.2**  Reach the base of St. Mary's Falls (GPS: 38.770870, -104.918409). (**Option:** If you continue up the trail to the top of the falls, go back to the junction and left. Hike for 0.2 mile to a viewpoint above the falls [GPS: 38.7706440, -104.9199320].)

**5.2**  Return to Gold Camp Road and go left on the closed road.

**6.4**  Arrive back at the trailhead and parking area.

# Gray Back Peak Trail

*This trail ends with great views from the summit of 9,288-foot Gray Back Peak on the southern edge of the Pikes Peak massif. The off-the-beaten-track hike offers moderate grades, is family friendly, and travels through pine, spruce, and aspen, providing lots of solitude and a real wilderness experience.*

**Start:** Gray Back Peak Trailhead on FR 371

**Distance:** 3.8 miles out and back

**Hiking time:** 2.5 to 3 hours

**Difficulty:** Moderate

**Elevation gain:** 538 feet

**Trail surface:** Singletrack dirt path

**Seasons:** Year-round. Apr through Nov is best. Trail can be icy and snow-covered in winter.

**Schedule:** Open daily

**Other trail users:** Horses on first section of trail. Occasional mountain bikers.

**Canine compatibility:** Dogs allowed

**Land status:** Pike National Forest

**Fees and permits:** None

**Map:** USGS Mount Big Chief quad

**Trail contact:** Pike National Forest, Pikes Peak Ranger District, 601 S. Weber St., Colorado Springs, CO 80903; (719) 636-1602; www.fs.usda.gov/psicc

**Special considerations:** Bring water; none is available on the trail. Get off the summit during thunderstorms.

**Finding the trailhead:** From I-25 take the Circle Drive exit (exit 138) and drive west on Circle Drive, which becomes Lake Avenue at its junction with CO 115. Continue west on Lake Avenue until it dead-ends at the Broadmoor Hotel. Turn right on Lake Circle and drive a quarter mile to a roundabout. Turn left at the roundabout on Mesa Avenue and follow it around the west side of the Broadmoor Hotel and golf course. At a four-way intersection, go left on El Pomar Road and drive up it to an angling right turn onto Old Stage Road. Follow the steep paved road until it turns to gravel at a sharp switchback. Continue up the twisting gravel road for about 6 miles to FR 371 at a sign for Emerald Valley Ranch. Turn left on FR 371 and drive 0.3 mile on the narrow road to a saddle. Park in a sloping parking area on the left that fits three vehicles (**GPS:** 38.731464, -104.906657). Use caution driving on Old Stage Road as it's steep, often busy with traffic, dusty, and can be muddy, icy, and slippery.

## THE HIKE

The Gray Back Peak Trail offers a marvelous backcountry hike that climbs to the rocky summit of 9,288-foot Gray Back Peak, a high peak on the southeast edge of the Pikes Peak massif. The summit yields great views of Emerald Valley to the west, Cheyenne Mountain to the northeast, and the brown plains below, stretching east toward Kansas. The gravel trail has generally moderate grades and is easy to follow. The first half of the trail is often used by horses from The Ranch at Emerald Valley so it is worn and eroded in places.

Begin from the parking area in the saddle at 8,750 feet. The trailhead is unmarked. Hike southeast on a narrow trail, slowly climbing up the western

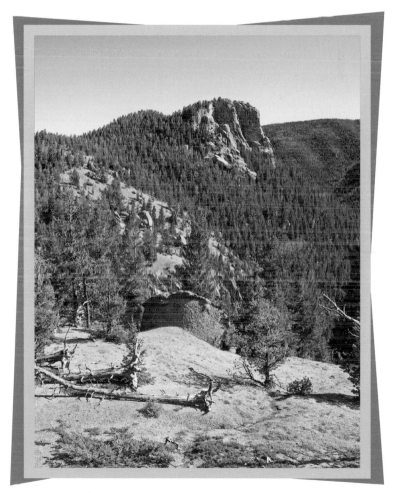

The Wicked Cliffs form a vertical bastion on the west side of Gray Back Peak.

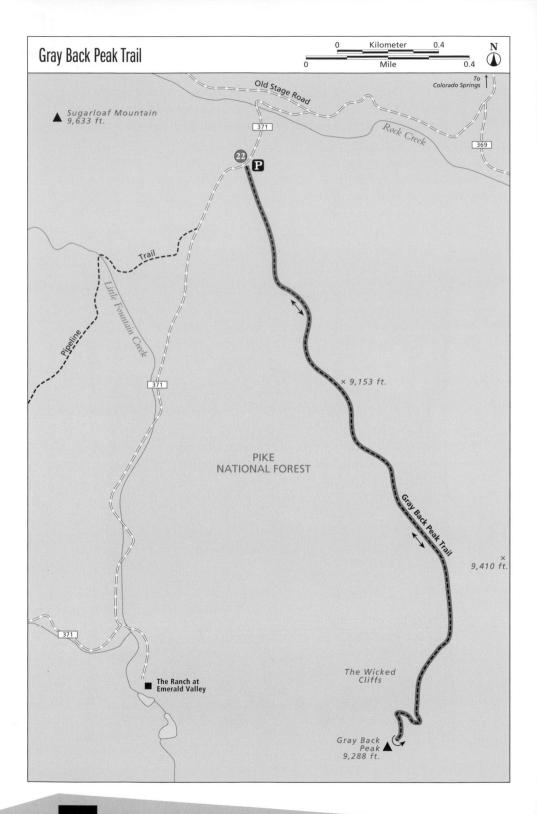

Gray Back Peak Trail

0 Kilometer 0.4
0 Mile 0.4

N

Old Stage Road

To
Colorado Springs

Sugarloaf Mountain
9,633 ft.

371

Rock Creek

369

22

P

Trail

Little Fountain Creek

Pipeline

371

× 9,153 ft.

PIKE
NATIONAL FOREST

Gray Back Peak Trail

×
9,410 ft.

371

The Wicked
Cliffs

The Ranch at
Emerald Valley

Gray Back
Peak
9,288 ft.

slope of a ridge. After 0.3 mile of steady uphill hiking, the trail passes a saddle and continues up the slope onto a broad ridge. At 0.7 mile you reach a 9,153-foot summit. It's a good spot to take a break and catch your breath. Check out the great views to the northwest of the abrupt cliffs on the east side of Mount Vigil.

Descend the loose gravel trail on the broad ridge to a saddle, then climb the ridge to a wooded knoll and drop down to a saddle at 1.3 miles. Take note of the trail junction at this saddle. A horse path continues up left, while the Gray Back Peak Trail goes sharply right (south). A cairn (stack of rocks) usually marks this junction. The next section from here to the summit offers excellent hiking through quiet woods on a good narrow trail.

Hike south on west-facing slopes with open views across Emerald Valley, and after 1.6 miles reach a high saddle between Gray Back Peak to the right and Peak 9,410, an unnamed and higher summit, to the left. Dense aspens interspersed with fir and spruce blanket the saddle. The trail heads south from the saddle, rising and switchbacking up the peak's steep east flank. After 1.9 miles of hiking, you finally emerge onto the airy 9,288-foot-high summit of Gray Back Peak.

Relax in the shade of twisted trees on the summit and enjoy the views. Below are sharp, remote canyons on the southern edge of the Front Range, and in the distance to the south rise the dark bulk of the Wet Mountains and the distant twin Spanish Peaks.

To return to the trailhead, follow the trail back down to the saddle then north to the trail junction. Remember to go left. You'll have a couple hills to climb on your way back to the parking area.

## MILES AND DIRECTIONS

**0.0** Start from the trailhead on the east side of the dirt road (GPS: 38.731474, -104.906631).

**0.7** Reach the rounded summit of the first hill.

**1.1** The trail reaches the second summit. Look south for some great views of Gray Back Peak to the south.

**1.3** Descend down to a wooded saddle and trail junction. Keep right on the main trail.

**1.6** Reach a saddle between Gray Back Peak and unnamed Peak 9,410.

**1.9** Follow switchbacks up the eastern face to the summit of Gray Back Peak (GPS: 38.7114, -104.8999).

**3.8** Arrive back at the trailhead via the same route.

# Emerald Valley Pipeline Trail

*The Pipeline Trail follows the old pipeline that carried water from Penrose-Rosemount Reservoir to the Broadmoor Hotel along the north side of Emerald Valley, a hidden valley on the south side of the Pikes Peak massif. The out-and-back hike is pleasant, passing through forest and meadows with minimal elevation gain.*

**Start:** Parking area on right side of FR 371 off Old Stage Road

**Distance:** 5.8 miles out and back

**Hiking time:** 2 to 3 hours

**Difficulty:** Moderate

**Elevation gain:** 175 feet total

**Trail surface:** Singletrack dirt trail

**Seasons:** Year-round. Apr through Nov is best. The trail may be icy in winter.

**Other trail users:** Mountain bikers, horseback riders

**Canine compatibility:** Leashed dogs only

**Land status:** USDA Forest Service public land

**Fees and permits:** None

**Schedule:** Open daily

**Map:** USGS Mount Big Chief

**Trail contact:** Pike National Forest, Pikes Peak Ranger District, 601 S. Weber St., Colorado Springs, CO 80903; (719) 636-1602; www .fs.usda.gov/psicc

**Special considerations:** Stay on the designated trail. Trail can be icy in winter; use caution and wear micro-spikes as needed.

**Finding the trailhead:** From I-25 take the Circle Drive exit (exit #138) and drive west on Circle Drive, which becomes Lake Avenue at its junction with CO 115. Continue west on Lake Avenue until it dead-ends at a roundabout at the Broadmoor Hotel. Turn right on Lake Circle and drive 0.25 mile to a roundabout. Turn left on Mesa Avenue and follow it around the west side of the Broadmoor Hotel and golf course. At a four-way intersection, go left on El Pomar Road and drive to an angling right turn onto Old Stage Road. Follow the steep paved road until it turns to gravel at a sharp switchback. Continue up the twisting gravel road for 6.25 miles to FR 371 at a sign for Emerald Valley Ranch. Turn left on FR 371 and drive 0.3 mile on the narrow road to a saddle (parking for Gray Back Peak Trail). Park in a small area on the right just past the saddle. The trailhead is 0.1 mile down the road on the right (**GPS:** 38.731474, -104.906631). Use caution driving on Old Stage Road as it's steep, often busy with traffic, dusty, and can be muddy, icy, and slippery.

## THE HIKE

The Pipeline Trail, sometimes called Emerald Valley Trail so it's not confused with another Pipeline Trail in North Cheyenne Cañon, is one of the best unknown hikes in the Pikes Peak region. The trail is close to the city, and the trailhead is relatively easy to reach from the Old Stage Road on the south side of the Pikes Peak massif.

The trail follows an old pipeline so it has minimal elevation gain. The singletrack path is generally wide and easy to follow as it threads across steep dry drainages and open wooded slopes on the northern edge of broad Emerald Valley. It's a perfect family hike on a summer afternoon when wildflowers dapple meadows or in early October when golden aspens blaze across mountain slopes.

To access the trailhead and hike, drive up the dirt Old Stage Road, a rough road that accesses the Broadmoor Stables, Emerald Valley Ranch, and the Gold Camp Road, which continues west to Cripple Creek. The road is sometimes busy, steep in places, and may be a rough washboard. Take your time driving and watch for cars on blind corners. The road is usually snowpacked and icy in winter; a four-wheel-drive vehicle is recommended in winter conditions.

Begin the hike by walking 0.1 mile down the dirt road from the parking area to the 8,618-foot trailhead on the right. Look for an exposed 10-inch metal pipe—the pipeline—in the trail. If you walk down the road to Emerald Valley

The Pipeline Trail traverses along the north side of Emerald Valley beneath Mount Vigil and San Luis Peak.

Ranch, now a Broadmoor Hotel property called The Ranch at Emerald Valley, you've gone too far.

The historic Emerald Valley Ranch area below the Pipeline Trail was the site of a sawmill in the late 1800s. Later it was an Episcopal retreat and Girl Scout camp before Spencer Penrose, founder of the Broadmoor, bought the property and used it as Camp Vigil for his friends. Later the ranch belonged to the City of Colorado Springs and was used by groups like the YMCA and the Boy Scouts. It was turned into a dude ranch in 1946 and operated until the Broadmoor bought it in 2011 and turned it into an exclusive retreat with expensive cabins.

Hike west on the mostly level trail, following a trail alongside an old pipeline. The pipeline, which delivered water from Penrose-Rosemount Reservoir to the Broadmoor Hotel below, was built around 1920. Just past the trailhead the trail swings past the wooden ruins of an old mine. Continue another 0.3 mile to a trail junction at Little Fountain Creek. Keep straight on the Pipeline Trail. This area around Cather Springs does have some private property so stay on the trail to avoid trespassing.

The right turn follows a rough trail for a half mile up the steep draw to Bear Trap Ranch and on to Mount Vigil, the prominent peak above that's ringed by tall granite cliffs. Some historians believe that this draw was descended by Lieutenant Zebulon Pike and his band of merry men when they retreated down to the prairie below after failing to climb his namesake mountain in November 1806.

The hike continues west on the Pipeline Trail, which dips in and out of shallow dry drainages and edges across steep gravel slopes. Broken granite cliffs loom above the trail. A stone wall composed of jumbled moss-covered boulders borders the pipeline and trail in places. Douglas fir and Engelmann spruce fill cool, shady vales while ponderosa pines spread across sunny well-drained slopes.

Emerald Valley, drained by an unnamed tributary of Little Fountain Creek, is bounded on the north by a high ridge of rocky mountains. Mount Vigil, an unranked 10,073-foot peak surrounded by tall cliffs, anchors the eastern edge of the ridge. In the middle of the ridge are 10,433-foot San Luis Peak and 10,450-foot Mount McKinley, while 10,490-foot Knight's Peak is at the west end above Penrose-Rosemount Reservoir.

After 1.8 miles, as the valley begins narrowing, the trail crosses a stone bridge and at 2.4 miles intersects FR 371 (which may be closed), a rough road that runs west up the valley from the ranch, at the site of the old Emerald Valley Boys Camp. Little remains of the camp except a stone fireplace from a now-vanished building and several foundations. Continue west on the trail, now following the four-wheel-drive road west up the valley.

The valley floor is open, with grassy meadows and groves of quaking aspen along a trickling creek. After 2.9 miles the trail reaches several beaver ponds. This is the turnaround point for this out-and-back hike. It is possible to continue

Emerald Valley Pipeline Trail

hiking west up the old road, which eventually becomes a rough trail that passes over a saddle southwest of Knight's Peak, descends down into East Beaver Creek's valley, and then climbs back northwest to the Gold Camp Road. Return to the trailhead and your vehicle by following the trail back east, making a 5.8-mile round-trip hike.

## MILES AND DIRECTIONS

**0.0** Parking lot on the right side of FR 371. Walk down the road to the trailhead (GPS: 38.731474, -104.906631).

**0.1** The trailhead is on the right side of FR 371. Look for a pipe with a concrete cover at the trailhead. After a couple hundred feet, you will hike past an abandoned mine.

**0.4** Pass a junction with a gravel road.

**0.5** Cross Little Fountain Creek to a trail junction. Continue straight ahead.

**1.0** Cross a dry creek bed and drainage.

**1.2** Cross a dry creek bed and drainage.

**1.4** Intersect a trail that goes left to the road. Continue straight.

**1.8** Cross an old stone bridge.

**2.4** Junction with FR 371. Continue straight on the trail.

**2.9** Reach beaver ponds on the left and the turnaround point. Turn around and hike back to the trailhead. The trail continues west from here, wrapping around Point 10,490, also called Squires, to the Gold Camp Road.

**5.8** Arrive back at the trailhead on FR 371.

# Beaver Creek Loop Trail

*The Beaver Creek Loop Trail, which actually follows three different trails, is one of the best and most rugged hikes in the Pikes Peak region. The hike follows deep canyons, climbs steep slopes and ridges, yields spectacular views, and offers wildlife viewing.*

**Start:** Trailhead on east side of parking area at the end of Fremont County Road 132

**Distance:** 7.0-mile lollipop

**Hiking time:** 4 to 7 hours

**Difficulty:** Moderate. Trail is steep in places and has uneven rocky footing. At least 1 creek crossing.

**Elevation gain:** Over 2,000 feet total

**Trail surface:** Double- and single-track dirt and rock trail

**Seasons:** Year-round. The trail has snow and ice in winter. Bring micro-spikes. In spring the creek runs high and may be very difficult to cross.

**Schedule:** Open daily

**Other trail users:** None

**Canine compatibility:** Dogs allowed, but the trail is not dog friendly since much of the trail surface is chip rock and hard on your dog's paws.

**Land status:** Beaver Creek State Wildlife Area (Colorado Division of Wildlife) and Beaver Creek Wilderness Study Area (Bureau of Land Management)

**Fees and permits:** None

**Map:** USGS Phantom Canyon

**Trail contacts:** Colorado Parks and Wildlife, 1313 Sherman St., 6th Floor, Denver, CO 80203; (303) 297-1192; http://cpw.state.co.us. Also Bureau of Land Management, Royal Gorge Field Office, 3028 E. Main St., Canon City, CO 81212; (719) 269-8500; www.blm.gov/co/st/en/fo/rgfo.html.

**Special considerations:** This hike is fairly strenuous, requires at least a half day to hike, and is not recommended for beginners since the terrain is rough and it is possible to get lost. The trail can be hot in summer so carry plenty of water, use sunscreen, and wear a hat. Rattlesnakes are often seen on the trail at lower elevations; be alert for snakes under rocks and in bushes off the ground alongside the trail. A couple of mandatory creek crossings are found on lower Beaver Creek. Use extreme caution when crossing, especially in spring when runoff is high and after heavy thunderstorms in the canyons to the north.

**Finding the trailhead:** Drive south from Colorado Springs on CO 115 toward Penrose and US 50. On the north side of Penrose, make a right (west) turn on Third Street / Fremont County Road 123 (signed "Brush Hollow Reservoir"). Drive west for 5.5 miles to Fremont County Road 132 and turn right (north). Follow this gravel road northwest for 12.5 miles to a parking lot at the end of the road (**GPS:** 38.570387, -105.012364). The trailhead is on the east side of the large parking lot. The last few miles of Road 132 can be muddy and impassable in winter and spring.

## THE HIKE

The Beaver Creek Loop Trail is a 7.0-mile lollipop hike that explores three remote and hidden canyons tucked into the southern slope of the Pikes Peak massif southwest of Colorado Springs. This excellent hike follows three trails—Beaver Creek, Trail Gulch, and Powerline—and traverses a variety of terrain, including hills covered with scattered piñon pine and juniper, steep craggy mountains, and two rugged canyons lined with granite cliffs that were carved by East and West Beaver Creeks.

The creeks and their canyons form the foundation of a proposed 28,069-acre wilderness area, which the Bureau of Land Management (BLM) designated as a wilderness study area in the 1980s. The BLM determined that the area met the criteria for federally protected wilderness but Congress has left it in limbo and not yet officially preserved what is the closest true wilderness to Colorado Springs. The rough, roadless terrain offers superb wilderness values. A 1987 environmental-impact statement said Beaver Creek "allows excellent opportunities for an individual to escape the sights and sounds of man."

The extreme ruggedness of the Beaver Creek canyons provides great opportunities for solitude and outdoor recreation, including hiking, backpacking, fishing, rock climbing, horseback riding, and wildlife study. The BLM estimates annual visitation to the study area is between 7,000 and 10,000 people a year.

Beaver Creek is a prime wildlife area, one of the best in Colorado. A study shows the area is home to over 7,000 mule deer, 300 bighorn sheep, and 1,200 turkeys, as well as black bears, foxes, beavers, cutthroat trout, falcons, rattlesnakes, and the largest population of mountain lions in Colorado. Biologists estimate that the area has a lion population of one cat per 5 square miles, compared to one lion per 10 to 20 square miles on other BLM lands in southern Colorado.

Begin the hike at the trailhead on the east side of the parking lot. Walk through an opening in a fence to a kiosk to your left that has a map of the wilderness study area. On the right side of the trail is another kiosk with three panels that interpret Beaver Creek Wilderness Study Area, riparian habitats, and area wildlife.

Continue east along a fence line next to a closed road for 500 feet to a fork. Keep left and hike down and across sandy Banta Gulch. The wide trail bends sharply left below a bluff and edges along the east side of a wide tallgrass meadow in flat bottomlands along Beaver Creek.

After 0.8 mile the trail reaches another fork with an old road going left along the creek and a broad trail that heads right. Take the right fork, which stays above the creek. The left fork stays low and requires several fords farther upstream. This route description makes a counterclockwise loop by following first the Trail Gulch Trail, climbing over a high ridge on the old Powerline Trail, and then following the Beaver Creek Trail back to this point. A wooden sign at the junction points left to "Creek" and right to "Trail." Go right and walk 50 feet to a colorful sign that introduces you to Beaver Creek State Wildlife Area and includes a map.

The 2,228-acre state wildlife area, lying mostly within the wilderness study area, is a long, thin property along West Beaver Creek from Skaguay Reservoir (9,206 feet) near Victor to the parking area at the lower mouth of Beaver Creek (5,720 feet).

Follow the right fork across a meadow on the right side of the valley, then ascend a stony hill on the wide trail to a sloping meadow studded with junipers

A hiker walks on Beaver Creek Trail below the junction of East and West Beaver Creeks.

and piñon pines. The trail passes under a rustic gateway of old juniper logs and descends to the wilderness study-area boundary, marked by a sign at a mile.

Continue downhill into Trail Gulch and a trail junction above the trickling creek. This is the start of the Beaver Creek Loop. The trail coming up from the creek to the left is the way you will return to this point. A sign here points west to "Beaver Creek" and south to "Parking Lot." Continue straight on the Trail Gulch Trail. This next trail segment is just over a mile long and gains over 400 feet to the junction with the Powerline Trail.

The trail follows the cliff-lined canyon northwest, threading along the narrow canyon floor. The lower part of the canyon is dry and rocky with scattered piñon and juniper and tall cottonwoods shading the creek. During wet seasons you make numerous boulder-hops, with as many as 20 crossings depending on the water level, across the creek as the trail gently climbs up the canyon. Eventually the canyon loses the cliffs and begins to widen.

The singletrack trail crosses meadows of wavering grasses, passes through open ponderosa pine forest, and after 2 miles reaches a junction with the Powerline Trail marked by a small cairn and a sign. This is a good place to sit down and have a sip of water and a snack. The next hike segment up the Powerline Trail climbs over 1,000 feet to the hike high point in 1.7 miles. Trail Gulch Trail itself continues up the canyon a few more miles to Rosemount Reservoir and the Gold Camp Road.

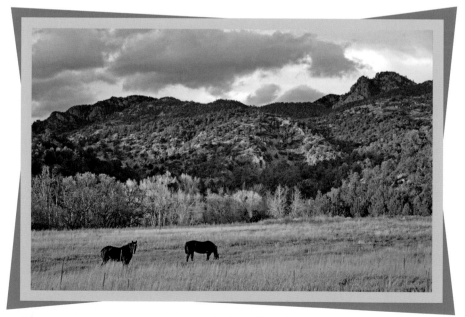

Horses graze in a broad meadow along Beaver Creek near the trailhead.

Go left from the junction on the Powerline Trail. The narrow gravel trail quickly gains elevation, switching back and forth on a blunt ridge. After a steep half mile, you can catch a breather at a good viewpoint that looks north up Trail Gulch. Continue up the trail to the top of the first summit, a rocky outcrop that allows a view down Trail Gulch to the parking lot and your vehicle to the south. Beyond are the wooded Wet Mountains and the ragged snowcapped Sangre de Cristo Mountains.

After 3 miles the trail reaches its high point, an open spot on a high ridge. If you want a close look at an old power-line pole erected some one hundred years ago, go right up the ridge a hundred yards to the double-trunked pole with two crossbeams. Broken glass insulators are on the ground below the power line.

From the ridgeline and high point, the narrow trail descends a steep mile, losing some 1,200 feet, to East Beaver Creek. The trail makes a series of wide switchbacks down the steep west side of the ridge, crossing gravel slopes dense with scrub oak thickets and a mixed woodland of ponderosa pine and Douglas fir on the shady north-facing mountainsides.

Eventually the slope eases and the trail easily descends down a draw, passing a small waterfall, until it reaches a trail junction marked with a cairn. This is the end of the Powerline Trail. Just below are the remains of an old prospector's cabin and an overlook just above East Beaver Creek. This is a good stopping point for a snack. You can scramble down to the creek to the right here if you want. The confluence of East and West Beaver Creeks and their deep canyons is a few hundred feet downstream.

The next 2 miles of the hike, following the Beaver Creek Trail, is simply spectacular, with soaring granite cliffs decorating the mountainsides and the roaring creek dashing through the walled canyon below the trail. At the trail junction go left (south) on Beaver Creek Trail from the Powerline Trail. The trail climbs through fir and scrub oak, then edges across steep dry slopes with cacti and grass above cliffs that drop down to the inner canyon and the creek.

The trail dips across dry ravines and rolls across hillsides before descending down to Beaver Creek. The trail parallels the creek, crossing rounded boulders before climbing back up slopes above the cliff-lined creek in the lower canyon. After 5.5 miles the trail reaches a 100-foot-high cliff that blocks progress. The creek bends right beneath the right side of the cliff, forming a deep pool.

In dry conditions you can traverse across the rock face above the pool, making few tenuous climbing moves to finish. Don't attempt it, however, if the water is high or you're unsure of your footing since a fall would be dangerous. Instead, look for a crossing farther upstream where the creek is shallower and wider. If the creek is full in springtime, be sure to find a sturdy pole to lean against in the current when you cross.

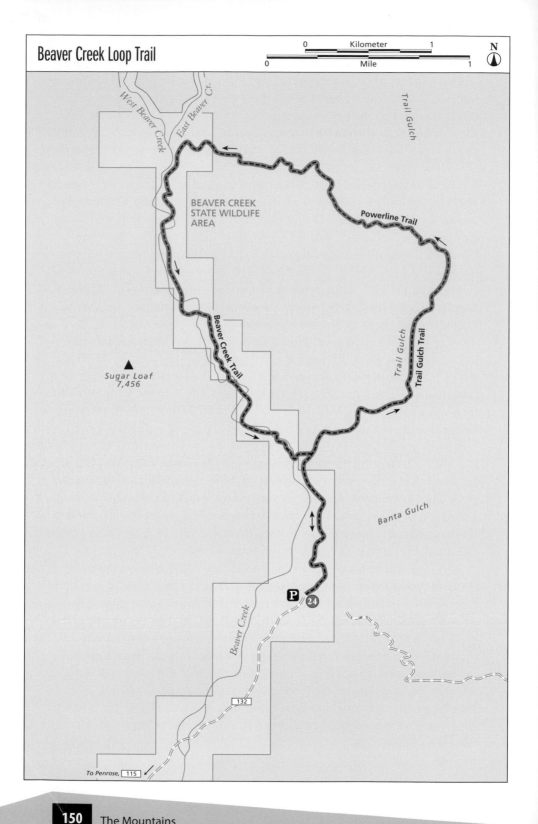

# Beaver Creek Loop Trail

0 Kilometer 1

0 Mile 1

N

BEAVER CREEK
STATE WILDLIFE
AREA

West Beaver Creek

East Beaver Cr.

Trail Gulch

Powerline Trail

Beaver Creek Trail

Sugar Loaf
7,456

Trail Gulch

Trail Gulch Trail

Banta Gulch

P 24

Beaver Creek

132

To Penrose, 115

Past the crossing, the trail climbs onto a flat ridge and crosses a short-grass meadow spiked with cholla cacti. It then edges shelf-like across a steep slope that drops directly down to the creek below and finishes by descending into lower Trail Gulch. Scramble up the south side of the canyon to the junction at the beginning of the loop at 6 miles. Go right (south) at the wooden sign that says "Parking Lot" and continue on the Beaver Creek Trail.

The last trail section retraces your original footsteps from the trail junction for 1 mile back to your vehicle in the parking lot.

## MILES AND DIRECTIONS

**0.0** Start at the trailhead on the east side of the parking area (GPS: 38.570727, -105.011986) and hike east on a closed road. After about 500 feet, reach a fork in the closed road. Go left (GPS: 38.571896, -105.010555).

**0.5** Reach another major fork. Go right on the wide Beaver Creek Trail (GPS: 38.573824, -105.01125). The left fork follows the creek north.

**0.9** Boundary of the Beaver Creek Wilderness Study Area.

**1.0** Junction of Beaver Creek Trail, which goes left up the canyon, and Trail Gulch Trail (GPS: 38.57980, -105.01167). Go right and head northeast up Trail Gulch Trail.

**2.0** Reach the junction with Powerline Trail (GPS: 38.59245, -105.00043). Go left on Powerline Trail and climb steeply uphill.

**3.7** Trail reaches the top of a ridgeline and the high point of the hike (GPS: 38.59776, -105.01090).

**4.7** Descend steeply down west-facing slopes and reach the bottom of the trail and the junction with Beaver Creek Trail (GPS: 38.59966, -105.02203). Go left on Beaver Creek Trail on slopes above and along the east side of Beaver Creek.

**6.0** Reach the junction with Trail Gulch Trail and the end of the hike's loop. Go right on Beaver Creek Trail and follow back to the trailhead.

**7.0** End the hike at the trailhead and parking area.

# Red Mountain Trail

*The Red Mountain Trail climbs 800 feet from Ruxton Avenue on the west side of Manitou Springs to the 7,361-foot-high summit of Red Mountain, a spur peak that rises directly over the picturesque town. The hike follows a good trail with easy grades to the remains of a long-abandoned incline railway and summit house and offers spectacular views of Manitou, Ute Pass, the Garden of the Gods, and Pikes Peak.*

**Start:** Iron Springs Trailhead by Iron Springs Chateau in Manitou Springs

**Distance:** 3.0 miles out and back

**Hiking time:** 1 to 2 hours

**Difficulty:** Moderate

**Elevation gain:** 800 feet

**Trail surface:** Double- and single-track dirt

**Seasons:** Year-round but best hiking is Mar through Nov. Icy in winter.

**Schedule:** Open daily

**Other trail users:** Mountain bikers on lower Intemann Trail; runners

**Canine compatibility:** Dogs permitted

**Fees and permits:** None

**Map:** USGS Manitou Springs

**Trail contact:** Manitou Springs Chamber of Commerce and Visitors Bureau, 354 Manitou Ave., Manitou Springs, CO 80829; (719) 685-5089 or (800) 642-2567; manitousprings.org

**Finding the trailhead:** The hike begins at the Iron Springs Trailhead by Iron Springs Chateau in Manitou Springs. From Colorado Springs drive west on US 24 and exit onto Manitou Avenue. This is the first Manitou exit on US 24. Drive west on Manitou Avenue to a roundabout and turn left onto Ruxton Avenue, following signs for the Pikes Peak Cog Railway. Follow Ruxton until it splits into a one-way road to the Cog Railway depot and a one-way street back to Manitou Avenue. Follow the right road to the depot and make a U-turn left onto the return one-way street. Find a place to park here or along the right side of Ruxton Avenue. The Iron Springs Trailhead for the Intemann Trail is on the right just before Ruxton becomes two-way (**GPS:** 38.857289, -104.927498).

## THE HIKE

Red Mountain, a low peak rising above Manitou Springs' south side, offers a great hike to a lofty lookout and great views of Manitou. Despite the mountain's steep slopes, the singletrack trail wends to the peak's 7,361-foot summit with gradual gentle grades that switchback across the steepest slopes. Besides fun hiking and great views, Red Mountain also offers a surprise ending—the abandoned concrete foundations of an old restaurant, casino, and summit house of an incline railway that, like neighboring Mount Manitou Incline, once carried tourists to the top.

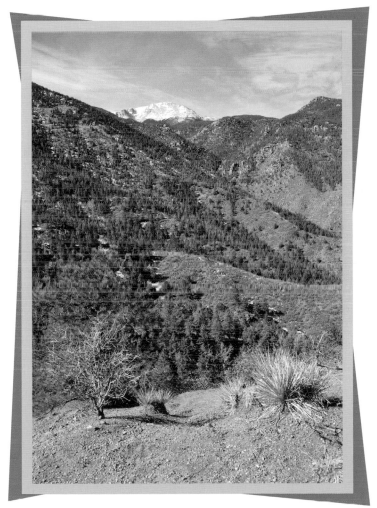

Pikes Peak and Engelmann Canyon lie west of Red Mountain's summit.

**25**

Begin your Red Mountain adventure at the Iron Springs Trailhead next to Ruxton Avenue below the Pikes Peak Cog Railway station and the Iron Springs Chateau. After finding a parking spot on either Ruxton Avenue or Iron Springs Road, which can be a problem during the busy summer tourist season, hike east on a trail along the south side of Ruxton Creek past the Iron Springs, a mineral spring under a pavilion on the north bank of the creek. Continue down the trail to Spring Road and turn right.

Walk up the dirt road to a gate and pass onto the Intemann Trail. The first half-mile segment of this hike follows the Intemann Trail, an incomplete trail that contours east above Manitou Springs to the Section 16 Trail above the Gold Camp Road. The trail is named for Paul Intemann, a Manitou Springs city planner who envisioned a network of trails above Manitou. He was killed in a car accident in New Mexico in 1986.

Follow the trail, a closed road that doubles as a fire road, up a draw, around a blunt ridge, and up a broad vale toward a couple of power poles. Look to the right before the poles for a sign marking the start of the Red Mountain Trail. This 1-mile spur trail, built by volunteers in 1999 and 2001, is on a swathe of Manitou Springs Open Space land.

Turn right (south) and hike up the Red Mountain Trail, which slowly climbs southwest in a mixed conifer forest of ponderosa pine and Douglas fir left of a steep ravine. Follow the trail as it switchbacks up the steep slope until it swings left and climbs to a saddle on a wooded ridgeline. This is the official end of the trail but not the hike.

Go left at the saddle and continue up the rocky trail, which threads above the steep eastern flank of Red Mountain. After gaining 50 more feet of elevation, the trail ends on the mountain's flat summit.

The spacious summit of 7,361-foot-high Red Mountain offers wonderful views. Below nestles Manitou Springs, with houses lining its hilly roads. The distant sounds of traffic, barking dogs, and music filters upward. To the east rise the red rocks at Garden of the Gods, and beyond spreads the distant prairie horizon. The westward view is spectacular. Pikes Peak rears high above. Lower are the pinnacles Gog and Magog perched on a long wooded ridge on the north slope of Cameron Cone.

The top of Red Mountain, however, is not just about great views. If you look around, you'll see the old concrete foundations of several buildings erected here in the early twentieth century. The Red Mountain Incline Railway, which competed with the nearby Mount Manitou Incline Railway, ferried visitors up the mountain's steep northeast face. The lower concrete footings mark where the railway ended and visitors disembarked. The upper foundations are the site of a restaurant, bar, and dance hall where both live music and whiskey flowed. Some

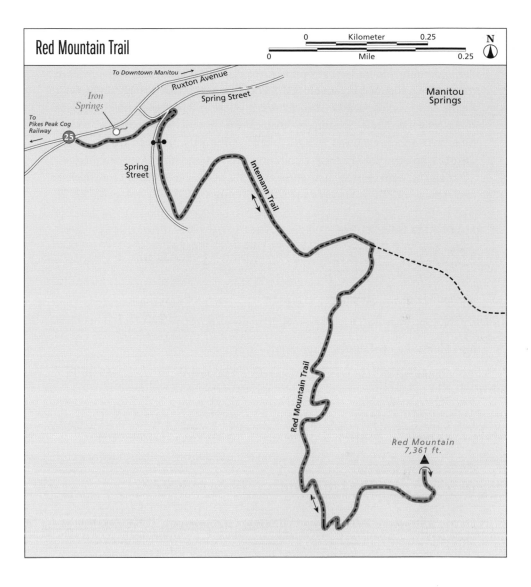

even say it was a casino and a gentleman's club, a polite way of saying it was a brothel, but that's just rumor.

Before the railway, the summit of Red Mountain was a gravesite. In the late nineteenth century, Manitou Springs was a healing place for tuberculosis patients who journeyed west for dry air and its healing mineral springs. A young lady named Emma Crawford came for the cure in 1889 but died on December 4, 1891, at the age of 19. She once hiked to the summit, where she had a vision and left a scarf tied on a tree by her chosen burial plot.

After Emma's death, her fiancé and twelve pallbearers carried her coffin up Red Mountain and buried her on the summit. In 1912 the coffin was moved to the south so the incline summit house could be built. After heavy rain in 1929, Emma and her coffin washed down the mountain, spilling her remains. She was reburied in a Manitou cemetery, but many locals say that her ghost still stalks Red Mountain, and some claim to have glimpsed the Victorian-clad specter. Every October Manitou Springs hosts a coffin race in her honor and remembrance.

After brooding on the summit about all this melancholic history, turn around and retrace your steps 1.5 miles back down the trail to the Iron Springs Trailhead.

## MILES AND DIRECTIONS

**0.0**  Trailhead for Paul Intemann Memorial Nature Trail on Ruxton Avenue (GPS: 38.857289, -104.927498).

**0.1**  Junction with Spring Road. Go right.

**0.2**  Junction with road. Go right on Intemann Trail.

**0.5**  Junction with Red Mountain Trail. Go right.

**1.5**  Summit of Red Mountain (GPS: 38.8514, -104.9212).

**2.5**  Return to junction with Intemann Trail. Go left.

**3.0**  Arrive back at the trailhead.

## The Red Mountain Incline Railway

An incline railway, or funicular, ran up the steep north side of Red Mountain to a summit house perched on its rock summit. The Red Mountain Incline Company was built in the first eight months of 1912 and the Red Mountain Scenic Railway opened in late summer. Tickets cost 50 cents round-trip and 25 cents for children. The incline, however, was extremely steep, making it too scary for many riders. Some riders actually refused to ride the incline down, preferring instead to safely hike down from the summit pavilion.

The incline brochure extolled the pleasures of a trip up Red Mountain: "This very experience is for you, yes—and with thrills, yes, but with absolute safety, comfort and pleasure. . . . Unlimited stopover at summit, free pavilion, picnic grounds, 'hike' trips, music, dancing, etc. See the beautiful sunset from the mountaintop." Sounds like fun! The railway, however, only lasted a few years before closing down.

# 26

# Mount Manitou Incline Trail

*The 0.9-mile Mount Manitou Incline Trail, rising directly above Manitou Springs along the abandoned route of a 1907 incline railway, is one of the most popular hikes in the Pikes Peak region. The trail goes straight up the steep mountainside, gaining 2,000 feet in less than a mile with an average grade of 41 percent and a maximum grade of 68 percent. The trail, usually just called "the Incline," offers a strenuous sustained uphill hike to the top of the grade below the summit of 9,250-foot Rocky Mountain and then returns 3.2 miles down gradual grades on Barr Trail to the trailhead for a 4.5-mile loop hike.*

**Start:** North side of Pikes Peak Cog Railway parking lot on west side of Manitou Springs
**Distance:** 4.5-mile loop
**Hiking time:** 1.5 to 3 hours
**Difficulty:** Very strenuous. Do not attempt this trail if you are overweight or have heart or other health problems. It is advisable to consult your doctor before hiking the Incline Trail.
**Elevation gain:** 2,011 feet. Starting elevation is 6,574 feet. Ending elevation is 8,585 feet.
**Trail surface:** Gravel and loose gravel with railroad-tie steps held in place by rebar
**Seasons:** Year-round
**Other trail users:** None
**Canine compatibility:** Dogs not permitted. Dog waste has been a serious problem on the trail.
**Land status:** Owned by 3 different entities. The lower 25 percent is owned by the City of Colorado Springs / Colorado Springs Utilities. The middle 50 percent is owned by the Manitou and Pikes Peak Railway. The upper 25 percent is public land in Pike National Forest.
**Fees and permits:** None
**Schedule:** Open daily, dawn to dusk
**Map:** USGS Manitou Springs
**Trail contact:** Pike National Forest, Pikes Peak Ranger District, 601 S. Weber St., Colorado Springs, CO 80903; (719) 636-1602; www .fs.usda.gov/psicc
**Special considerations:** Use at your own risk. No pets. Practice a No Trace ethic; trash cans are at the trailhead. It is recommended for uphill use only to avoid downhill accidents and trail crowding.

**Finding the trailhead:** To reach the Incline Trailhead from I-25, take the Cimarron Street/US 24 exit and drive west on US 24 for 5.4 miles to the first Manitou Springs exit. The exit ramp circles down to Manitou Avenue. Go west on Manitou Avenue for 1.4 miles, following signs for "Cog Railway." At a roundabout at the junction of Manitou Avenue and Ruxton Avenue, go west on Ruxton and drive 0.7 mile to the cog railway depot. Park at the Barr Trailhead lot farther up Ruxton; along legal parking spaces on Ruxton Avenue; or at a Manitou Springs public parking lot where you can take a free shuttle to the Incline Trailhead in summer. The trailhead is on the north side of the Cog Railway parking lot (**GPS:** 38.856934, -104.931457). Do not park in this lot. It is reserved for cog patrons only and illegally parked vehicles will be towed.

## THE HIKE

The Mount Manitou Incline Trail, which actually ascends 9,250-foot Rocky Mountain, is an almost mile-long trail that climbs straight up the mountainside above Manitou Springs for 2,011 feet with an average grade of 41 percent and a short, steep section of 68 percent. The trail, often called the Incline or the Manitou Incline, is one of the most popular trails in the Pikes Peak region, with more than 350,000 trail users annually.

It's recommended that after you reach the top of the Incline Trail, you descend 3.2 miles down Barr Trail for a 4.5-mile round-trip hike. Descending the Manitou Incline is not only dangerous because of loose gravel footing and rusted pieces of metal rebar anchoring railroad-ties steps, but also because it creates traffic jams and disturbs uphill hikers.

The Incline is often used as a cardio workout by local athletes, including Olympians training at the US Olympic Training Center in Colorado Springs, as well as local soldiers and cadets. The current uphill record belongs to triathlete Mark Fretta, who ran up it in 16 minutes, 42 seconds, while Olympic short-track speed-skating gold medalist Apolo Ohno did it in 17 minutes, 45 seconds. Most hikers do the ascent in 40 to 50 minutes, although many take up to 2 hours to reach the top.

Use caution, however, before attempting to hike up the Incline Trail. A sign at the beginning of the trail reads: "WARNING: This is an EXTREME TRAIL. Consult with your doctor before adding the Incline to your exercise routine. If you need medical attention on the Incline, it could take First Responders over an hour to get to you."

The Mount Manitou Incline Trail began as an incline railway, or funicular, in 1907, that allowed access to a small hydroelectric plant and water pipes at the mountaintop, providing water to Manitou Springs below. The steep railroad and its stunning panoramic views quickly became a tourist attraction, and a summit house was built in 1914 and then remodeled in 1958. The Pikes Peak Cog Railway operated the Incline Railway, which took 16 minutes to climb from base to summit house, during the last decades of the twentieth century, until a flash flood and rock slide erased part of the rail bed. The Cog decided not to make expensive repairs to get the Incline going again.

As the Incline Railway fell into disrepair, dedicated athletes began using its steep, relentless grade for training. One such notable athlete was Matt Carpenter, a Manitou Springs city councilman but also a twelve-time winner of the Pikes Peak Marathon, an up-and-down 26-mile endurance race on Barr Trail.

The Mount Manitou Incline Trail follows a straight-up path on the old grade of an incline railway.

Pike National Forest and some locals wanted to have the railway's scar, a vertical stripe visible from Colorado Springs, rehabilitated and replanted with trees. Also at issue was that the Incline was private property and everyone using it as a hiking workout was trespassing. Eventually several thorny issues regarding the Incline were worked out, mostly regarding parking problems, since many Incline users parked in the private Cog Railway lot, at the small Barr Trail lot, or clogged Manitou city streets, including Ruxton Avenue, below the Incline Trail.

The Incline Trail's legal battles and parking woes were addressed over many years, and in early 2013 the cities of Colorado Springs and Manitou Springs along with the USDA Forest Service reached an agreement to authorize use of the recreational trail. This included a Forest Service Special Use Permit pushed through Congress to abandon the trail corridor as a railroad; make needed safety improvements to the Barr and Incline Trailheads and to improve and stabilize the trail; and create parking management and regulations. The trail officially opened on February 1, 2013.

Parking, not trespassing, is the big problem now for Incline hikers. It's possible to park at the lot for Barr Trail farther west from the trailhead but the lot is

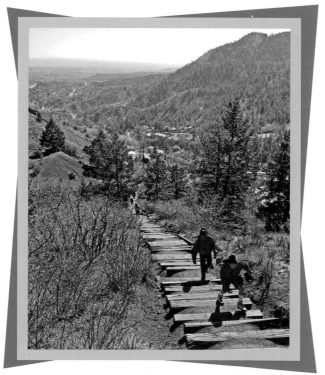

The middle section of the Mount Manitou Incline Trail eases off before the final steep grade.

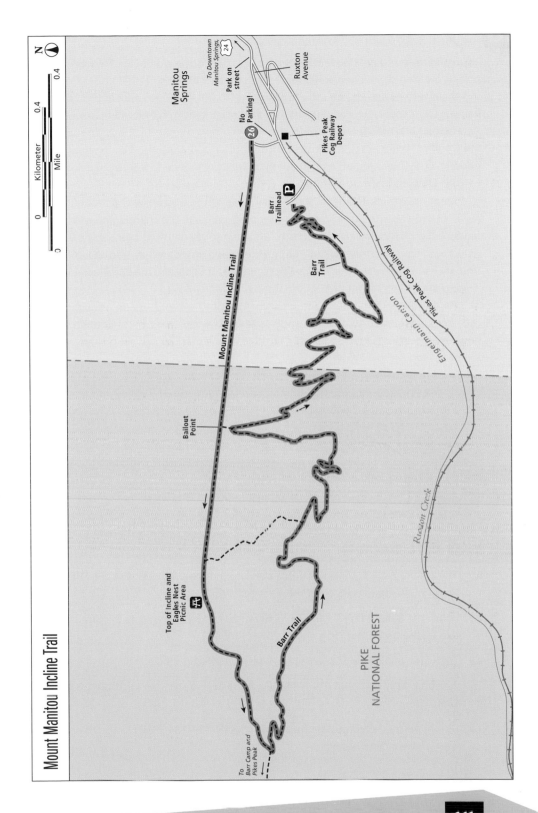

# Mount Manitou Incline Trail

N

Kilometer
0        0.4        0.4

Mile
0        0.4

Manitou Springs

To Downtown Manitou Springs, 24

Ruxton Avenue

Park on street

26 No Parking!

P

Pikes Peak Cog Railway Depot

Barr Trailhead

Barr Trail

Mount Manitou Incline Trail

Pikes Peak Cog Railway

Engelmann Canyon

Bailout Point

Ruxton Creek

Top of Incline and Eagles Nest Picnic Area

Barr Trail

PIKE NATIONAL FOREST

To Barr Camp and Pikes Peak

small and there is a parking fee. Hikers can also park down on Ruxton Avenue or one of the side streets and walk up to the trailhead. Make sure that your parking space is legal and not on private property. Do not, however, park at the Cog Railway lot. It is only for Cog patrons and illegally parked vehicles will be towed. An alternative is to take a free shuttle from downtown Manitou Springs through the summer. It runs every 20 minutes for 12 hours a day, stopping at all the public parking areas (fee charged) then heading up Ruxton Avenue to a drop-off at Iron Springs Chateau below the trailhead.

From the Incline Trailhead at the north side of the Cog Railway parking lot (GPS: 38.856934, -104.931457), begin stepping upward. The trail begins with a gradual climb that quickly steepens to an average grade of 40 percent. At 0.6 mile the trail reaches the Bailout Point, where you can exit left a short distance from Incline Trail to Barr Trail. You can descend Barr Trail back to the Barr Trailhead if you don't feel up to completing the steeper section above.

Past the Bailout the trail continues steeply with an abrupt grade of 68 percent before angling back to what appears to be the top. Don't be discouraged, however, since this is a false summit. Continue to one more steep section and the top of the Incline Trail. Woohoo!

While you catch your breath and have a drink of water, enjoy the spectacular views across the mountains and Manitou Springs tucked in the valley far below. You earned each of the 2,000 steps of that 2,000-foot elevation gain.

Now it's time to head back down. Descending back down the Incline Trail is discouraged since the steep trail, with a loose gravel surface in places, is dangerous. Instead make it a loop hike by following a steep social trail down south to Barr Trail and descending it back to the base. Alternatively you can hike west on Eagle's Nest Trail from the Incline summit to a trail junction at No Name Creek. Go right and descend Barr Trail back to Manitou Springs for a 4.5-mile round-trip loop hike.

## MILES AND DIRECTIONS

**0.0** Start at the trailhead on the north side of a parking lot opposite the Pikes Peak Cog Railroad (GPS: 38.856934, -104.931457).

**0.6** Reach the Bailout Point (GPS: 38.857904, -104.94238). Go left to Barr Trail to exit off the trail.

**0.9** Top of the Incline (GPS: 38.858421, -104.947789).

**1.3** Junction with Barr Trail (GPS: 38.856434, -104.954918). Go left down Barr Trail.

**4.5** Reach the trailhead for Barr Trail (GPS: 38.855751, -104.933911) above and west of the Incline Trailhead.

# Heizer Trail

*This is a steep, old trail that climbs the northeast flank of Cascade Mountain above the town of Cascade and US 24 in Ute Pass.*

**Start:** Small parking area on south side of the town of Cascade
**Distance:** 5.6 miles out and back
**Hiking time:** 3 to 5 hours
**Difficulty:** Strenuous due to steepness. Trail climbs for 2.5 miles before the grade lessens.
**Elevation gain:** 1,750 feet
**Trail surface:** Singletrack dirt path
**Seasons:** Year-round
**Schedule:** Open daily
**Other trail users:** Runners, mountain bikers
**Canine compatibility:** Dogs allowed

**Land status:** Pike National Forest
**Fees and permits:** None
**Map:** USGS Cascade
**Trail contact:** Pike National Forest, Pikes Peak Ranger District, 601 S. Weber St., Colorado Springs, CO 80903; (719) 636-1602; www.fs.usda.gov/psicc
**Other:** It's best to park below the trailhead and walk up Anemone Hill Road to the trailhead.
**Special considerations:** Trail is slick and icy in winter; wear microspikes for traction.

**Finding the trailhead:** From Colorado Springs and Manitou Springs, drive west on US 24 to the town of Cascade. Turn left (west) at a traffic light, following signs for the Pikes Peak Highway. After exiting the highway, turn left immediately on Emporia Avenue. Follow it to another left turn onto Park Street, which leads to Anemone Hill Road. Park at a pullout by a sign that reads "Snow Plow Turn Around," or in winter park below the road on one of the other streets and hike up to the trailhead, which is at the end of Anemone Hill Road (**GPS:** 38.895249, -104.972694).

The Heizer Trail is an old path that steadily ascends steep wooded slopes from the small town of Cascade to the summit of 9,387-foot (2,766 meters) Cascade Mountain. Cascade is a rounded mountain that overlooks a long slicing valley called Ute Pass, named for the old Ute Indian trail that once followed it. The trail connected the bubbling mineral springs in Manitou Springs as well as the sacred Garden of the Gods with the Ute's mountain homeland. The Ute Trail, extending west to Utah, was later used by mountain men, trappers, and then miners who flocked to Cripple Creek in the 1890s in search of elusive gold.

The town of Cascade, named for several small waterfalls, began as a rest stop for freighters and travelers who had just navigated the steep canyon below. After the Colorado Midland Railway came through in 1887, the town thrived as a tourist destination with several grand hotels, including the elegant Hotel Ramona with a conical dome and big verandas. David Heizer, the mayor of Colorado Springs, got involved in Cascade at that time and was involved in the construction of the Pikes Peak Carriage Road, Hotel Ramona, as well as the trail that now bears his name.

Cascade Mountain, with 296 feet of prominence, is an unranked summit that offers great views for the intrepid hiker. Bulky Pikes Peak towers above its

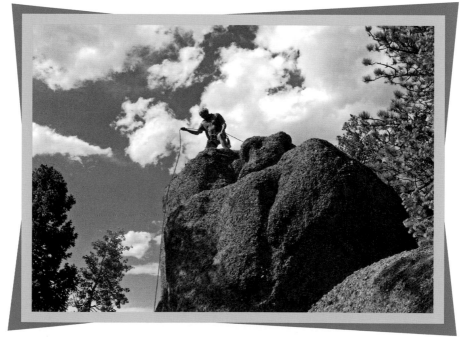

The author prepares to descend off the rocky summit of Cascade Mountain.

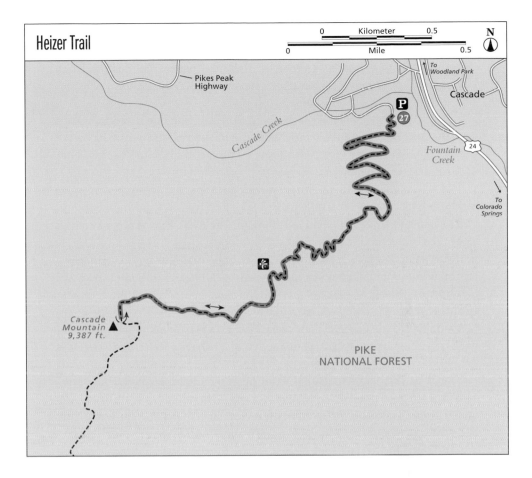

## Heizer Trail

0 Kilometer 0.5
0 Mile 0.5

N

To Woodland Park

Pikes Peak Highway

Cascade

**P**
**27**

Cascade Creek

Fountain Creek

24

To Colorado Springs

Cascade Mountain 9,387 ft.

PIKE NATIONAL FOREST

boulder-strewn summit, while the stream of traffic on US 24 in Ute Pass is a distant hum below. Heizer Trail and Cascade Mountain offer a private wild experience. Don't plan on seeing anyone else on this backcountry hiking gem.

The Heizer Trail is a great workout trail for runners, comparable with the first part of Barr Trail up Mount Manitou. The trail's steady uphill grade offers few spots to catch your breath without stopping. The good news is that after you reach the summit, it's a fast downhill run back to the trailhead. Few mountain bikers use Heizer Trail due to its steepness and occasional sections of gravel.

The Heizer Trailhead is located at the top end of steep Anemone Hill Road on the south side of Cascade just west of US 24. Park by a sign that says "Snow Plow Turn Around" if it is not winter. If no parking is available, it is best to park down in the bottom of the valley by a small park and hike up the road to the trailhead.

The Heizer Trail begins quickly climbing, following a series of wide switchbacks up steep mountain slopes. There are plenty of scenic points for rest stops, with dramatic views up the pass to the slowly turning Ferris wheel at Santa's Workshop and the Pikes Peak Highway. This first trail section has moderate grades with a good gravel surface. It can, however, be icy and slippery in winter since it doesn't get much sunshine.

After about a mile the trail reaches a group of large granite boulders, swings onto the sunny east flank of the mountain, and passes through dense thickets of Gambel oak. Above here the trail features more switchbacks with steeper grades and occasional patches of slippery gravel.

After a couple miles the trail moves back onto the shaded north slopes and reaches a lofty vantage point above some tall cliffs. This is a great stop for resting and having some needed liquid refreshment. The Pikes Peak Highway crosses slopes across the broad canyon below the overlook.

The trail continues up the mountain but the grade lessens. Eventually it reaches a clump of tall boulders surrounded by a forest of quaking aspen, firs, and spruces. The high point of Cascade Mountain is atop one of those granite boulders west of the trail. If you are a true highpointer and need to tag the mountain's summit so you can say you actually reached the high point, then you have to do a climbing problem up the boulder. It's best to have a short rope, especially for getting down off the summit.

While you are up there though, enjoy great mountain views with the northeast flank of Pikes Peak dominating the vista. The trail continues south from here, gently descending into a shallow valley. Look for a sign that points the way to Trail 703. Follow orange ribbons on trees to join it and continue south to Barr Trail.

To return to the trailhead, simply follow the Heizer Trail back down the mountain. Take your time on the steep sections since the gravel can be slippery and you don't want to fall.

## MILES AND DIRECTIONS

**0.0** Begin at the trailhead on Anemone Hill Road (GPS: 38.895249, -104.972694).

**2.8** Rocky summit of Cascade Mountain is reached by scrambling (GPS: 38.8883, -104.9853).

**5.6** Arrive back at the trailhead.

# Catamount Trail

*The Catamount Trail is an out-and-back hike that begins in Green Mountain Falls, follows a road through a residential area to Catamount Falls, then switchbacks through open woods to the Garden of Eden, a hidden valley. The hike ends below South Catamount Reservoir on the north slope of Pikes Peak before returning to Green Mountain Falls.*

**Start:** Junction of Ute Pass Avenue and Belvidere Avenue in Green Mountain Falls

**Distance:** 6.4 miles out and back

**Hiking time:** 2 to 4 hours round-trip

**Difficulty:** Moderate

**Elevation gain:** 1,400 feet

**Trail surface:** Paved road to closed dirt road to singletrack dirt trail

**Seasons:** Year-round. The trail has snow and ice in winter. Bring micro-spikes.

**Schedule:** Open daily

**Other trail users:** Mountain bikes and horses are allowed but rarely seen on the rocky trail.

**Canine compatibility:** Leashed dogs only

**Land status:** Green Mountain Falls and Pike National Forest

**Fees and permits:** None

**Map:** USGS Woodland Park

**Trail contact:** Town of Green Mountain Falls, www.gmfco.us. Also Pike National Forest, Pikes Peak Ranger District, 601 S. Weber St., Colorado Springs, CO 80903; (719) 636-1602; www.fs.usda.gov/psicc

**Other:** Parking for the hike is along Ute Pass Avenue in Green Mountain Falls. There is no public parking on either of the 2 streets that access that start of the trail. Illegally parked cars may be towed.

**Finding the trailhead:** From downtown Colorado Springs and I-25, take the Cimarron Street / US 24 exit (#141) off I-25. Drive west on US 24 for 15.5 miles to the second Green Mountain Falls exit. Go left across the westbound lanes of US 24 and follow Ute Pass Avenue southwest for 0.7 mile into the town of Green Mountain Falls. Park on Lake Street to the left on the north side of a small lake (**GPS:** 38.933954, -105.014739) or in one of several roadside parking lots along the east side of Ute Pass Avenue north of Lake Street. The trailhead is the junction of Ute Pass Avenue and Belvidere Avenue a couple blocks north of Lake Street (**GPS:** 38.935764, -105.0177).

## THE HIKE

The popular Catamount Trail is one of the Pikes Peak region's hiking gems. The 3.2-mile trail, an out-and-back hike from Green Mountain Falls in Ute Pass to South Catamount Reservoir off the Pikes Peak Highway, offers a well-maintained trail, waterfalls and cascades, granite cliffs and boulders, and a gorgeous hidden valley filled with tall grass and birdsong on summer afternoons. The hike, despite ascending steep slopes, has an amenable grade and is easily completed in 4 hours. The trail, creek, and waterfall are named for the elusive catamount, another name for the mountain lions that inhabit Colorado.

Two roads—Belvidere and Hondo Avenues—allow access from Ute Pass Avenue to the beginning of Catamount Trail on a closed dirt road that leads to a waterworks building just below Catamount Falls and the actual trailhead for Catamount Trail. Both Belvidere and Hondo, however, have no public parking; only residents are allowed to park along the streets. There is no parking at the gated end of either street and violators will find their cars towed. To reach the trail, you must park at the Gazebo Lake on Lake Street or in one of several roadside parking areas on the east side of Ute Pass Avenue north of Lake Street. The roads were closed for hiker parking after years of cars clogging the narrow streets, blocking driveways, and lining the streets below the gates.

The hike starts at the junction of Ute Pass Avenue, the main street through Green Mountain Falls, and Belvidere Avenue, which goes left (west) from Ute Pass

Catamount Trail crosses meadows below granite cliffs in the Garden of Eden.

Avenue on the north end of town. After parking your vehicle on Lake Street or at one of the lots on the east side of Ute Pass Avenue, walk north to the road junction and the unofficial trailhead for the hike.

Walk west up paved Ute Pass Avenue, passing rustic old cabins and residences along gurgling Catamount Creek, for 0.7 mile until the road ends at the forest and a gated dirt road. Houses of note along the narrow, quiet street include the 1889 House of Seven Gables at the junction of Belvidere and Ute Pass Avenues; the Willomere House, built in 1888 for early settler George Howard; the first log house in Green Mountain Falls, built in 1887; and at the end of the road, the Hummingbird, a small house built by a groom for his bride. He was tragically killed in a railroad accident before the wedding.

Belvidere Avenue dead-ends at a gate that blocks a dirt road that goes left (south) up to a waterworks area and Catamount Falls. Go around the left side of the gate and hike up the road for 0.3 mile to the start of the Catamount Trail, a bridge over the creek, and a small tumbling waterfall, the lowest of a series of falls that make up Catamount Falls. The lowest falls are seen from a bridge over the creek, while the rest of Catamount Falls are seen from Catamount Trail. A mile to the south is Crystal Falls on Crystal Creek, which again is several small falls that cascade over boulders. For more information on both falls, read *Hiking Waterfalls in Colorado* (FalconGuides, 2013).

After a mile of walking, you reach the official trailhead for the Catamount Trail at the north side of the wooden bridge over the creek. A weathered sign marks the trailhead. Follow the blue dots nailed to trees to stay on the path at important junctions. There are two options to reach the Garden of Eden, a verdant hidden valley above the falls and behind the ridge above the trail. The old trail steeply follows the creek into the valley, while the described and preferred route follows a trail built between 1990 and 2000 up the mountainside north of the falls. This route, with lots of switchbacks, gradually gains elevation, is easy to follow, and offers two short trails to overlooks.

From the trailhead and road, scramble up the steep stony trail. Take care stepping on water-worn cobbles in the trail. A junction, marked by a post with two small signs, one yellow and one blue, is reached after a couple hundred feet. Go right on the blue dot trail and pass beneath Dome Rock, a 100-foot-high cliff.

One option is to take a left turn on the yellow dot trail. This follows the old trail up to the Garden of Eden as well as offers access to upper Catamount Falls and the Thomas Trail, which traverses south from Catamount Creek across steep slopes to Crystal Falls before dropping down Boulder Street to Ute Pass Avenue and the lake. It's almost 3 miles if you hike this loop from town to falls and back.

Catamount Trail heads north, gently climbing through a forest of spruce and fir while switchbacking up the steep mountainside. Partway up, a side trail traverses 300 feet south to rocky Town Overlook, a scenic viewpoint. Return to the main blue-dot trail and continue hiking upward. The trail gains over 700 feet from the road to a gravel saddle at 8,850 feet on a high ridge. Another short trail, marked with light-blue dots, goes southeast for 400 feet to Valley Overlook and great views of Green Mountain Falls nestled in the valley below.

The trail gently descends 100 feet down into the eastern end of the Garden of Eden, a moist hidden valley filled with wildflowers, honeybees, and birdsong in summer. Broken granite cliffs hem in the valley on the north while a dense woodland of Engelmann spruce and Douglas fir blanket the cooler south side. The long ridge on the south is 9,461-foot Mount Rebecca. Towering ponderosa pines grow alongside the trail as it threads west alongside willow-lined Catamount Creek.

The valley slowly pinches down as it bends southwest. The trail crosses the creek, climbs over some big boulders, and passes through a maze of fallen trees. Farther along, the creek tumbles over granite blocks, forming small waterfalls and noisy cascades. Continue hiking along the rocky trail above the creek until it passes through a broken fence and makes a sharp right turn to a gravel road and a small diversion dam. Walk up the road for 100 yards to a good utility road at about 9,000 feet that provides access to the South and North Catamount Reservoirs' dams. This is the end of the hike. From here you turn around and retrace the trail back to your car parked down on Ute Pass Avenue.

Another option is to extend the hike to the reservoirs and get a view of Pikes Peak. Take the right fork of the service road, then the middle fork, and follow it up South Catamount Creek for 0.3 mile. Finish by climbing up the road between the rock rubble dam and spillway to the top of the dam at 9,225 feet. South Catamount Reservoir along with neighboring North Catamount Reservoir and Crystal Reservoir comprise the 2,267-acre North Slope Recreation Area, a Colorado Springs watershed area managed for outdoor recreation. Most folks come to fish in the high lakes, catching brook, rainbow, and cutthroat trout as well as lake trout up to 30 inches long. There is also picnicking but no water sports, wading, or swimming in the city water supply.

## MILES AND DIRECTIONS

**0.0** Trailhead on the east side of Ute Pass Avenue in Green Mountain Falls (GPS: 38.935728, -105.017427).

**0.7** Gate at the west end of Belvedere Road (GPS: 38.937259, -105.03131). Go left through the gate and up the closed dirt road.

**1.0** Reach the junction of Catamount Trail and the dirt road (GPS: 38.93394, -105.02989). Go right on the trail past a couple small waterfalls.

**1.1** Hike a short distance up the trail to a junction (GPS: 38.93330, -105.03018). Go right on Catamount Trail. A left turn follows the old trail up steep slopes alongside the creek.

Catamount Trail

**1.6** Junction with overlook trail (GPS: 38.93409, -105.03292). Go left to the first overlook, then return to the main trail and continue uphill.

**1.8** Reach the top of a ridge (GPS: 38.93398, -105.03541). Go left to the upper overlook (purple blazes), then return to the trail. Go left (west) and descend into the upper valley.

**3.2** Turnaround point of the hike at the utility road (GPS: 38.930752, -105.045846).

**6.4** Arrive back at the trailhead.

## Green Mountain Falls and Catamount Trail

The town of Green Mountain Falls was named in December 1887 by William J. Foster for the waterfalls on Catamount Creek as well as Crystal Falls to the south. The area was previously part of a ranch owned by George Howard, who settled here in 1881. Foster bought the valley off Howard in 1887 with the intention of making a resort town beside the Colorado Midland Railroad, which was built up Ute Pass at that time. In 1888, streets were platted, the lake was excavated and a gazebo was built on a small island, and over one hundred tent cabins, rented for $4 to $7 a week, were erected for summer guests escaping the lowland heat.

The following year a couple of hotels, the seventy-room Green Mountain Falls Hotel and Lakeside Hotel, opened, and a train depot made the town an official stop. The town, incorporated in 1890, flourished as a lakeside resort. The Catamount Trail was built back in those early days for vacationers—men in suits and bowler hats and women in Victorian hoop skirts—to hike up to the falls for a picnic and game of cards. Many also hiked beyond the falls to the summit of Mount Rebecca.

Now the vacation cabins have been converted to year-round residences, and Green Mountain Falls, with 640 residents, has lapsed into a quiet reverie as a Colorado Springs bedroom community. The network of trails that connected the town to the waterfalls and mountains were ill-defined and fell into disrepair, especially the popular trail alongside Catamount Falls. The steep trail became a mess of slick boulders and a hike to the valley beyond required balance and sturdy shoes. By the late 1980s, after several hiking injuries and rescues, a town committee decided to build a better trail. Work began in 1990 on a new Catamount Trail, which, instead of following the creek, angled up slopes to the north. The trail, with twenty-two switchbacks and 770 feet of elevation gain, was finished in 2000 after ten years of work done by hundreds of volunteers. Much of the work was completed in 1997.

## THE HIKE

The Crags Trail (FS Trail #664) on the northwest flank of Pikes Peak may be the perfect summer hike in the Colorado Springs region. The trail slowly ascends up gentle grades in a lush subalpine valley along Fourmile Creek, which originates on the north slope of 14,115-foot Pikes Peak and eventually empties into the Arkansas River near Cañon City to the south.

The hike, rambling below granite cliffs and dark forested mountainsides, offers all the views of a mountain ascent, but your thighs and lungs won't feel the burn like climbing a real fourteener (14,000-foot peak). Expect not only scenic views but also crisp mountain air, wildflower-strewn meadows, and plentiful wildlife, including deer and elk.

Columbines, the Colorado state flower, bloom along the Crags Trail.

From the trailhead by the restrooms on Teller County Road 62, the Crags Trail crosses Fourmile Creek and the most difficult part of the hike begins. The trail switchbacks up a steep hillside, quickly gaining elevation before leveling off above the Crags Campground. Curve southeast around a hillside and drop back down to a trail junction at 0.6 mile. Keep to the left, minding the trail marker for the Crags, and begin hiking alongside tumbling Fourmile Creek.

The trail passes through a jumbled boulder field before opening into a broad grassy expanse. The trail then heads east up the narrowing valley and reaches a wider meadow. The creek makes wide meanders across the valley floor, its banks densely lined with willows. Outcroppings of granite line the hillside to the left. Groves of aspen trees shade the trail while tall Engelmann spruce and subalpine fir trees stand sentinel-like along the edge of the meadow. Pangborn's Pinnacle, a mighty granite dome, towers above the broad valley to the east.

The Crags Trail briefly jogs to the left, climbing higher before dropping back into the meadow. The trail splits just before a large granite dome on the left. Keep to the right-hand track with the cliff to your left. The trail then tracks across the edge of a swampy marshland before climbing back to solid ground.

The bare northwest shoulder of Pikes Peak, Colorado's thirty-first-highest mountain, looms to the right. Tall cliffs and crags dot the steep forested slopes above the valley. As the valley narrows, the trail passes a cliff to the right. The shady north side the cliff makes an excellent rest stop on bedrock slabs. Sit down and enjoy the trickle of the creek and take in the valley up which you just hiked. This is also a good turnaround point since the next half-mile trail segment gains lots of elevation and is heavily wooded.

Continue hiking up a narrow wooded canyon on the rustic trail, then climb up an abrupt, steep gully. Keep an eye on the trail since it can be easy to lose as it switches back and forth over tree roots and lumpy boulders. Eventually the trail reaches a high saddle at 2.3 miles.

The trail goes left here and climbs to a small summit at 10,800 feet with a big view and the trail's end point at 2.5 miles. This is a great place to linger and enjoy breathtaking expansive views. To the east is the backside of a huge granite buttress called Old Ironsides; farther east twists the Pikes Peak Highway, a couple reservoirs, and the flat top of the Rampart Range. On a clear day you can even see the distant prairie horizon. Also check out the ancient weathered limber pines that inhabit this windswept ridge.

To return, retrace the trail for 2.5 miles back to the trailhead. Remember to stay on the trail as you descend the wooded gully below the saddle.

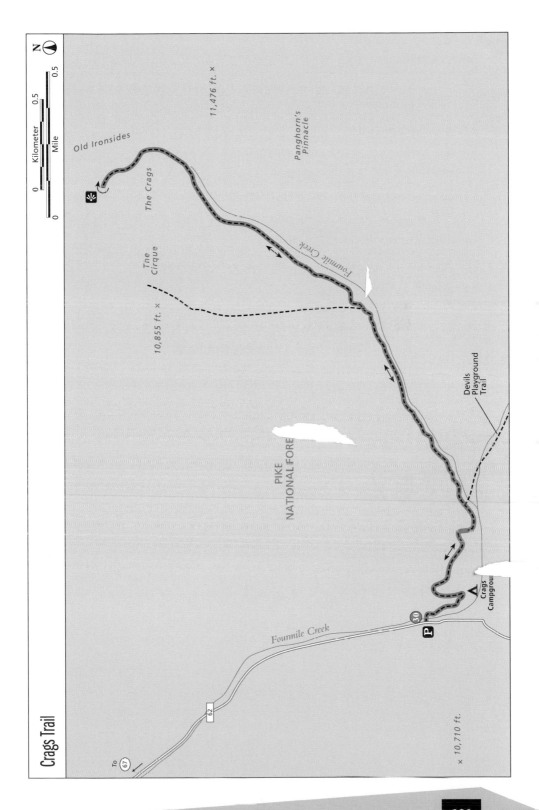

Crags Trail

N

Kilometer
0          0.5

Mile
0          0.5

Old Ironsides

The Crags

11,476 ft. ×

Panghorn's
Pinnacle

The
Cirque

10,855 ft. ×

Fourmile Creek

PIKE
NATIONAL FORE

Devils
Playground
Trail

Crags
Campgrou

Fourmile Creek

62

To 67

× 10,710 ft.

## MILES AND DIRECTIONS

**0.0** Start from the trailhead (GPS: 38.873633, -105.123719) on the east side of CR 62 and opposite the parking area.

**0.6** Junction with trail from the campground. Continue straight (east).

**1.4** Reach the west side of a wide valley. Trail heads east along the north edge of the willows and meandering creek.

**2.0** Junction with trail that goes left to the Cirque. Continue straight on the main trail.

**2.3** Reach the saddle. Go left up a ridge.

**2.5** End of trail at a viewpoint (GPS: 38.888471, -105.097989).

**5.0** Arrive back at the trailhead.

### 1806: Pike Attempts the Peak

Lieutenant Zebulon Pike led a detachment of fifteen men to explore the southern boundary of the newly acquired Louisiana Purchase in 1806. The valiant expedition, exploring unmapped territory, attempted to climb what Pike called "Grand Peak" in late November. Pike and three of his men, clad in summer clothes, failed in snow and cold, turning back after climbing one of the smaller mountains southeast of the great peak, possibly Mount Rosa. The lieutenant famously wrote in his journal that the mountain would never be climbed, but a close examination of the text reveals that he thought it was impossible in the 22°F temperatures and waist-deep snow that his party encountered.

# Devils Playground Trail

*The Devils Playground Trail is the standard hiking route up Pikes Peak. The 13.8-mile round-trip hike up the northeast side of the Peak is easily done round-trip in a day by competent, fit hikers and offers spectacular views, fun hiking, and a diverse variety of terrain and ecosystems.*

**Start:** Crags Trailhead on east side of Teller County Road 62

**Distance:** 13.8 miles out and back

**Hiking time:** 10 to 14 hours

**Difficulty:** Strenuous. Class 2 with mostly trail hiking but some scrambling up a boulder field below the summit.

**Elevation gain:** 4,100 feet

**Trail surface:** Singletrack dirt trail with some doubletrack trail in places

**Seasons:** Year-round

**Other trail users:** Runners

**Canine compatibility:** Dogs allowed

**Land status:** Pike National Forest

**Fees and permits:** None

**Schedule:** No restrictions.

**Map:** USGS Pikes Peak

**Trail contact:** Pikes Peak Ranger District, 601 S. Weber St., Colorado Springs, CO 80903; (719) 636-1602; www.fs.usda.gov/psicc

**Other:** Camping is allowed along the trail. Campsites must be 300 feet from all water sources.

**Finding the trailhead:** From Colorado Springs drive west on US 24 up Ute Pass to Woodland Park and then on to Divide. Turn south in Divide on CO 67 and drive 4.1 miles. Just past the Mueller State Park turnoff on the right, look for a left turn onto dirt Teller County Road 62, marked with a small sign for Crags Campground. Follow the rough road east and south, passing through a Mennonite camp, for 3 miles to a large marked parking lot on the right and a trailhead on the left. Park in the lot (**GPS:** 38.873753, -105.123929). The turnoff for the Crags Campground, a good summer campsite, is 0.1 mile farther south on the left side of the road.

## THE HIKE

The 6.9-mile-long (one-way) Devils Playground Trail, climbing the northwest side of 14,115-foot Pikes Peak, is an excellent hike up one of America's most famous mountains. The trail is easily hiked round-trip in a day, generally easy to follow, and much shorter than 13.0-mile Barr Trail up the east side of the mountain. Devils Playground Trail is considered the standard hiking route on the Peak.

Pikes Peak, the historic landmark of the Rocky Mountains and the biggest skyscraper in Colorado Springs, stands east of the main bulk of the Colorado Rockies. This huge, conspicuous mountain dominates the Front Range landscape like no other mountain. Rising abruptly from the high plains, Pikes Peak is easily seen from over 100 miles away. Its distinctive silhouette is glimpsed from north of Denver and from far out on the undulating eastern prairie, where its snow-capped countenance appears like a distant mirage. Standing apart from other high mountains, Pikes Peak was a symbol and beacon for prospectors and pioneers journeying westward in the 1850s "Pikes Peak or Bust" gold rush.

The bulky mountain that explorer Zebulon Pike and his band of merry men could not climb on a snowy November day in 1806 now has more people reach its airy summit—via trail, highway, and cog railroad—than any other high mountain in North America and probably the world, except for Mount Fuji in Japan.

The Devils Playground Trail passes through a granite gap at Devils Playground with distant views of the Continental Divide.

Every August thousands of runners gather in Manitou Springs to race up Barr Trail to the summit, doing the ascent only, while the next day hundreds run up and down the Peak for a grueling 26-mile marathon. Race cars negotiate the curving loops of the Pikes Peak Highway in an annual Race to the Clouds. On New Year's Eve members of a local group, the Ad-a-Man Club, trudge through snow to set off midnight fireworks from the summit.

While it is easy to drive in comfort to the summit on the Pikes Peak Highway or to take the cog railroad, the most satisfying and exhilarating way to get there is on foot. Because of its easy access, fame, and Front Range dominance, more hikers reach Pikes Peak's summit than any other 14,000-foot peak in Colorado.

A lot of prospective hikers ascend the mountain on the 13.0-mile-long Barr Trail, which begins in Manitou Springs and climbs the eastern side of the mountain. Barr Trail is, despite its easy grades and well-manicured surface, a difficult trail to both ascend and descend in a 26-mile round-trip day. A lot of hikers either stop overnight at Barr Camp or hike to the summit one-way and either are picked up on top or take the cog railroad back down. If you want to hike Pikes Peak in a day, then the Devils Playground Trail is the hike for you.

Start your Pikes Peak ascent at the 10,000-foot Crags Trailhead, also the trailhead for the Devils Playground Trail, on the east side of the road and opposite a large parking area (GPS: 38.873626, -105.123637). A pit toilet is at the trailhead. Cross Fourmile Creek on a good bridge and follow the trail up a couple of switchbacks on a steep hillside, then contour east above Crags Campground. After 0.6 mile the trail reaches a junction with the original Crags Trail coming in from the right, from the campground. Walk another 75 feet to another major junction and go right on the signed Devils Playground Trail (Trail #753). The Crags Trail goes left and up the main valley into the Crags area.

## Expect Extreme Weather

You need to be prepared if you plan to hike up Pikes Peak on either the Devils Playground Trail or Barr Trail. A hike up Pikes Peak is not to be taken lightly. It's a high-altitude hike, and the weather, temperature, and oxygen level dramatically change from the base of the mountain in Manitou Springs to the summit over 8,000 feet higher. It's possible to leave the lower elevations, even the 10,000-foot-high trailhead for Devils Playground Trail, in a summery climate and find yourself on the summit in winter with snow, wind, and below-freezing temperatures. This dramatic change can occur in every summer month. Don't be lulled into complacency, and be prepared for every condition to be safe.

From this junction to the summit, the trail is easy to follow and well worn by numerous boots. Cross Fourmile Creek again on a split-log bridge and begin hiking up the rocky trail on gentle slopes alongside a small unnamed creek and through a dense fir and spruce forest. The trail slowly gains elevation for the next 1.5 miles with a few steep sections, crossing a log bridge at 0.9 mile and passing a couple obvious granite formations on the left including Banana Rock at 1.3 miles.

After the last creek crossing over stones at 1.6 miles, the trail passes an open meadow at 10,900 feet and begins switchbacking up a steep rocky slope covered in weather-beaten limber pine trees, reaching timberline at about 11,800 feet. Take a rest here on some boulders besides the trail and enjoy the view west down the valley you just hiked up. Beyond stretches a vast panorama of mountains, including most of the fourteeners in the Sawatch Range 80 miles to the west.

From timberline the trail works up steep slopes for another thousand feet without any switchbacks to relieve your legs before finally emerging onto a high, grassy ridge at 12,750 feet. After reaching the top of the flat ridge, take a rest at one of the large cairns that mark the trail. These cairns, or stacked piles of rocks, are especially useful to locate where the trail descends from the ridgetop in bad weather such as summer thunderstorms or if the wind whips snow into a ground blizzard in spring. You can easily spot the rest of the hike from the flat ridge, with the trail heading west around the cliffed south flank of Devils Playground Peak and then the long north ridge of Pikes Peak, creased on its west side by the Pikes Peak Highway, a paved 19-mile-long auto route to the summit.

The hike continues east on the wide doubletrack trail, here an old Jeep road. The trail dips down and then gently gains elevation below 13,070-foot Devils Playground Peak, an unranked summit with only 140 feet of prominence but the highest point in Teller County. The trail passes through Devils Gate, a gap between two granite cliffs, and then swings around the squat peak to the Pikes

## Adjust to the Elevation

First make sure that you are properly acclimated to the altitude. If you fly into Colorado Springs from some sea-level city, take a few days to adjust to the elevation. Do some lower-elevation training hikes before attempting Pikes Peak. It's easy to get altitude sickness, especially above 13,000 feet, so take it easy when you are hiking. Set a slow, steady pace and stop frequently to catch your breath and hydrate. If you begin to feel dizzy, develop a headache, and are nauseous, then there is a good chance that you are developing altitude sickness. The best cure is to immediately descend to a lower elevation where more oxygen will make you feel better.

# Pancake Rocks and Horsethief Falls Trails

*This popular classic hike climbs into a high glaciated valley below Horsethief Falls and Sentinel Point, with an optional hike to the falls. Then it continues higher to Pancake Rocks, a collection of rock stacks on a ridge, and expansive views across southern Colorado.*

**Start:** CO 67 past a road cut that bypasses an old railroad tunnel
**Distance:** 6.4 miles out and back
**Hiking time:** 3 to 6 hours
**Difficulty:** Moderate
**Elevation gain:** 1,400 feet
**Trail surface:** Singletrack dirt path
**Seasons:** Year-round. May through Oct is best. The trail is icy and snowpacked in winter. Bring snowshoes, micro-spikes, and a GPS unit so you don't lose the trail in the trees.

**Schedule:** Open daily
**Other trail users:** Runners, mountain bikers
**Canine compatibility:** Dogs allowed
**Land status:** Pike National Forest
**Fees and permits:** None
**Map:** USGS Pikes Peak
**Trail contact:** Pike National Forest, Pikes Peak Ranger District, 601 S. Weber St., Colorado Springs, CO 80903; (719) 636-1602; www.fs.usda.gov

**Finding the trailhead:** From I-25 take the Cimarron Street / US 24 exit and head west. Drive up US 24 through Ute Pass and Woodland Park to Divide. Go left in Divide on CO 67. Drive 9.2 miles south on CO 67 and pass a closed-off tunnel on the left. After going around a curve, the gravel parking area and trailhead are on the left at the other end of the old Little Ike Tunnel (**GPS:** 38.834283, -105.137462). Use extreme caution pulling in and out of the parking area since traffic can be heavy on the highway.

## THE HIKE

The 6.4-mile Pancake Rocks Trail (FS Trail #704), with an optional short side excursion up to Horsethief Falls, is one of the finest day hikes in the Pikes Peak region. The trail offers it all—spectacular mountain scenery, willow-lined beaver ponds, hillsides of shimmering golden aspen in late September, far-reaching views, and unusual granite rock formations. It is also a popular winter hike since the thick forest holds snow for most of the winter. Bring snowshoes for deep unconsolidated snow as well as micro-spikes for your boots for traction on icy trail sections.

The trailhead is located on the east side of CO 67, the well-traveled highway that runs south from Divide to the historic gold-mining towns of Cripple Creek and Victor. Now, of course, Cripple Creek mines another type of gold from the pockets of gamblers who come to test their luck at cards and slot machines on Bennett Avenue. The highway itself follows the bed of an old railroad that carried passengers and gold ore from what was once called the "World's Greatest Gold Mining Camp." The trailhead and parking for about twenty cars is at the south end of the now-closed Little Ike Tunnel.

The Pancake Rocks Trail and its companion Horsethief Falls Trail (FS Trail #704B) offers the raw beauty of the Colorado Rockies to hikers. The first part of the hike to the falls is often busy with the clump of boots, but those who venture up to aptly named Pancake Rocks find solitude. The trail is mostly singletrack dirt

Hikers cross granite bedrock at Pancake Rocks above Oil Creek Valley.

although part of the first section to the falls follows an old abandoned road bed. The hike to Horsethief Falls is a great short outing for families and kids, although the relentless uphill in the first 0.6 mile will test their endurance.

The trail departs from the south side of the parking lot at 9,740 feet. Climb briskly up the trail above the highway to a switchback and continue uphill. At 0.1 mile the trail bends east onto shady north-facing slopes above a deep valley and quickly leaves the highway sounds behind. The wide track steadily ascends, traversing across a steep slope. Granite boulders, covered with green moss, scatter across the mountainside in an evergreen forest of fir and spruce. The distant sound of rushing water filters up from the valley floor below.

After scrambling over a short section of boulders, the trail levels out at 0.6 mile and enters broad Horsethief Park, an open glaciated valley filled with willows and reflective beaver ponds. At this point the trail also intersects the Ring-the-Peak Trail, a 64-mile-long compilation of footpaths that encircle 14,115-foot Pikes Peak. At the time of this writing in 2014, the trail is about 80 percent complete, with several sections needing both a trail and landowner permissions. The Ring-the-Peak Trail heads north from this junction toward the Crags on the northwest flank of Pikes Peak. Continue straight on Trail 704.

The trail skirts along the southern edge of the broad valley, passing placid ponds. To the north on low hills are stands of quaking aspen, the most widely distributed tree in North America. If you hike in late September, expect to see the autumn gold leaves of the aspens spreading color across the landscape. Rocky 12,527-foot Sentinel Point, a prominent pointed summit on the west side of Pikes Peak, looms east above the basin.

At 0.7 mile there is an obvious trail junction marked with an old wooden sign. Go right on the Pancake Rocks Trail (Trail 704). (**Option:** If you are only hiking to Horsethief Falls, continue straight on Trail 704B for 0.3 mile to the falls, then return to the trailhead by the same route. If you are hiking to Pancake Rocks, however, it's best to visit the falls on the return hike.)

The trail heads south and begins a sustained climb up a steep north-facing slope blanketed with dense forest. The trail section can be slow going in winter with deep, unconsolidated snow. The trail makes five big switchbacks, gaining about 800 feet of elevation, until it levels out between a couple of rocky points. Hike south on the open trail through short-grass meadows and scattered fir and spruce trees. Look for a short spur trail that climbs up left to a knobby overlook that offers views of Sentinel Point.

Continue south and then descend the trail below steeper slopes and broken cliffs (don't confuse these with the real Pancake Rocks) before huffing it back up a hill to the trail's 11,088-foot high point on a ridge crest. Descend the trail for the last quarter mile down gradual slopes to Pancake Rocks, a collection of rock stacks on granite slabs at 10,935 feet. The granite here is fractured horizontally rather than vertically, forming the unusual layered pancake rocks. Even without syrup and butter, they are still quite a delectable sight.

The Pancake Rocks, 3.2 miles from the trailhead on CO 67, are the end of the trail, so find a comfortable rock shelf and have a sip of water and nibble on an energy bar or sandwich while you enjoy the wide views. To the east is a deep valley floored by Oil Creek. The valley's steep slopes are blanketed with aspen, forming a gorgeous autumn tapestry, while granite cliffs, including the King, Queen, Rook, and Great Dihedral perch below a rocky ridgeline. To the south are more aspen-covered mountains and beyond are the landmark Spanish Peaks over 100 miles away, the Wet Mountains, and the long ragged spine of the Sangre de Cristo Range. A close look reveals four fourteeners (14,000-foot peaks) clustered in the range's central section, including Crestone Peak, Crestone Needle, Kit Carson Peak, and Humboldt Peak.

After catching your breath and rehydrating, retrace your footsteps back to Horsethief Park. There are two short uphill sections but lots of downhill so the

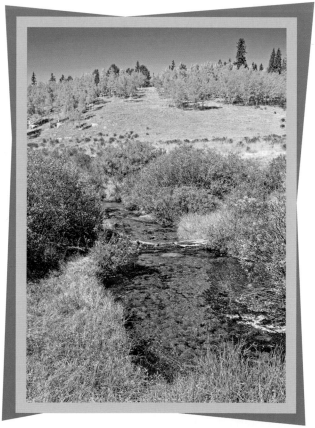

A clear stream runs between willow-clad banks in Horsethief Park.

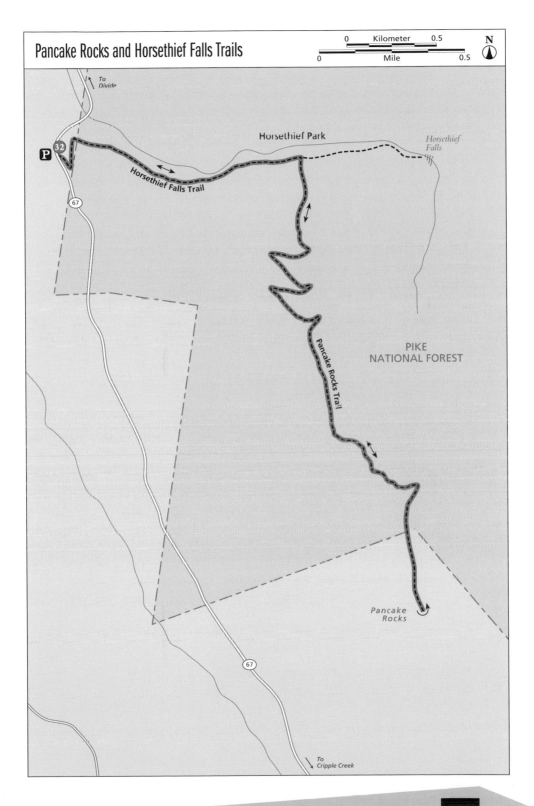

# Pancake Rocks and Horsethief Falls Trails

0    Kilometer    0.5
0    Mile    0.5

N

To Divide

Horsethief Park

Horsethief Falls

P 32

Horsethief Falls Trail

67

Pancake Rocks Trail

PIKE NATIONAL FOREST

Pancake Rocks

67

To Cripple Creek

hike down goes quickly. Watch your feet on a few steep trail sections since loose gravel, acting like marbles underfoot, scatters on top of hard ground.

At the junction of the two trails in Horsethief Park, go left to descend 0.7 mile back to the parking lot or, for full value, go right and hike a short 0.3 mile up to Horsethief Falls.

Trail 704B heads east along the edge of the forest and the willow-filled valley floor, slowly climbing uphill to the base of Horsethief Falls. Here the chilled stream rushes over a worn boulder and cascades down a slabby cliff of granite bedrock. At the base, cross logs over the stream to sit on rocks on the north side of the falls, or clamber up the hillside for 0.1 mile to a lofty perch above the falls at 10,200 feet. Either choice is great for a quiet picnic or a nap in the afternoon sunshine. It is best to view the falls in May and June when rapidly melting snow on Sentinel Point fills the creek. In dry years only a thin sheen of water slides down the falls.

After relaxing at Horsethief Falls, it's a quick mile hike back to the parking area and the trailhead. It's all downhill and goes fast.

## MILES AND DIRECTIONS

**0.0**  Parking area and trailhead on the east side of CO 67 just south of closed Little Ike Tunnel (GPS: 38.834283, -105.137462).

**0.6**  Steep climb ends and trail reaches Horsethief Park. Junction with Ring the Peak Trail (GPS: 38.83355, -105.12663). Go straight.

**0.7**  Trail junction with Pancake Rocks Trail (GPS: 38.83395, -105.12358). Go right on Trail #704, labeled with a Ring the Peak marker. Hike up a steep wooded hillside with five switchbacks. (*Option:* If you are only hiking to Horsethief Falls, continue straight on Trail 704B for 0.3 mile to the falls, then return to the trailhead by the same route.)

**1.9**  The trail flattens out at the top of the hill (GPS: 38.82572, -105.12325). Continue south, passing a spur trail that climbs to a rocky lookout to the east.

**3.2**  Reach Pancake Rocks and the end of the trail (GPS: 38.81343, -105.11655).

**5.7**  Return to the trail junction with Trail #704B to Horsethief Falls. (*Option:* Go right to the falls [0.6 mile round-trip].)

**6.4**  Reach the trailhead, parking area, and CO 67.

# Mueller State Park Loop

*A popular loop hike that descends Outlook Ridge past three scenic overlooks and then returns up a wooded valley past Lost Pond to the park road.*

**Start:** Outlook Ridge Trailhead on west side of parking lot just north of park visitor center

**Distance:** 3.3-mile lollipop

**Hiking time:** 1 to 2 hours

**Difficulty:** Moderate. Some elevation gain and loss on good trails.

**Elevation gain:** 400 feet

**Trail surface:** Single- and double-track dirt path

**Seasons:** Year-round. Winter can be icy; wear spikes on your boots.

**Schedule:** Park open daily 5 a.m. to 10 p.m. for day use

**Other trail users:** Mountain bikers

**Canine compatibility:** Dogs not permitted

**Land status:** Public land in Mueller State Park

**Fees and permits:** Daily fee required to enter the park

**Maps:** USGS Divide. Mueller State Park trail map at website.

**Trail contact:** Mueller State Park, 21045 CO Highway 67, PO Box 39, Divide, CO 80814; (719) 687-6867; www.parks.state.co.us/parks/mueller

**Finding the trailhead:** Take the Cimarron St./US 24 exit (exit 141) from I-25. Drive west on US 24 up Ute Pass and through Woodland Park. Continue west on US 24 to the town of Divide. Turn left (south) on CO 67 toward Cripple Creek. Drive 3.8 miles to the park entrance and turn right (west) into the park. After paying your entrance fee, follow Wapiti Road for 1.5 miles to the Outlook Ridge parking area and trailhead on the left (south) side of the road. Restrooms, picnic tables, and water are available at the trailhead (**GPS:** 38.881137, -105.181298).

## THE HIKE

The 3.3-mile-long Outlook Ridge and Lost Pond Loop hike combines seven park trails into a single hike. The trail mileage can be shortened, depending on the optional hikes out to the three overlooks along the way. Each of those out-and-back trails to the overlooks is 0.6 mile long. The four main trails the hike follows are the Outlook Ridge Trail (Trail #7), Geer Pond Trail (Trail #25), Lost Pond Trail (Trail #11), and Revenuer's Ridge (Trail #1). The entire route is easy to follow and well marked by posts with trail numbers and blue arrows.

The loop hike, divided into two distinct sections, follows a rounded ridge west from the park road past three scenic overlooks of valleys below and then returns up a wooded valley past a small pond and back to the road. The ridge trail section offers picture-perfect views of snowcapped Pikes Peak to the east and the surrounding landscape of wooded hills and vales, while the second segment threads up a short steep valley that is filled with tall conifers, groves of quaking aspen, birdsong, and, in summer, a colorful array of wildflowers.

Mueller State Park, lying west of CO 67 just south of Divide, spreads across 5,120 acres with an average elevation of 9,600 feet on the northwest side of 14,115-foot Pikes Peak. The park, a showcase of natural wonders and wildlife, offers over 55 miles of hiking on thirty-six trails that explore its shady valleys,

The western slopes of Pikes Peak rise beyond rolling wooded hillsides along the Outlook Ridge Trail.

humped ridges and mountains, and granite cliffs and domes. Many of the trails lead to scenic overlooks with far-ranging views of the jagged Sangre de Cristo and Sawatch Ranges, home to Colorado's highest mountains.

The park's web of well-maintained trails, with generally little elevation gain and loss, can be easily linked together to form excellent loop hikes of varying lengths and difficulties. The comprehensive trail system is organized by numbers. Trails range from short and easy to long and challenging. Pick up the park's trail map when you enter the park, at the visitor center, or download a copy from the park's website to plan other Mueller adventures beyond the hikes described here.

Mueller also has 132 campsites and is renowned as the best wildlife-watching area in the Pikes Peak region, with lots of large mammals including black bears, elk, and mule deer roaming the backcountry, as well as raptors like golden eagles and red-tail hawks. The park's sheer size and lack of roads ensure lots of seclusion, peace, and isolation for hikers.

The Outlook Ridge and Lost Pond Loop hike begins at the Outlook Ridge Trailhead and parking area at 9,680 feet on the west side of Wapiti Road just past the park visitor center. Picnic tables, restrooms, and water are available here. Sign the register on the trailhead kiosk and study the trail map. The smooth double-track trail, an old ranch road, heads west down Outlook Ridge and after 0.1 mile reaches a trail junction with Revenuer's Ridge Trail (Trail #1), the return trail for the last leg of the hike. Go straight.

The trail dips and rolls, with occasional views south into Hay Creek Valley to the south, and after 0.5 mile reaches a junction with Raven Ridge Overlook Trail (Trail #8) on a slight uphill. Go left (south) on Trail #8 for great views. Raven Ridge Trail traverses a meadow and then drops steadily for 0.3 mile to a spectacular overlook of wide granite benches that drop abruptly below. Watch children here since the overlook is unfenced. This is the best viewpoint on the hike, with Pikes Peak looming to the east. After enjoying the expansive view, return 0.3 mile uphill to the Outlook Ridge Trail and turn left.

Hike down a broad ridge through aspen groves and conifers. After another 0.3 mile you reach the junction with Red Tail Overlook Trail (Trail #9) on a bend. Go left (south) on Red Tail and hike 0.3 mile downhill on the doubletrack-to-singletrack trail to a timber staircase and end at another spectacular overlook. This point, lower than Raven Ridge Overlook, is a smooth granite slab perched above cliffs and Brook Pond. Again, after enjoying the view, retrace your steps uphill to Outlook Ridge Trail and go left.

The trail descends steeply for another 0.3 mile and reaches the junction with the Long Eagle Overlook Trail (Trail #10), the third overlook, at a bench. Go left on Long Eagle, climbing a short hill and then following a level ridge to another great viewpoint at 0.3 mile. Return back to the junction with Outlook Ridge Trail and turn left (northeast).

Follow the doubletrack trail for 100 feet to a junction on the left with a sign that reads "Trail 7 Bypass to Avoid Steep Hills." Go left on the Trail #7 bypass—this path avoids the steep hill ahead of you and a descent on the other side by contouring northeast across wooded slopes. Follow the singletrack trail through dense spruce and fir forest for 0.2 mile to a junction with the alternative steep Trail #7. Continue straight for 0.1 mile, crossing a trickling creek, to a major trail junction with Geer Pond Trail (Trail #25) and the end of the Outlook Ridge Trail (Trail #7). Go right on Trail #25.

The next 0.8-mile trail segment follows Geer Pond Trail for 0.4 mile, which then becomes Lost Pond Trail (Trail #11). The hike initially ascends a steep hill out of the drainage on a doubletrack trail. From the top of the climb, traverse above the shady valley. The rustic roadbed narrows in a swampy area fringed with dense forest, and the trail reaches Lost Pond after 3.5 miles. The small, quiet pond tucks in a pastoral pocket of forest and meadow.

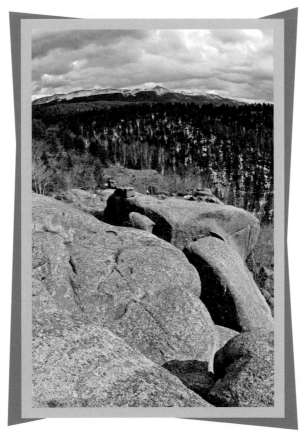

Granite cliffs and slabs spill down below Raven Ridge Overlook.

# Mueller State Park Loop

Leave the pond by climbing north on the wide trail, which is now Lost Pond Trail (Trail #11), to the head of a shallow valley. Bend right and continue climbing east to a trail junction 0.3 mile from Lost Pond. Continue climbing another 0.1 mile to the Lost Pond Trailhead and parking area. Below the parking area and park road, however, is a junction with Revenuer's Ridge Trail (Trail #1). Go right (south) on Trail #1.

The last hike segment travels 0.5 mile south along Revenuer's Ridge Trail, dipping through draws and crossing tree-shaded slopes until it intersects Outlook Ridge Trail (Trail #7). Go left to finish on Trail #7 for 0.1 mile to the Outlook Ridge Trailhead and parking area after 3.3 miles of hiking.

## MILES AND DIRECTIONS

**0.0** Begin at the Outlook Ridge Trailhead on the west side of the parking area by restrooms.

**0.1** Junction with Revenuer's Ridge Trail (#1) on right. Go straight.

**0.5** Junction with Raven Ridge Overlook Trail (#8) (GPS: 38.879316, -105.188835). Go left on #8 to overlook (GPS: 38.876004, -105.190744). Return to Outlook Ridge Trail (#7) and go left (west).

**1.1** Junction with Red Trail Overlook Trail (#9) (GPS: 38.879859, -105.193309). Go left for 0.3 mile on #9 to overlook (GPS: 38.87538, -105.194277). Return to Outlook Ridge Trail (#7) and go left (west).

**1.5** Junction with Lone Eagle Overlook Trail (#10) (GPS: 38.880496, -105.194939). Go left for 0.3 mile on #10 to overlook (GPS: 38.877082, -105.198316). Return to Outlook Ridge Trail (#7) and go left (northeast). In a few hundred feet you will come to the junction with #7 bypass. Go left.

**1.9** Junction with Geer Pond Trail (#25) (GPS: 38.88116, -105.191887). End of #7. Go right on #25.

**2.3** Reach Lost Pond (GPS: 38.882895, -105.185359). End of #25. Continue straight on Lost Pond Trail (#11).

**2.7** Reach Lost Pond Trailhead (GPS: 38.882698, -105.181915) and junction with Revenuer's Ridge Trail (#1). Go right on #1.

**3.2** Junction with Outlook Ridge Trail (#7). Go left on #7 for 0.1 mile to trailhead.

**3.3** End the hike at the trailhead.

# Vindicator Valley Trail

*The Vindicator Valley Trail makes a 2-mile loop through what was once one of the most active and richest mining districts in Colorado. The trail explores the area's gold rush history, passing numerous old mines including the Theresa and Vindicator mines.*

**Start:** Trailhead and parking lot on west side of CR 81 north of Victor

**Distance:** 2.0-mile lollipop

**Hiking time:** 1 to 2 hours

**Difficulty:** Easy with gentle grades

**Elevation gain:** 250 feet

**Trail surface:** Single- and double-track dirt trail and closed road

**Seasons:** Year-round. It can be icy and snowy in winter.

**Schedule:** Open daily

**Other trail users:** Mountain bikers, cross-country skiers, horseback riders

**Canine compatibility:** Leashed dogs only

**Land status:** Public and private

**Fees and permits:** None

**Map:** USGS Cripple Creek South

**Trail contact:** Victor Chamber of Commerce, http://ccv chamber.com

**Other:** The first part of the trail to the Theresa Mine is wheelchair accessible.

**Special considerations:** The trailhead is at 10,000 feet so altitude can cause problems. Stay hydrated by drinking plenty of water and use ibuprofen for altitude headaches. The trail crosses an unsafe mining area — stay on the trail, keep children under control, and keep your dog leashed.

**Finding the trailhead:** From Colorado Springs and I-25, drive west on US 24 up Ute Pass and Woodland Park to Divide. Turn left (south) on CO 67 and drive south through Cripple Creek to Victor. In the center of Victor, turn left (north) off CO 67/Victor Avenue on Fourth Street. Drive 1 block and turn right on Diamond Avenue/CR 81, which runs east and then north out of Victor. Drive 1.7 miles north through Goldfield and turn left into a parking lot at the trailhead (**GPS:** 38.725185, -105.123413). An alternate trailhead (**GPS:** 38.727447, -105.127256) is farther north at the Vindicator Mine—continue up CR 81 another 0.4 mile and turn left on CR 831. Drive 0.4 mile to the trailhead on the left at the top of the trail loop.

## THE HIKE

The 2-mile-long Vindicator Valley Trail, one of the Trails of Gold near Victor behind Pikes Peak, is an interpretative trail that explores the area's colorful 1890s gold rush days. The wide gravel trail, with a smooth walking surface, makes a wide loop on the southeast flank of Battle Mountain north of the town of Victor, nicknamed the "City of Mines." The easy hike, with gradual uphill grades, passes old mines and crumbling historic buildings. Numerous signs along the trail detail the area's rich mining history. The first trail section to the Theresa Mine is wheelchair accessible.

The trail has two trailheads—an upper one on Teller County Road 831 and a lower one on Teller 81. Begin your hike at the lower trailhead on the south side of a dirt parking area off the paved road just north of Goldfield.

Hike southwest on the wide trail, which is lined by a split-rail fence, toward the obvious Theresa Mine on the skyline. A trail junction is reached after 0.1 mile. Keep right on the main trail. The left trail is where you return after hiking the loop.

The trail reaches the north side of the Theresa Mine after a quarter mile. The mine's head frame towers above the trail, its metal sheath rattling in the wind and dark with rust. An ore house adjoins the head frame. Just past the mine, look up right at an old metal-sided outhouse that undoubtedly offered one of the area's best latrine views. A sign explains the photogenic mine's history.

A powder magazine alongside the trail was used by crews at the Anna J Mine.

The Theresa Mine began operating in 1895, just north of Winfield Scott Stratton's famed Independence Mine, the richest gold mine in the Cripple Creek–Victor Mining District. It operated until 1915 when low gold prices caused by World War I forced it to close. The mine was idle until 1930 when it reopened with surging prices in the Great Depression and the main shaft was dug to 1,620 feet. A fire destroyed the Theresa's wood structures in 1934 and the buildings were reconstructed with steel and the metal sheath seen today. The mine operated until 1961 before closing for good, although starting in 1981 the mine's waste dump rock was removed for heap leaching, a modern process to separate gold from low-grade ore. The Theresa Mine produced an estimated 120,000 ounces of gold, valued at over $196 million at current gold prices.

A good viewpoint, looking southwest toward the distant Sangre de Cristo Mountains, is west of the mine as the trail bends right. In the valley below is the old town of Goldfield, now a collection of houses but a town of miners in 1900 with a population of 3,000 and two newspapers. The dilapidated Anna J Mine sits on the west side of the trail 0.1 mile west of the Theresa. Gold was dug from the Anna J from the 1890s until it closed in 1947. Weathering has exposed the mine's wooden head frame and torn much of the corrugated metal sheeting off its buildings. Piles of waste rock surround the site.

A trail junction is just past the Anna J Mine at 0.4 mile. A short spur path goes right to building ruins above the Theresa. On the east side of the junction, however, is an interesting small structure used to store explosives. The stone-and-brick building, with a half-moon roof, was a storage magazine with a heavy steel door. Most mines had two magazines—one for explosives and one for detonators to lessen the possibility of accidental explosions. This magazine was used by Anna J miners.

Continue hiking up hill, passing numerous mine ruins as well as the abandoned bed of a railroad spur that served the Vindicator Mine and others on Battle Mountain. The trail is fenced to keep hikers from crossing dangerous slopes with open mine shafts since this is still considered an active mining area. Also, stay on the trail to avoid damaging the fragile historic buildings.

After 0.7 mile the trail reaches the upper trailhead and parking lot on CR 831 / Independence Road. The numerous mine buildings at this trail high point include the towering steel head frame of the famed Vindicator Mine and the adjoining mill. The Vindicator, with multiple shafts, was a huge production. In old photographs from 1900, the humming Vindicator complex looks like a small busy city, with heaps of dump rock, a railroad line, an ore-sorting house, and a couple of enclosed head frames.

The hike continues past the trail high point at the Vindicator by heading west across the head of the bowl-shaped valley and then gently descending open slopes past more mine ruins and abandoned mine shafts. The western rim of the

0    Kilometer    0.25

0    Mile    0.25

N

81

831

P

Vindicator
Mine

P

34

Anna J
Mine

Theresa
Mine

81

Goldfield

To
Victor

🐛 **Green Tip:**
*Don't take souvenirs home with you. This means natural*
*materials such as plants, rocks, and wildflowers as well as*
*historic artifacts such as fossils and arrowheads.*

valley is the upper edge of the Cripple Creek & Victor Gold Mining Company, a subsidiary of AngloGold Ashanti and Colorado's largest gold producer. The company is excavating a deep pit, the largest open pit mine in Colorado, below what was the old Cresson Mine, and recovering low-grade gold with grades as little as 1 gram of gold from a ton of rock. While the Cresson opened in 1892, the current pit operation began in 1995.

As the trail descends, stop and check out the numerous mine buildings and catch a breather at various scenic overlooks. After 1.5 miles the trail bends left and begins its return back to the trailhead by traversing across gentle slopes below the Theresa Mine. At 1.9 miles you reach the original trail junction. Keep right on the broad path and return to the parking area and the end of a historic hike.

## MILES AND DIRECTIONS

**0.0** Begin at the trailhead at the south side of a parking lot on the west side of CR 81 just north of Goldfield (GPS: 38.724947, -105.123505). Hike southwest on the wide trail.

**0.1** Reach a trail junction (GPS: 38.724462, -105.124169). Keep right on the wide trail. The left trail is the return at the end of the loop hike.

**0.3** The Theresa Mine towers above the trail (GPS: 38.723093, -105.12605).

**0.4** The Anna J Mine is on the left side of the trail. In a few hundred feet, you reach a trail junction (GPS: 38.723996, -105.127301). A spur trail goes right to an overlook of mine ruins. Keep left on the main trail. Check out a stone-and-brick magazine on the east for storing explosives. Continue hiking up the trail.

**0.7** Reach the upper trailhead and parking area on CR 831 (GPS: 38.727422, -105.12724). The Vindicator Mine head frame and building ruins are just west of the trailhead. The trail begins descending here.

**1.5** After passing numerous mine ruins, the trail bends sharply left and crosses gentle slopes (GPS: 38.721581, -105.128937).

**1.8** Pass below the Theresa Mine.

**1.9** Reach the original trail junction. Keep right on the main path.

**2.0** End the hike at the trailhead and parking area.

# Dateline 1890: Bob Womack Discovers Gold

Bob Womack, a 46-year-old cowboy described in *Hamptons'* magazine as an "amiable, riotous, and irrepressible prospector," discovered one of the world's greatest gold bonanzas in a dry gulch southwest of Pikes Peak in 1890. Womack, aware of rumors that there was gold near Pikes Peak, herded cows across grassy hills along Cripple Creek, always keeping his eyes on the ground as he rode his horse. Bob looked for telltale rocks and outcroppings that might indicate the presence of gold or silver. In 1878 he had a piece of gray rock assayed—it came back as gold at $200 a ton. But no one believed the assay, especially after an 1884 gold claim on nearby Mount Pisgah proved to be a fraud, with salted ore. In 1890 Womack struck pay dirt with his El Paso Lode, located above his cabin in Poverty Gulch. While experts in Colorado Springs again greeted his claim with skepticism, other miners quietly filed their own claims on the hills.

By 1891 everyone believed Bob Womack and the gold rush was on. Almost overnight the town of Cripple Creek sprang up in the valley below Poverty Gulch and by 1900 the area boasted a population of 50,000 and was Colorado's fourth-largest city. While Cripple Creek was the financial and social center of the mining district, its sister city Victor, dubbed the "City of Mines," was the mining center, with the area's greatest gold producers, including the Independence, Ajax, and Portland mines, spread across the slopes of Battle Mountain above the town.

The Cripple Creek and Victor Mining District had more than 500 operating mines by 1900, and during its boom years, over $340 million of gold was extracted at the prevailing price of $20.67 an ounce. The district offered 150 saloons, forty-one assay offices, ninety-one lawyers, forty-six brokerage houses, and fourteen newspapers, along with dance halls, brothels, hotels, theaters, restaurants, and shops. Few gold camps in the world have surpassed the wealth dug from Cripple Creek's mines. Over half of Colorado's total gold production has come from the district, which produced more than fifty millionaires. Since 1890 over 23 million ounces of gold have been dug from the rolling hills with a 2012 value of $37 billion.

Bob Womack would have been proud. Bob, however, never became a millionaire. He sold his interest in the El Paso Lode for $300; a few months later that interest was worth $15,000, and the mine eventually produced over $5 million in gold. Bob moved down to Colorado Springs, staying at his sister Eliza's boarding house, before dying in 1909.

# Florissant Fossil Beds National Monument Trails

*The Petrified Forest Loop Trail, along with the optional wheelchair-accessible Ponderosa Loop Trail, explores the Florissant Fossil Beds National Monument Trails unique fossil record, passing massive petrified tree stumps and old fossil quarries that have yielded some of the world's best fossil insects, butterflies, and leaves.*

**Start:** Trailhead east of Florissant Fossil Beds National Monument visitor center
**Distance:** 1.0-mile loop
**Hiking time:** About 1 hour
**Difficulty:** Easy
**Elevation gain:** Minimal
**Trail surface:** Dirt trails
**Seasons:** Year-round
**Schedule:** Open daily, sunrise to sunset
**Other trail users:** None. Hikers only.

**Canine compatibility:** Dogs not permitted
**Land status:** National Park Service
**Fees and permits:** Park entrance fee required
**Maps:** USGS Lake George. Monument trail map.
**Trail contacts:** Florissant Fossil Beds National Monument, 1 Teller County Rd. 62, Divide, CO 80814; (719) 748-3253; www.nps.gov/flfo

**Finding the trailhead:** From I-25 and downtown Colorado Springs, take the Cimarron Street/US 24 exit (exit 141) and drive west for 35 miles, passing through Woodland Park and Divide, to the town of Florissant. Turn left (south) on Teller County Road 1, and drive 2 miles to the visitor center road. Turn right (west) and drive 0.2 mile to a parking area at the visitor center (**GPS:** 38.913541, -105.284764). An admittance fee is charged.

## THE HIKE

These two excellent and informative easy hikes—the 1-mile Petrified Forest Loop Trail (featured route) and the optional, wheelchair-accessible 0.5-mile Ponderosa Loop Trail—explore the unique geological record that is preserved and protected by 5,998-acre Florissant Fossil Beds National Monument, a stone repository of ancient life.

The hikes, which are easily combined into a loop that begins and ends at the monument visitor center, not only offer fun hiking, they are also educational. Interpretive signs are regularly scattered along both trails, giving insight into both yesterday's fossil record and today's forest and grassland ecosystems. These easy walks are kid friendly and ideal for family adventures.

Florissant Fossil Beds is simply one of the best and richest fossil locales in the world. Buried beneath the meadows and woodlands is an extensive record of a lush lost world from 34 million years ago. The fossils here are of two types: the minute and the huge. There are the massive petrified stumps and trunks of towering redwood trees, buried by volcanic mudflows that also dammed the valley, forming Lake Florissant, that capture our imagination.

But it is small, delicate fossils of tiny insects, animal remains, and fragments of plant life hidden within thin shale layers that make the Florissant Fossil Beds singular. More than 1,500 insect species have been uncovered here, including

The Big Stump is the petrified remains of a giant redwood that once grew along the edge of ancient Lake Florissant.

almost all the fossilized butterflies found in the Western Hemisphere as well as the only fossil of a tsetse fly, now found only in equatorial Africa.

Start your fossil hikes at the visitor center. You can pick up a trail map and self-guiding booklet and look at fossils in the center before heading out. Exit out the back door of the visitor center to a paved path and a kiosk with safety information. Remember that you're at 8,400 feet here and may feel the altitude if you're coming from a lower elevation. Bring water, use sunscreen, and keep an eye on the weather in summer. Lightning and thunderstorms are common in the afternoon.

To hike the Petrified Forest Loop Trail, walk from the visitor center to the stump shelter. Go right (north) from the Y junction on the north side of the stump shelter. The trail goes north along the west edge of a broad valley, crossing large meadows fringed with glades of ponderosa pine. Another trail junction is 100 feet north of the fork. Keep straight on the doubletrack trail. Many interpretative signs are scattered along the trail, offering lots of information about the fossils, ancient ecosystems, park geology, and monument history.

The trail reaches a trail junction after 0.3 mile and the aptly named Big Stump, one of the monument's largest fossils. Big Stump is the remains of a massive redwood tree that was as tall as 230 feet and more than 750 years old when volcanic mud buried its base, smothering the tree's roots and depriving them of oxygen. Besides the twelve excavated stumps seen today, remote sensing reveals at least forty stumps that still remain buried here along the edge of ancient Lake Florissant.

(**FYI:** While it's not available on a self-guided tour, Scudder Pit is about 0.1 mile to the left. This fossil excavation site was named for early paleontologist Samuel Scudder, who collected in the pit area, amassing more than 600 fossil species of insects, most of which are now in Harvard University's Museum of Comparative Zoology. In 1890 Scudder's definitive *Tertiary Insects of North America*, detailing Florissant's astonishing fossils, was published. You're not allowed to collect any fossils here. To see Scudder Pit, you must take a ranger-led tour.)

After viewing the colorful Big Stump, head east on the trail, passing a couple more stumps, to a hillock dotted with ponderosa pines. The trail turns right here and heads southwest back to the visitor center and parking. More signs detail the area's early history, when competing fossil pits vied for customers, who paid to view the stumps or to dig fossils. Near the visitor center, an obscure trail to the Hornbek Homestead cuts sharply left. Keep straight to the trail's end at the parking lot and visitor center.

## MILES AND DIRECTIONS

**0.0**   Start of Petrified Forest Loop (GPS: 38.913829, -105.286467).

**0.3**   Trail junction to Scudder Pit on left (GPS: 38.918142, -105.286025). Visit only on ranger-led tour.

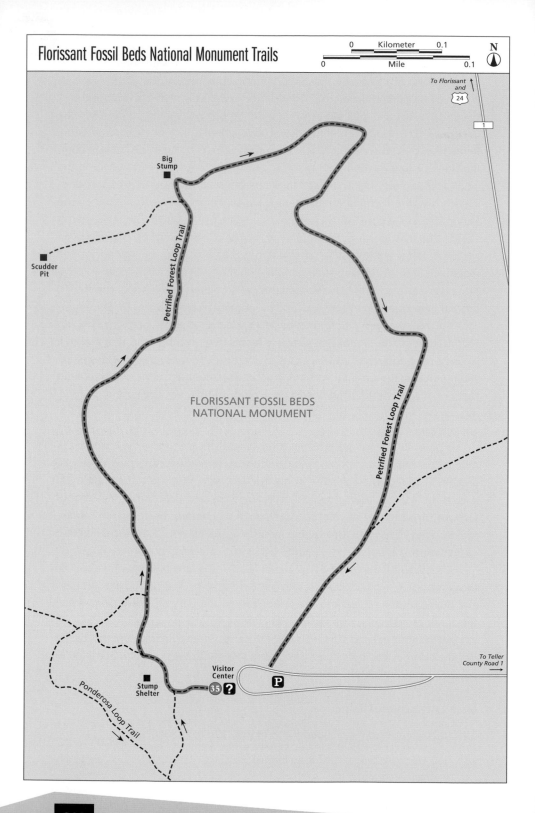

# Florissant Fossil Beds National Monument Trails

Kilometer 0 — 0.1

Mile 0 — 0.1

N

To Florissant and 24

1

Big Stump

Scudder Pit

Petrified Forest Loop Trail

FLORISSANT FOSSIL BEDS
NATIONAL MONUMENT

Petrified Forest Loop Trail

To Teller County Road 1

Visitor Center 35 ?

Stump Shelter

P

Ponderosa Loop Trail

**0.4**   Reach Big Stump on the left (GPS: 38.918384, -105.286089).

**1.0**   Finish the loop at the paved trail at the back of the visitor center (GPS: 38.913702, -105.285830).

### Options

The wheelchair-accessible Ponderosa Loop Trail has lots of interpretative signs, some benches, and a couple of buried petrified stumps. Follow the short 0.5-mile trail counterclockwise, passing some big petrified stumps and exploring the hillside above. The first stump is straight ahead under a canopy. Continue to the next stump pavilion for interesting exhibits and two large redwood stumps, including one with three trunks from a common root system. After climbing stairs out of the stump pit or taking the paved walk around the pit, follow the trail 50 feet to a Y junction. Go left on a smooth gravel path. A signpost between trails points the way.

The rock-lined, doubletrack trail travels up and left across a gentle hillside covered with fir, spruce, and pine. At the only trail junction, keep left on the wide trail. The right fork connects to longer loop hikes. Return to the large stump shelter and amphitheater and hike back to the Y fork on its north side. Keep straight to return to the visitor center.

### Ponderosa Loop Trail Miles and Directions

**0.0**   Start at the trailhead behind the monument visitor center (GPS: 38.913491, -105.285657).

**0.1**   Reach a Y trail junction north of stump shelter (GPS: 38.913835, -105.286475). Go left on the Ponderosa Loop Trail.

**0.4**   End the Ponderosa Loop hike at the Y junction north of large stump shelter. Go straight to return to the visitor center. (**Option:** Go right at the junction to start the 1-mile Petrified Forest Loop.)

**0.5**   Finish your hike when you reach the visitor center.

### More Florissant Fossil Beds Trails

For extra credit, Florissant Fossil Beds offers six other excellent trails that total almost 14 miles. You can pick up a detailed trail map and get info from a park ranger in the visitor center. All the trails are well maintained and moderate in difficulty. They have minimal elevation loss and gain, making all the trails ideal for kids or beginning hikers. Among the trails you may choose are the 3.8-mile Hornbeck Wildlife Loop (keep an eye out for elk); the 2.8-mile Boulder Creek Trail, which ends at a jumble of granite boulders; and the 2.3-mile Twin Rock Trail, with its aspens, meadows, and rock formations.

# Twin Rocks Trail

*This moderate out-and-back hike explores broad grassy valleys and humped ridges coated with a pine and fir woodland. It follows a good trail to the far northeastern boundary of Florissant Fossil Beds National Monument and South Twin Rock, a rounded granite dome.*

**Start:** Trailhead on west side of Florissant Fossil Beds National Monument visitor center

**Distance:** 7.0 miles out and back

**Hiking time:** 2 to 4 hours

**Difficulty:** Moderate because of length

**Elevation gain:** About 500 feet. Total gain is 1,100 feet.

**Trail surface:** Dirt trail

**Seasons:** Year-round. Best months are Apr through Oct. The trail is icy and snowy in winter; good for snowshoeing and cross-country skiing.

**Schedule:** Day use only; Memorial Day to Labor Day, 8 a.m. to 6 p.m.; early Sept to late May, 9 a.m. to 5 p.m.

**Other trail users:** None. Hikers only.

**Canine compatibility:** Dogs not permitted

**Land status:** National Park Service

**Fees and permits:** Park entrance fee required. Pay at the visitor center.

**Maps:** USGS Lake George and Divide quads. National Monument trail map (available at visitor center or on the park website).

**Trail contacts:** Florissant Fossil Beds National Monument, 1 Teller County Rd. 62, Divide, CO 80814; (719) 748-3253; www.nps.gov/flfo

**Finding the trailhead:** From I-25 and downtown Colorado Springs, take the Cimarron Street/US 24 exit (exit #141) and drive west for 35 miles, passing through Woodland Park and Divide, to the town of Florissant. Turn left (south) on Teller County Road 1, and drive 2 miles to the marked visitor center road. Turn right (west) and drive 0.2 mile to a parking area at the visitor center (**GPS:** 38.913541, -105.284764). An admittance fee is charged. The hike begins on the west side of the visitor center before the first stump pavilion.

## THE HIKE

The Twin Rocks Trail is a wonderful hike that explores the backcountry at Florissant Fossil Beds National Monument. The 7-mile out-and-back hike, following four separate trails, sees little hiking traffic, with most walkers doing the shorter Ponderosa Loop and Petrified Forest Loop Trails. The hike traverses broad grasslands and shallow valleys lined with ponderosa pines and aspen glades, and finishes up a wide valley to South Twin Rock, double granite domes perched on the national monument's northeast boundary.

The hike offers easy walking with minimal elevation gain except for an uphill section above Grape Creek; the moderate difficulty rating is due to the length of the hike. The trails are singletrack paths that mostly follow old ranch roads that are covered with grass. Carry drinking water, since no potable water is found along the trail, and a raincoat, since drenching thunderstorms often occur on summer afternoons. A pair of binoculars is also a good addition to your pack since elk, mule deer, and other wildlife is often seen on this lonesome hike.

The Hornbek Homestead, which lies on the west side of CR 1, is a must-stop either before or after you do the Florissant hikes. The house and surrounding buildings, listed on the National Register of Historic Places as a prime example of a nineteenth-century homestead, was built in 1878 for Adaline Hornbek, who

The slabby face of South Twin Rock, the highest point at Florissant Fossil Beds National Monument, towers above the Twin Rocks Trail.

settled here as a widowed rancher with four children. The two-story log house had glass-pane windows; outbuildings included a milk house, chicken coop, and stable.

The hike begins on the west side of the visitor center, just past a half-moon-shaped plaza and before the first stump shelter. Go right (north) between two ponderosa pine trees on the Petrified Forest Loop Trail and hike northeast across a wide flat meadow, passing the top of a petrified stump that juts out of the ground. After 0.2 mile go right on Hornbek Wildlife Loop Trail. The next 0.9-mile section follows this trail to its junction with Shootin' Star Trail.

The singletrack trail continues northeast through a grove of pines on a hillock and descends to Teller County Road 1 at 0.3 mile. After crossing the road the trail gently drops down to a wooden bridge over trickling Grape Creek at 0.45 mile, swings left under a low granite cliff, and climbs a wooded hillside over a ridge to a higher ridgeline and a trail post at 0.9 mile.

Descend the cooler north side of the ridge through a Douglas fir forest and reach a signed trail junction after 1.1 miles. The Hornbek Wildlife Loop goes left here for 0.7 mile to the Hornbek Homestead. The hike, however, continues straight on the marked Shootin' Star Trail. The trail heads northeast along the edge of a ponderosa pine forest on the right and wide grasslands on the left.

Hike on the level trail and reach another major trail junction after 0.3 mile. The Twin Rocks Trail begins at this junction on the east side of an old dam built for a stock pond by early ranchers. The Shootin' Star Trail, named for elegant shooting star flowers found along the path in summer, goes right (southeast) for 1.6 miles to Barksdale Picnic Area off Lower Twin Rock Road.

Go left on the singletrack Twin Rocks Trail from the junction and hike northeast on a gradual grade. The trail continues following the edge of the pine forest and broad meadows, which dip gently westward to the historic Hornbek Homestead and Teller County Road 1. The trail crosses the grasslands and passes through open piney woods. Stop to enjoy good views west across the national monument to the Puma Hills and the rough Tarryall Range in Lost Creek Wilderness Area to the northwest. Also watch for herds of elk and mule deer grazing in the meadows west of the trail and in the open valleys farther east.

After hiking 0.7 mile from the last trail junction, you dip down into a shallow valley and cross a small creek on a wooden bridge. The last leg of the Twin Rocks Trail heads east up this valley along an unnamed creek for 1.7 miles to the eastern boundary of Florissant Fossil Beds National Monument and the end of the trail.

Hike east on the north side of the shallow valley through open meadows. The floor of the valley on your right is bound by the west-flowing creek, lined with willows and groves of aspen. After hiking 0.3 mile from the bridge, you reach an old stock pond, the creek blocked by a small earthen dam. Cattails and willows clot the dam, while the pond's still water reflects sky, clouds, and, in autumn, golden quaking aspen trees.

Continue hiking east up the widening valley, passing pine-clad hillsides studded with granite boulders. At 2.7 miles the trail passes beneath an 80-foot-high granite outcropping capped by an overhanging block. Look at the bottom of the cliff for a thick band of white quartz. The next half mile of hiking is up the wide valley through open meadows, passing overgrown roads that once led to now-abandoned ranches and homesteads, to a boardwalk that crosses a short marshy section along the creek.

The trail heads east across an open meadow toward 8,963-foot South Twin Rock, a rounded granite dome cleaved by vertical cracks separated by steep slabs. The rock, the high point of Florissant Fossil Beds National Monument, rises in the far northeast corner of the monument property. Just north of South Twin Rock is Upper Twin Rock Road and North Twin Rock, an 8,975-foot knob that overlooks US 24.

Pass just south of the rugged dome and walk through an aspen grove. This is especially gorgeous in autumn when golden leaves shimmer on the quaking aspens. Continue on the trail under a slabby cliff and, after 3.5 miles of hiking, reach the end of the trail at a fence and gate that marks the northeastern boundary of the national monument. A sign notes "Trail Ends: Private Property Beyond This Point."

This is a great spot for lunch on dense grass alongside the trail or on a granite slab on the hillside above. After a proper rest, gather your pack together and return back to the visitor center, retracing your steps along the three trails for a 7.0 mile long hike.

**Green Tip:**
*Observe wildlife from a distance. Don't interfere in their lives—both of you will be better for it.*

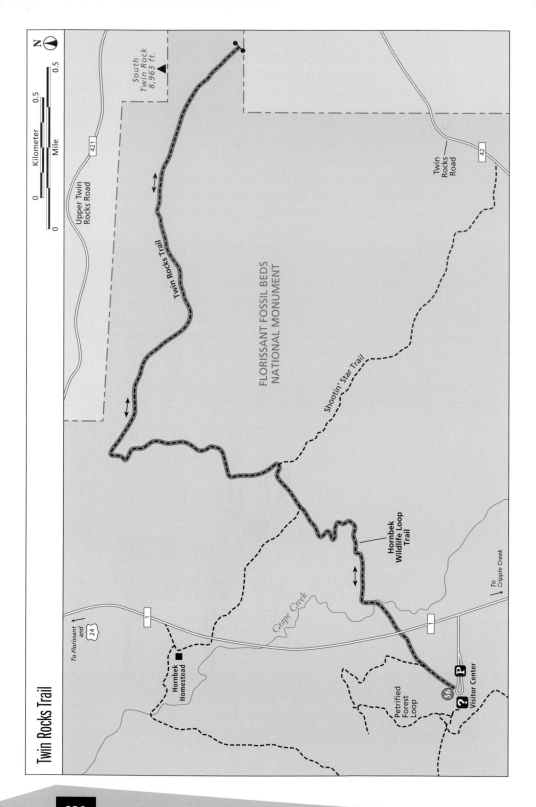

Twin Rocks Trail

South Twin Rock
8,963 ft.

FLORISSANT FOSSIL BEDS
NATIONAL MONUMENT

Twin Rocks Trail

Upper Twin
Rocks Road

421

Twin
Rocks
Road

42

Shootin' Star Trail

Hornbek
Wildlife Loop
Trail

Grape Creek

To Florissant
and

24

1

Hornbek
Homestead

1

To
Cripple Creek

Petrified
Forest
Loop

3.6

P

2

Visitor Center

N

Kilometer
0        0.5

Mile
0        0.5

## MILES AND DIRECTIONS

**0.0** Start at the trailhead on the west side of the visitor center. Go right from the paved trail on the Petrified Forest Loop Trail (GPS: 38.913704, -105.285824).

**0.2** Turn right on the Hornbek Wildlife Loop Trail (GPS: 38.914945, -105.283688).

**0.3** Cross Teller County Road 1. Descend east across a valley to a bridge.

**0.5** Cross the bridge over marshy Grape Creek (GPS: 38.917334, -105.279847) and begin hiking uphill.

**0.9** Reach the top of a high ridge marked with a post (GPS: 38.919248, -105.276067), then descend forested north-facing slopes.

**1.1** Reach a major trail junction (GPS: 38.920750, -105.274266). Go straight on the Shootin' Star Trail. Follow the edge of a wide valley. A left turn is the continuation of the Hornbek Wildlife Loop Trail.

**1.3** Reach another major trail junction on the east side of an old earthen dam (GPS: 38.921892, -105.271702). Go left on marked Twin Rocks Trail. Right is Shootin' Star Trail.

**2.0** Reach a wooden bridge over a creek (GPS: 38.929569, -105.271187). The trail bends east up a wide valley.

**2.3** Reach an old stock pond lined with cattails and willows (GPS: 38.928560, -105.267547).

**2.7** Trail passes below a south-facing granite cliff.

**3.1** Cross a boardwalk across a short marshy area or scramble across a granite slab above it (GPS: 38.926862, -105.253259).

**3.3** Pass through an aspen grove below South Twin Rock and continue east below a slabby cliff.

**3.5** Reach a gate on the eastern boundary of the national monument and the end of the trail (GPS: 38.923750, -105.246886). The land beyond the fence is private property. Turn around here and hike back.

**7.0** Arrive back at the visitor center and the hike's end.

# Goose Creek Trail

*An excellent out-and-back hike on Goose Creek Trail up a scenic valley to historic buildings and a final overlook in the heart of Lost Creek Wilderness Area.*

**Start:** Goose Greek Trailhead (#612) just west of Mutakat Road / Park County Road 211
**Distance:** 9.2 miles out and back
**Hiking time:** 6 to 8 hours
**Difficulty:** Moderate
**Elevation gain:** 900 feet
**Trail surface:** Singletrack dirt trail
**Seasons:** Year-round. Trail is snowy and icy in winter. The access road to the trailhead may be impassable in winter.
**Schedule:** Open daily
**Other trail users:** Equestrians, backpackers. No mountain bikes or motorized vehicles allowed.

**Canine compatibility:** Dogs are allowed off-leash.
**Land status:** Public land in Lost Creek Wilderness Area, Pike National Forest
**Fees and permits:** A free permit for each group is at the trailhead and must be filled out and deposited in a steel box. No fees are required.
**Map:** USGS McCurdy Mountain
**Trail contact:** South Platte Ranger District, Pike National Forest, 19316 Goddard Ranch Ct., Morrison, CO 80465; (303) 275-5610; www.fs.usda.gov

**Finding the trailhead:** Drive west on US 24 from Colorado Springs through Woodland Park and Divide to Lake George. Continue west from Lake George on US 24 for 1.2 miles and turn right (north) on paved Park County Road 77. Follow CR 77 for 7 miles and turn right (north) on FR 211. Follow dirt FR 211 for 11 miles to FR 558. Turn left (west) and drive 1.9 miles to the Goose Creek Trailhead and a large parking area (**GPS:** 39.173117, -105.375202).

## THE HIKE

The popular and wildly scenic Goose Creek Trail travels west up a gorgeous mountain valley into the heart of the Lost Creek Wilderness Area from its eastern trailhead for 9.4 miles to its northern trailhead in Wigwam Park. This hike, 4.6 miles one-way, is half of the trail's total distance, making it a great day-hiking excursion from Colorado Springs. The trail is often busy, especially on weekends, with hikers and backpackers, so come during the week for more solitude, quiet, and inspiration.

The 119,790-acre Lost Creek Wilderness Area protects most of the 25-mile-long Tarryall Range, a swath of wooded mountains west of Colorado Springs. Only a couple of mountains in the Tarryalls break the above-timberline elevation mark—12,432-foot Bison Peak, the range high point, and 12,164-foot McCurdy Mountain. The magic of the Tarryall Range and the wilderness range, however, is not in majestic snowcapped peaks but in bold outcroppings of pink Pikes Peak granite. The range is a metropolis of architectural forms—castles, spires, spikes, domes, minarets, mosques, house-size boulders, and cliff-lined corridors.

The Lost Creek Wilderness Area, an enclave of deafening silence an hour west of the bustle of Colorado Springs, is named for Lost Creek, one of Colorado's most unusual water courses. Lost Creek, originating on the west side of

The old engine at the shafthouse is all that remains of a proposed dam project on Lost Creek.

the Tarryalls, twists through wide willow-filled valleys and down rocky canyons and in at least nine places disappears underground or becomes "lost" beneath huge jumbles of fallen boulders. After its final disappearance, a half-mile forested stretch that this hike crosses to a viewpoint, Lost Creek emerges from the boulder sink and becomes Goose Creek.

The ancient Pikes Peak granite, a rough, coarse-grained granite, was deposited over a billion years ago in a huge batholith beneath the earth's crust. The molten rock slowly solidified and cooled underground. Later this bedrock was uplifted by the Ancestral Rocky Mountains and today's Rocky Mountains, and then ensuing eons of erosion stripped away surface layers, exposing the granite core. Weathering and erosion, including frost-wedging and flowing water, chiseled and sculpted the granite, leaving today's fanciful wonderland of rock forms and shapes.

Begin the hike at the 8,220-foot Goose Creek Trailhead a hundred yards southwest of the parking lot on the west side of the dead-end access road. Before starting the hike, someone from your hiking party must fill out a wilderness permit at a register box at the trailhead. Deposit the lower portion of the permit in a metal box and keep the other half in your possession while in Lost Creek Wilderness Area. The free permit allows the national forest to keep an accurate count of wilderness users.

Just past the permit station is a sign marking the wilderness boundary as well as a 1979 plaque designating Lost Creek Scenic Area, an area within the wilderness, as a prestigious National Natural Landmark. A two-panel interpretative sign has an area map, rules and regulations, safety info, what to bring on your hike, and the basic Leave No Trace ethic.

The singletrack trail (Trail #612) descends from the wilderness boundary, heading southwest down a mountain slope covered with dead tree snags. The area at the trailhead and to the south and southwest up Hankins Gulch was decimated by the Hayman Fire in 2002. The hillside is slowly regenerating with shrubs and wildflowers filling across the slope. Dead snag trees, still black from the fire, gauntly stand tall, although many have snapped off in high winds. Beware of toppling snags if you are hiking in the burn area when it's windy.

After descending for a quarter mile, the trail crosses Hankins Creek on a slippery log. Continue a few feet to a trail junction. Go right on the signed Goose Creek Trail. A left turn goes up Hankins Pass Trail to Hankins Pass in the south part of the wilderness area. The trail heads north above the creek and in half a mile reaches the edge between the burn area and the forest. Enter the pine and fir forest and turn left on the trail at Goose Creek. At 0.7 mile the trail crosses to the north bank of the creek on a sturdy steel bridge with plank flooring and turns west.

The next 0.4 mile of trail threads through a mixed conifer forest of ponderosa pine, Douglas fir, and Engelmann spruce beside Goose Creek. In spring the creek is swollen with snowmelt, but usually it's a pleasant tumbling stream;

trout swim in its deep hole. Eventually the valley widens and the creek meanders among boulders and pools in still beaver ponds lined with willows. Granite slabs and faces stair-step up a couple unnamed mountains that tower to the south.

After 1.3 miles the trail leaves the creek and begins climbing steep slopes above Goose Creek. The next 3.5-mile trail segment gently climbs for a couple miles to 8,700 feet before dipping and rolling through a series of dry shallow valleys that drain south into Goose Creek. The initial hill is steep and rutted in occasional places before traversing across mountain slopes.

At about 2 miles look up left through a gap in the trees toward a big sweeping slab with a thin pinnacle called the Organ Pipe beside it. On the right side of the slab and pinnacle at 8,960 feet is one of the Tarryalls' most unusual rock formations: Harmonica Arch (GPS: 39.19100, -105.39483). One of the longest unsupported granite arches in the United States, Harmonica Arch is 85 feet long, 30 feet high, 18 feet wide, and 15 feet thick. The arch is reached from the trailhead by a 4.8-mile round-trip hike that gains a net 740 feet. The trail to it leaves the bottom of the valley where the Goose Creek Trail begins going uphill.

Continue west on the wide, well-used trail along the north side of the valley. Occasional overlooks allow good views up the valley toward the heart of the wilderness area. The trail descends hills, crosses shallow valleys, and climbs back over ridges.

After 3.9 miles the trail reaches a junction in the bottom of a shallow valley. A wooden sign designating the Goose Creek Trail also points left to a spur trail that leads to "Historic Buildings." Go left down this rocky path for 0.1 mile to a collection of dilapidated buildings alongside a meadow and the junction with the Shafthouse Trail, which you will take shortly.

These ramshackle buildings were built in the 1890s to house workers for the Antero and Lost Creek Reservoir Company, which was attempting between 1891 and 1910 to build a dam at the boulder jumble just to the south of here. The largest was a two-story bunkhouse with plank floors and a stone fireplace on the first floor. The walls were made of big logs, hewn to a square shape, with the gaps between logs chinked with mortar. The back of the house was apparently a kitchen and dining room for feeding the hungry employees. Next door is another, smaller log cabin, and across the trail on the east side of the meadow are the remains of other cabins. Nearby is the gravesite of a 1930s prospector named Palmer, his grave outlined with rough chunks of white quartz.

The last leg of the hike goes 0.7 mile from the historic buildings to the shafthouse site and on through boulders to a spectacular overlook on top of giant boulders. From the signed trail junction at the north side of the bunkhouse, go west on the trail marked "Shafthouse."

The singletrack trail goes west, crosses a trickling creek, then bends southeast and traverses across a gravelly hillside to a high point below a granite dome.

Descend the trail through giant boulders to the bottom of the valley, which at this point is the top of a massive jumble of boulders covered with soil, gravel, trees, and grass. Lost Creek tumbles through secret rock passages over 100 feet below the surface here.

The trail heads west here, 0.6 mile from the buildings, and reaches the site of the old shafthouse. A rusted piece of machinery—an old steam engine—sits here on a gravel pad below a slabby cliff. This is the site of a cable pulley used to raise and lower tools, supplies, workers, and waste tailings from a shaft that was dug here to the creek far below the ground surface. The workers housed in the buildings were hired to drill a shaft through the bedrock to Lost Creek. The idea then was to pump the underground void full of concrete to dam the creek and form a proposed Lost Park Reservoir in the gorgeous valley just upstream. Technology in 1900, however, was not up to the task and the project failed by 1910. Just imagine the work that it took, though, just to haul all the bits of the steam engine back to this remote spot.

Beyond the shafthouse the trail winds through boulders and then passes across a quiet meadow surrounded by towering cliffs and domes. Continue into a catacomb of giant boulders and either scoot down a big log in a narrow corridor on the left or squeeze through a slot into another narrow corridor on the right. Both passageways lead west for a couple hundred feet to the hike's end at 4.6 miles and a dramatic overlook perched on the edge of a cliff. Be careful scrambling onto the rounded viewpoint above the cliff since there are deep drops in wide cracks as well as a precipitous cliff to the west. This is not a good spot for unsupervised children or those with an aversion to heights. Be prepared for some route-finding dilemmas and possible backtracking to find the best way to the overlook.

The scenic view is simply spectacular. Lost Creek twists across the valley floor, meandering between banks clotted with dense willows. Steep mountain slopes blanketed with fir and spruce climb south above the creek. Immense granite domes, abrupt cliffs, compact outcrops, and boulder piles cover the mountainsides and line the valley's edge. This hidden valley, not seen from the final trail section, is a fitting end to one of the best and wildest hikes in Pikes Peak country. It's a mysterious place that doesn't readily give up its secrets except to those willing to walk into the wilderness.

After savoring the view and enjoying your packed lunch, retrace your steps for 0.8 mile back through the boulder field to the shafthouse ruin and on to the cabins and trail junction. Go right on Goose Creek Trail and hike 3.8 miles back to the trailhead and your car. Most of the trail is downhill so the hiking goes quickly. There are few key junctions on the way, so stick to the well-worn path and you'll be back in a couple of hours.

## The Hayman Fire

The Hayman Fire, the largest in Colorado's recorded history, began south of Lost Creek Wilderness Area and Goose Creek near Lake George on June 8, 2002, and wasn't under control until July 18. The fire torched 138,114 acres in the South Platte River drainage between Lost Creek Wilderness Area and CO 67 north of Woodland Park. Fortunately the fire only burned along the eastern edge of the wilderness area, saving the area's old forests and beauty from ravaging flames. Most of the river canyon east of the wilderness boundary was severely burned, although the area is slowly regenerating, with groves of colonizing aspen spreading across hillsides and riparian growth along creeks. An ongoing study found that 80 percent of the forest understory, including perennial flowers like Front Range beardtongue, Fendler's ragwort, and some exotic species including mullein, quickly regenerated within a couple of years on the burned forest floor.

Towering granite formations rise above Lost Park.

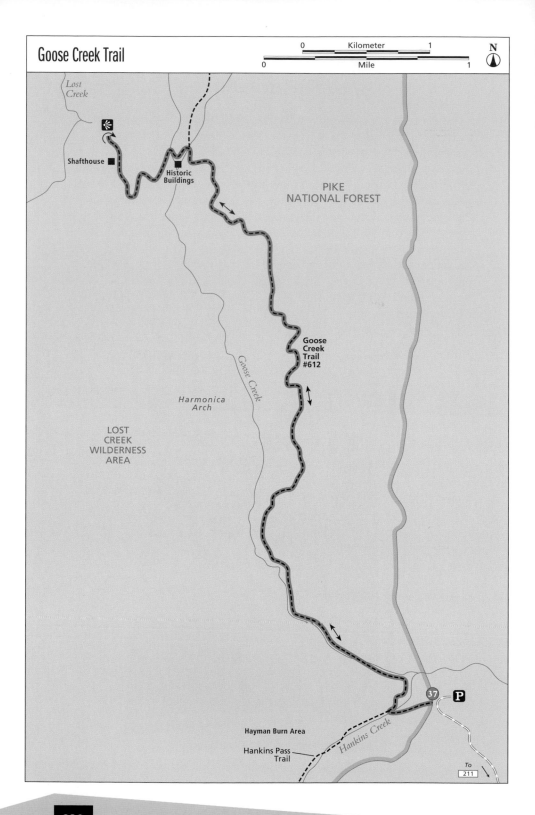

# Goose Creek Trail

Kilometer
0        1

Mile
0        1

N

*Lost Creek*

Shafthouse

Historic Buildings

PIKE NATIONAL FOREST

Goose Creek Trail #612

*Goose Creek*

*Harmonica Arch*

LOST CREEK WILDERNESS AREA

Hankins Creek

Hayman Burn Area

Hankins Pass Trail

37

P

To 211

## MILES AND DIRECTIONS

**0.0** Begin at the Goose Creek Trailhead west of the parking area (GPS: 39.172640, -105.376266).

**0.2** Descend through a burn area and cross a bridge over Hankins Creek to a junction with Hankins Pass Trail. Go right on the west side of the creek (GPS: 39.171997, -105.379996).

**0.5** Reach edge of forest after burn in lower Hankins Gulch.

**0.7** Cross Goose Creek on a bridge to the north bank and go west (GPS: 39.175296, -105.381742).

**1.3** Reach meadows along the creek and start going uphill above the creek GPS: 39.181905, -105.389631.

**3.9** Junction of the Goose Creek Trail and the side trail (GPS: 39.208469, -105.397790) to the historic buildings and overlook. Go left down the valley to the buildings. When you reach the historic buildings, go right toward the overlook (GPS: 39.207586, -105.397718) or straight to the buildings. If you continue down a trail from the buildings to Goose Creek and then walk upstream a few hundred feet, you can see where Lost Creek emerges from the boulder sink and becomes Goose Creek.

**4.5** Reach the old shafthouse (GPS: 39.207310, -105.402288). Continue through a meadow and a boulder field.

**4.6** Overlook (GPS: 39.208953, -105.403264) of Lost Creek and valley.

**5.4** Return to Goose Creek Trail. Go right (east) on the main trail.

**9.2** End the hike at the trailhead. The parking lot is to your left down the access road.

# Blodgett Peak Trail

*A steep hike up a rough trail leads to the summit of Blodgett Peak, an unranked summit that looms over the suburbs of northwest Colorado Springs.*

**Start:** Trailhead at Blodgett Peak Open Space parking area on west side of Woodmen Road

**Distance:** 6.4 miles out and back

**Hiking time:** 4 to 6 hours depending on physical condition

**Difficulty:** Moderately strenuous. Trail is steep, eroded in parts, and has uneven footing.

**Elevation gain:** 2,681 feet

**Trail surface:** Closed gravel road; double- and singletrack dirt trail

**Seasons:** Year-round. Trail has snow and ice in winter. Bring micro-spikes.

**Schedule:** Open daily, dawn to dusk.

**Other trail users:** None

**Canine compatibility:** Leashed dogs allowed on the lower trail section in the city parkland

**Land status:** City of Colorado Springs and Pike National Forest

**Fees and permits:** None

**Map:** USGS Cascade

**Trail contact:** Colorado Springs Parks, Recreation and Cultural Services, 1401 Recreation Way, Colorado Springs, CO 80905-1975; (719) 385-5940; www.springs gov.com

**Finding the trailhead:** From I-25 in Colorado Springs, exit west at the Garden of the Gods Road exit (#146). Drive west on Garden of the Gods Road for 1.1 miles to Centennial Boulevard and turn right (north). The next driving leg follows Centennial north for 4.8 miles to the trailhead. Follow Centennial north through Piñon Valley subdivision to Vindicator Drive, a major road that goes east to I-25 to Woodmen Road and the Woodmen Road exit (#149). Continue north on Centennial, which becomes West Woodmen Road at Orchard Valley Road. Continue on West Woodmen another half mile to the obvious parking lot and trailhead on the left (west) side of the road for Blodgett Peak Open Space (**GPS:** 38.94892, -104.886095).

## THE HIKE

Blodgett Peak, rising to a rocky 9,423-foot summit on the northwest edge of Colorado Springs, offers a steep trail to a small summit with spectacular views of the city spreading out below, the Air Force Academy, and Pikes Peak towering to the southwest. The 3.2-mile trail, gaining almost 2,700 feet of elevation from parking lot to summit, is a strenuous hike for most people.

Expect parts of the trail to be difficult to follow, particularly with numerous social trails branching off; slopes eroded from too many footsteps; and loose gravel and rock sections. The upper part of the mountain also has lots of dead trees that were torched in the 2012 Waldo Canyon Fire, which swept across high ridges and the mountaintop. Use caution and watch for falling branches if you

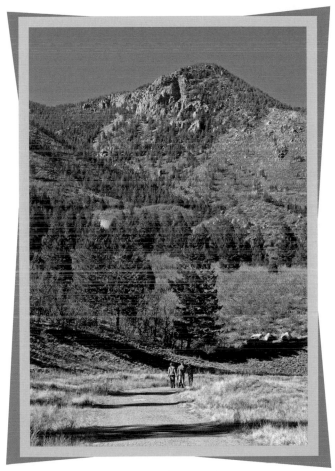

Blodgett Peak towers above a closed road near the water tower.

are hiking in windy conditions. Some hikers will prefer using trekking poles for balance on the difficult trail sections.

Before fitness seekers began inundating the Mount Manitou Incline for a stair-stepping workout, there was Blodgett Peak. The hike up Blodgett, once commonly used by Air Force Academy cadets for training, is still a great workout hike and, better yet, has none of the Incline's crowds. The peak has a loyal following of local hikers who regularly trek to its summit. Anyone who considers themselves an experienced Pikes Peak country hiker needs to climb Blodgett Peak at least once.

The hike starts at a trailhead at a small parking lot on the west side of Woodmen Road on the edge of Blodgett Peak Open Space, a 167-acre Colorado Springs city parkland. There are ten parking spaces plus a spot for people with disabilities and a toilet and information kiosk at the trailhead parking lot. Additional parking is found along the paved shoulder on the west side of West Woodmen Road, beside the parking lot.

Blodgett Falls spills down a vertical granite cliff.

Begin your Blodgett summit adventure from the obvious trailhead at the west end of the parking area. A bench facing toward Blodgett Peak honors Patrick Niedringhaus, an 18-year-old climber and hiker who died in an avalanche on Torreys Peak in the Colorado Rockies in 2004. Blodgett was one of Patrick's favorite local hikes. Before taking your hike, take a minute to sit on the bench to remember young Patrick and to scout the hike ahead of you.

Look northwest from the bench and trailhead to Blodgett Peak, the obvious high, pointed mountain with tall granite cliffs on its south-facing slopes. The true summit of Blodgett is behind the false summit you see from here. Note several obvious landmarks on the south flank of the mountain that mark the hiking route. Scouting the hike in advance allows you to locate the landmarks so that you are not lured off the best trail by social trails that usually end in brush and boulders.

To stay on track, these are the landmarks to locate on the trail: a round green water tower; a steep unnamed canyon on the south side of Blodgett Peak; a cliff band halfway up the canyon that ascends the mountain slope to the right; a large boulder field that spills down below the largest cliffs below Blodgett's summit; and a high south-facing cliff on the ridge west of the summit.

From Patrick's Bench and the trailhead, hike west for 0.6 mile up the wide closed road (which provides utility access to the water tower) to the fourth and last switchback before the tower. Go left on the doubletrack Hummingbird Trail at a junction on the left side of the switchback.

The Hummingbird Trail makes a wide bend to the south before contouring north across shady slopes clad with pine, fir, and spruce. At 1.4 miles this pleasant trail section ends at a wide gravel spot in the bottom of a dry canyon. A couple of trail options are found here. Do not go straight up the steep slope to the north, although a popular social trail heads up this way to an old road. If you go this way, be prepared for some serious bushwhacking through dense scrub oak thickets if you lose your chosen path or it ends. Instead, go left on a singletrack trail up the bottom of the canyon. A large granite boulder with a slabby south face and vertical face above the trail is 100 feet up the trail.

The next trail segment continues up the steep canyon for almost a mile to a steep cliff band and a 50-foot-high waterfall. This continuously steep trail section is easy to follow but has some eroded sections with unsure footing. A pair of trekking poles and a few tree branches to grab are handy to keep your balance. Water often runs across bedrock in the upper part of the canyon and down the waterfall. Avoid getting sidetracked from this trail and going onto scree slopes on the north side of the canyon on social trails and shortcuts. They are more difficult to follow and overuse of them will lead to continued erosion. The trail up the canyon could use some trail love in the form of rebuilding eroded sections and placing rock steps and water bars to lessen erosion.

After reaching trickling Blodgett Falls and the cliff band at 2.3 miles, go right on a steep trail section at the base of the cliffs, which runs north up the mountainside. To your right here is Blodgett's infamous boulder field. Some hikers prefer to boulder-hop up the long, steep boulder field, but it is best to keep left of it to avoid shifting boulders and twisted ankles.

Above the cliff band after climbing a steep 0.1 mile, the trail goes left and contours across a hillside with open woods for a hundred yards. Again, some hikers will go right above the cliff band and clamber up the upper boulder field, which is hemmed in by cliffs on either side, to a false summit east of Blodgett's main summit. The easier alternative is to keep left and follow the well-beaten trail.

Past a large pointed boulder, the trail bends right and begins zigzagging up a steep mountain slope studded with ponderosa pine and Douglas fir. At 2.6 miles the trail enters the Waldo Canyon burn scar. During the massive wildfire in June 2012, the upper slopes of Blodgett Peak were toasted by flames, killing almost all the trees from here to the summit. Pick your way up the steep trail, stepping over loose rocks and falling trees and keeping right of a high broken cliff to your left. At 3.0 miles the trail reaches a broad saddle. The summit of Blodgett Peak is directly east from here.

The last 0.2-mile trail segment heads northwest from the saddle, scrambling up through boulders surrounded by tall burnt trees. It's advisable to use extreme caution or turn around if you are on the upper section of Blodgett Peak in high winds since the dead snag trees can topple or break, which would be fatal if one hit you. After 3.2 miles of uphill hiking, the trail ends on Blodgett's rock-strewn summit.

The mountaintop offers spectacular panoramic views of the Pikes Peak region. Below you spreads the northwest suburbs of Colorado Springs, while the city center rises to the southeast. Pikes Peak, usually snow covered much of the year, towers 11 miles to the southwest. The reservoir and dam visible to the northwest is Rampart Reservoir, a popular fishing and recreation spot and part of the Colorado Springs water supply. The Air Force Academy lies to the north, tucked against the soaring escarpment of the Rampart Range.

Take a few minutes to relax on Blodgett Peak's summit, enjoy that great view, and have a hearty drink of water or energy drink. Now it's time to head back down. Follow the same route down the mountain. Watch your footing since you will encounter gravel and loose rock. Allow about half the time it took you to climb the mountain to get back to the trailhead and your car.

## MILES AND DIRECTIONS

**0.0** Trailhead at parking lot on West Woodmen Road (GPS: 38.948995, -104.886334). Hike west up the looping closed gravel road, gradually gaining elevation toward a round water tower.

# Blodgett Peak Trail

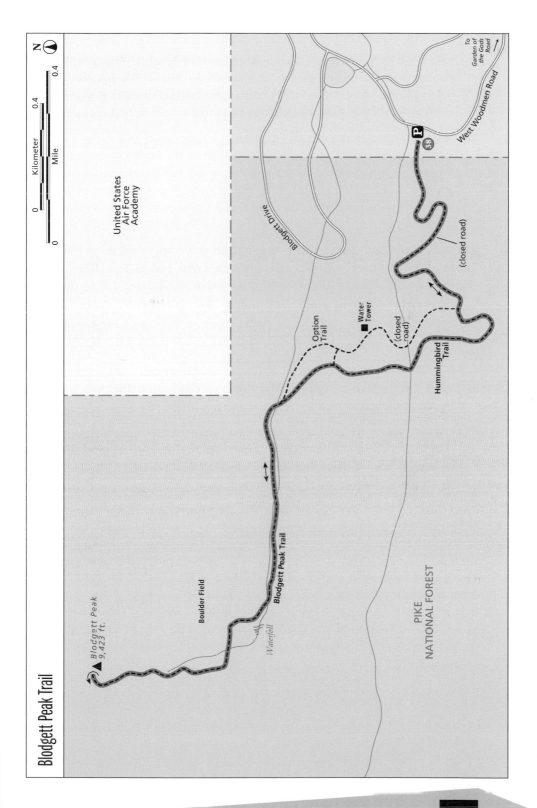

**0.6** Before reaching the water tower, turn left on Hummingbird Trail, a broad doubletrack trail, on the outside of a wide switchback. This junction is marked with a sign on a post for Hummingbird Trail and Blodgett Peak Trail (GPS: 38.94780, -104.892866). (See "Option" below.)

**1.4** The doubletrack Hummingbird Trail ends at a wide gravel area in the bottom of a dry canyon. A social trail goes straight up the brushy hill ahead—avoid going this way since several trails begin and end on the steep slopes above. Instead, go left and follow a singletrack trail up the bottom of the canyon, passing a large boulder 100 feet up the canyon (GPS: 38.953636, -104.897178).

**2.3** Reach a 50-foot-high waterfall and cliff band that blocks the canyon after following the steep trail along a mostly dry creek bed (GPS: 38.953965, -104.904639). Go right just below the falls and hike up a steep trail section between the cliff on the left and the boulder field on the right.

**2.4** The trail reaches a knoll where the cliff band ends. Go left and follow the good trail through woods for a few hundred feet to a pointed boulder. The trail goes north up steep wooded slopes here.

**2.6** You reach the Waldo Canyon wildlife burn area. Continue up the steep trail through a burned forest with tall blackened tree trunks.

**3.0** The trail reaches a wide gravelly saddle in the burned area (GPS: 38.957847, -104.907382). Hike northeast along the rocky trail, which can be easily lost among boulders, through more burned forest.

**3.2** Summit of 9,423-foot Blodgett Peak (GPS: 38.959627, -104.907629). After enjoying the view, descend the same trail back to the parking area.

**6.4** End the hike at the Blodgett Peak Open Space parking lot.

### Option

A less scenic alternative to Hummingbird Trail is to continue up the road for another 0.4 mile to the green water tower. Scramble up a steep singletrack trail left and above the tower, then follow the trail north through forest until it meets up with the Hummingbird Trail at a flat gravel area in the canyon floor. A side path (GPS: 38.95142, -104.89448) goes west for 250 feet to Hummingbird Trail in a scrub oak forest.

## THE HIKE

his 3.8-mile-long hike follows three trails—Palmer Reservoir, Swank, and Ice Cave Creek Trails—and makes a lollipop route west of the Town of Palmer Lake along North Monument Creek and Ice Cave Creek. Half of the hike follows a closed road that allows utility access to two reservoirs for the Town of Palmer Lake, while the other half threads through Ice Cave Creek's narrow, boulder-filled canyon before climbing over a wooded ridge.

Most of the hike is moderate and includes walking on the reservoir access road, hiking on rough terrain along the creek, and following an old jeep road. Grades are generally moderate with few steep uphill sections. The first half of the hike gains elevation, while the second half loses that elevation.

*Option:* For extra credit, do the Cap Rock loop hike (see below) by wandering farther up Ice Cave Creek before scrambling through a boulder field and up granite slabs to the airy summit of Cap Rock, a local landmark. This short loop is the most difficult route in this book.

Winter ice and snow covers Upper Palmer Reservoir below the trail.

The Palmer Reservoirs Loop hike begins at a trailhead signed "Reservoir Trailhead," on the west side of a switchback on Old Carriage Road, on the north side of North Monument Creek, and at the entrance to a steep-walled canyon. Plenty of parking is available at the trailhead and along the south side of the road just east of the trailhead. A sign at the trailhead details the area rules—all dogs must be leashed, no pets in the water, and no swimming, firearms, or horses.

The first hike segment goes 0.8 mile up Palmer Reservoir Trail from the trailhead to its junction with Ice Cave Creek Trail at the first reservoir.

Hike west on the trail up the narrowing canyon and, after a quarter mile, climb steeply up a short slope to a closed utility road. Follow the road up the bottom of the canyon, passing through a large gate, which is usually open. The hike climbs steadily up the road and reaches the dam at Lower Palmer Reservoir at 0.6 mile. A concrete dam, split by a spillway, forms a picturesque lake tucked into the narrow canyon and surrounded by a pine and fir forest. Enjoy the scenic view of the lake from the road, but remember that people and dogs are not allowed in the reservoir and fishing is prohibited.

Continue up the road along the north edge of the lake and in another 0.1 mile cross over Ice Cave Creek, which tumbles through a mass of fallen boulders in its lower canyon before emptying into a wetland at the west end of the reservoir. Just past the creek, follow the road up around a corner and look right at 0.8 mile for the start of the Ice Cave Creek Trail. The next trail segment follows Ice Cave Creek northwest for 0.6 mile to its junction with Swank Trail.

The next trail section follows Ice Cave Creek Road for 0.6 mile from the road to Swank Trail. The narrow singletrack trail, rebuilt by the Colorado Mountain Club in 2013, traverses across slopes covered with fir and spruce above the creek's rocky canyon. Numerous boulders of all sizes have fallen into the creek, creating watery caves and grottos beneath the granite blocks. The caves, receiving little direct sunlight, often hold ice flows in their dark depths through late May. This trail section is snowy and icy in winter so come prepared with spikes for your shoes for traction.

After you hike 0.4 mile from the road, the trail splashes across the creek and follows the open north bank west. Dense willows and grass clot the creek's banks and a couple openings in the forest cover give views northwest to Cap Rock, a pointed rock formation that towers above the canyon. After another 0.2 mile the trail bends away from the creek and reaches a junction with Swank Trail, an abandoned old road. Go left at this junction, 1.5 miles from the start of the hike.

Swank Trail heads across a hillside and descends down to an open grassy meadow along Ice Cave Creek and a trail junction on the north side of the meadow. Swank Trail goes south here across the creek. The Cap Rock Trail continues west up the canyon. A tall ponderosa pine stands sentinel on the west side of the meadow, and a squat granite boulder sits next to the creek.

While the standard hike continues on Swank Trail, this is where you decide if you want to climb Cap Rock. (See below.)

From the junction of the Cap Rock and Swank Trails, go south on Swank. Step across the creek and follow the old rutted Jeep road up a shallow valley blanketed in a spruce and fir forest. The trail slowly climbs and after a half mile reaches the top of a ridge and a junction with the Winding Stairs Trail, which follows the ridge west for almost 3 miles to Winding Stairs Road and the top of the Rampart Range.

Descend down the southwest side of the ridge on Swank Trail. The old road drops steeply down the mountainside before leveling out in a valley filled with grass and willows. At 0.35 mile from the ridgetop, the Swank Trail ends when it reaches Reservoir Trail and Inlet Trail on the north shore of the Upper Palmer Reservoir.

The last hiking segment runs 1.4 miles from the inlet on the reservoir back to the trailhead. Follow the Palmer Reservoir Trail, a closed utility road, east along the north shore of the upper lake. The trail climbs up from the shoreline and runs across the hillside above a curved concrete dam. Continue hiking past the lake and downhill, passing the junction with Ice Cave Creek Trail at 3 miles and the first dam at 3.2 miles. The road drops quickly down the lower canyon, passes through the gate, and reaches the first junction. Go right and descend a short singletrack trail to the bottom of the canyon. Follow the wide trail through piney woods back to the trailhead and parking lot.

## MILES AND DIRECTIONS

**0.0** Start from the trailhead on Old Carriage Road in Palmer Lake (GPS: 39.118669, -104.921208). Hike west on Palmer Reservoir Trail, a closed road, up North Monument Creek's canyon.

**0.3** Climb a short singletrack trail and reach a utility road (GPS: 39.118686, -104.925534). Hike up the road (Palmer Reservoir Trail), pass through a gate, and continue up the steep road.

**0.6** Reach the dam at Lower Palmer Reservoir (GPS: 39.117136, -104.931337). Hike west on the road along the north side of the lake.

**0.7** Reach the west end of the lake and cross over Ice Cave Creek.

**0.8** Reach Ice Cave Creek Trail on the right (GPS: 39.115932, -104.933794) at 7,600 feet. Go right on the singletrack trail on steep slopes above the creek.

**1.2** Dip down and cross Ice Cave Creek.

**1.4** Cross Swank Creek. After a couple hundred feet, you come to a junction with Swank Trail (GPS: 39.12228, -104.94193). Go left across a hillside and then west to an open meadow.

**1.5** Reach the junction of Swank Trail and Ice Cave Creek Trail on the edge of a meadow (GPS: 39.12195, -104.94372). Go left on Swank Trail and cross Ice Cave Creek. Continue south uphill on the rutted old road.

**2.0** Junction with Winding Stairs Trail on top of a ridge (GPS: 39.11780, -104.94193).

**2.4** Junction with Palmer Reservoir Trail and Inlet Trail on the north side of the upper reservoir (GPS: 39.11393, -104.94322). Continue south and then east on the wide Palmer Reservoir Trail above the north side of the lake.

**3.0** Junction with Ice Cave Creek Trail. Continue straight on the road.

**3.2** Reach the first dam.

**3.6** Leave the road and descend down to the trail in the bottom of the valley.

**3.8** Reach the trailhead and parking area.

### *Cap Rock Trail Option*

The Cap Rock Trail is a rough backcountry hiking adventure and the most difficult hike in this book. Hikers should be skilled at route finding, able to execute easy rock-climbing moves, and willing to make judgment calls for the group's safety. It adds 1.5 miles, 450 feet of elevation gain, and as much as 3 hours to the Palmer Reservoir Trails.

The trail is hard to follow at times since it winds among boulders along the creek before scrambling up a steep hill to a boulder field below Cap Rock's east face. A good sense of direction and strong route-finding skills are essential. Bring a map and compass or use a GPS unit and plug the "Miles and Directions" coordinates in it to stay on route. The return hike from the summit descends the west side of Cap Rock before returning down a crude path along the creek.

Start the Cap Rock Trail at the meadow where Swank Trail crosses Ice Cave Creek. Locate the Ice Cave Creek Trail, which goes west from the meadow and Swank Trail past a tall ponderosa pine. The trail winds among boulders on the hillside north of the creek and after 0.3 mile reaches a large blocky boulder on the right above the trail.

Scramble past the big boulder and then up the hillside, keeping left of the boulder field. Aim for a couple tall pines left of a huge pointed boulder below the southeast corner of Cap Rock, which looms above. Scramble and climb across boulders below the pointed block; use caution if there is snow on the rock surfaces. A couple places require careful foot placements and perhaps even a fixed rope to use as a hand line on tricky sections. Careful route finding is required to find the easiest route through the boulders. Do not get lured into traversing the boulder field below you—instead stay high.

Past the largest boulders, continue scrambling up right. Squeeze between boulders, edge up short slabs, and grab tree branches to pull past slippery gravel

# Palmer Reservoirs Loop with Cap Rock Option

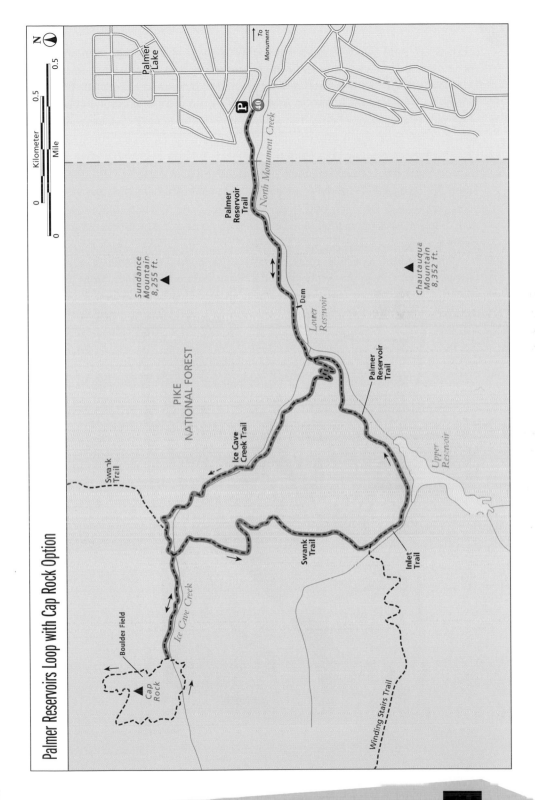

sections. Eventually the terrain becomes easier and you reach the base of a long granite slab that gently ascends south above the steep east face of Cap Rock. Scramble up the slab. The easiest line is up the middle between the granite on the left and trees on the right. Higher, step left onto the main slab and climb up its low-angle face to a high ledge below the final summit cap. This is a good spot to leave your pack and have a drink of water and snack. Look around too for a cache box.

The final pitch to Cap Rock's airy summit is up a 60-foot crack and groove on the north side. A couple easy climbing moves lead to a gentle slab to the summit. Stand on top and give a yodel—you earned that peak. After enjoying the view across Ice Cave Creek Valley and North Monument Creek Valley to Mount Herman, descend back down to your pack. It's easiest to descend by facing out and climbing down like a spider.

While you can reverse your ascent path to descend back to the creek, it's best to descend down the west side of Cap Rock and do a loop hike. From the shoulder below the summit, scramble down an angled slab to the west above

Chisel Point is a dramatic granite pinnacle west of Cap Rock.

Cap Rock's west face. Pick the line of least resistance to descend. If possible, it's easiest to stay on the rock surface of the wide ramp rather than in the forest to the right. Straight ahead towers the sharp pinnacle of Chisel Point.

At the bottom of the ramp, go left around a big rounded boulder and then squeeze between two boulders. Look to your left below here and locate a gully that descends south. Go down the gully, then edge down a slab to the left. Below is a short drop-off into another rock gully, which leads to more boulders. Thread your way through the boulders, which may require some backtracking to avoid getting cliffed off, until you reach gentle slopes below. Hike through open forest past a 45-foot-high boulder split by a wide crack and, after a mile of hiking from Swank Trail, reach the rough Ice Cave Creek Trail.

Go left (east) on the singletrack path and cross the creek through a dense stand of willows. Follow the trail east along the south bank of the creek, stepping over deadfall and loose rocks. The trail eventually peters out in a massive area of deadfall and giant boulders. Find a good way to cross the creek and scramble up steep slopes on the north side to find the trail again. Continue east and after 0.2 mile from the first creek crossing, you reach the large boulder where you began the ascent.

Follow the trail east from here for 0.3 mile back to the junction with Swank Trail in the meadow. Using the directions above, follow the Swank Trail to the Palmer Reservoir Trail and then back to the trailhead.

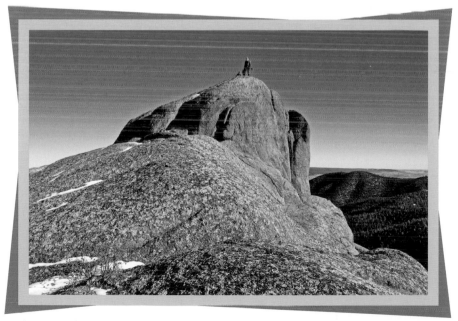

The summit of Cap Rock is a granite knob that overlooks the Rampart Range.

**Option: Cap Rock Miles and Directions**

**0.0**  At mile 1.5 under "Miles and Directions" above, leave Swank Trail at the meadow (GPS: 39.12195, -104.94372) and hike west on Ice Cave Creek Trail along the north bank of the creek.

**0.3**  Reach a large boulder above the trail and start uphill toward Cap Rock's southeast corner (GPS: 39.12202, -104.94895).

**0.4**  Scramble up a rough trail to the south side of a boulder field below Cap Rock's east face. Continue through the boulders, climbing over some and squirming past others. After a few hundred feet, reach the base of the east face after scrambling and climbing over boulders. Continue hiking north along the base of the face.

**0.5**  When possible, climb up left on steep wooded slopes to a granite ramp that slants up south. After about another 300 feet, you will reach the base of the rock ramp (GPS: 39.12463, -104.95067) and either climb steep wooded slopes to the right or scramble directly up the clean granite slab.

**0.6**  Reach the base of Cap Rock's knobby summit. Climb a crack and groove for 65 feet to the small summit of Cap Rock (GPS: 39.123454, -104.950675). Return to the base and head west down a sloping granite ramp at the top of the west face.

**0.8**  Reach the bottom of the ramp on the west side and scramble past some big boulders. Look for a groove to go down to the left. Follow the easiest way down brushy gullies below the west face of Cap Rock to the valley floor (GPS: 39.12278, -104.95238). Route finding is difficult here.

**1.0**  Reach Ice Cave Creek and a rough trail below the west face of Cap Rock. Cross the creek and follow the trail east along the south bank of the creek. After about 300 feet, cross the creek wherever it is possible and scramble up through rocks to the large boulder and return path to Swank Trail on the north bank.

**1.2**  Rejoin the return trail below the boulder (GPS: 39.12202, -104.94895) and follow it back to Swank Trail.

**1.5**  Reach Swank Trail at a meadow at a large tree (GPS: 39.12195, -104.94372). Go right on Swank Trail and follow the above directions back to the trailhead. At this point you will have hiked 3 total miles. (**Option:** For a 4.5-mile out-and-back hike, retrace your steps across Ice Cave Creek Trail back to the trailhead.)

# Appendix A: Further Reading

D'Antonio, Bob. *Hiking Colorado's Front Range* (2nd Edition). Guilford, CT: FalconGuides/Globe Pequot, 2012.

Duvall, Linda, and Marty Banks. *Insider's Guide to Colorado Springs* (2nd Edition). Guilford, CT: Globe Pequot, 2011.

Galas, Judith, and Cindy West. *Walking Colorado Springs.* Guilford, CT: FalconGuides/Globe Pequot, 1997.

Gaug, Maryann. *Best Hikes Near Denver and Boulder.* Guilford, CT: FalconGuides/ Globe Pequot, 2010.

Green, Stewart M. *Best Easy Day Hikes Colorado Springs.* Guilford, CT: FalconGuides/ Globe Pequot, 2011.

Green, Stewart M. *Rock Climbing Colorado* (2nd Edition). Guilford, CT: FalconGuides/Globe Pequot, 2010.

Green, Stewart M. *Scenic Driving Colorado* (3rd Edition). Guilford, CT: FalconGuides/ Globe Pequot, 2008.

Green, Stewart M. *Scenic Routes & Byways Colorado* (4th Edition). Guilford, CT: Globe Pequot, 2013.

Paul, Susan Joy. *Touring Colorado Hot Springs* (2nd Edition). Guilford, CT: FalconGuides/Globe Pequot, 2012.

Paul, Susan Joy. *Hiking Waterfalls in Colorado: A Guide to the State's Best Waterfall Hikes.* Guilford, CT: FalconGuides/Globe Pequot, 2013.

Sprague, Marshall. *Money Mountain: The Story of Cripple Creek Gold.* Lincoln: University of Nebraska Press, 1979.

Sprague, Marshall. *Newport in the Rockies: The Life & Good Times of Colorado Springs.* Chicago: Swallow Press, 1988.

Waters, Frank. *Midas of the Rockies: The Story of Stratton & Cripple Creek.* Chicago: Swallow Press, 1972.

# Appendix B: Restaurants, Brewpubs, and Accommodations

## RESTAURANTS

Colorado Springs offers well over 1,000 restaurants, from the Broadmoor Hotel's five-star option, including the Penrose Room and Charles Court, to humble curbside trucks that vend burritos with homemade tortillas. There are numerous standout restaurants in the Springs that offer a huge variety of cuisines, styles, and prices. This listing is the beginning of your culinary exploration and includes the author's favorite dining experiences. Try any of these restaurants after your day of hiking and you will surely be satisfied, happy, and ready to hit the trail again tomorrow. Bon appétit!

### Adam's Mountain Café
26 Manitou Ave.
Manitou Springs, CO 80829
(719) 685-1430
adamsmountain.com
A Manitou Springs tradition serving breakfast, lunch, and dinner with lots of vegetarian and vegan meals, no prepared foods, no microwaves, and organic local ingredients.

### Amanda's Fonda
3625 W. Colorado Ave.
Colorado Springs, CO 80904
(719) 227-1975
amandasfonda.com
Popular Mexican restaurant with creek-side dining in west Colorado Springs. Thirty-five flavors of tequila, lunch and dinner, and gluten-free menu available. Also a location at 8050 N. Academy Blvd.

### The Blue Star
1645 S. Tejon St.
Colorado Springs, CO 80905
(719) 632-1086
thebluestar.net
A popular and busy restaurant in an old Furr Foods grocery store with a varied menu, good service, and extensive wine list, one of the largest in the Springs.

### Green Line Grill

230½ Pueblo Ave.

Colorado Springs, CO 80903

(719) 964-1461

greenlinegrill.com

Chef Bobby serves up a tasty onion-"fried" burger straight out of central Oklahoma, topped with El Reno Slaw and served with hand-cut fries. Also a great veggie burger.

### Hungry Bear Restaurant

111 E. Midland Ave.

Woodland Park, CO 80863

(719) 687 5912

hungrybearcolorado.com

Hiking behind Pikes Peak? Visit the Hungry Bear, a family-style diner with traditional breakfasts and salads, burgers, and soups for lunch.

### Il Vicino

11 S. Tejon St.

5214 N. Nevada Ave.

(719) 475-9224, (719) 590 8633

ilvicino.com

Contemporary pizzeria with wood-fired artisan pizzas, calzones, flatbread sandwiches, salads, and award-winning ales.

### King's Chef Diner

131 E. Bijou St.

110 E. Costilla St.

Colorado Springs, CO 80903

(719) 636-5010

kingschefdiner.com

One phrase describes this classic downtown diner: green chile. It's hot and tasty, plus there's a vegetarian version. Open for breakfast and lunch. Eat at the tiny purple-castle diner on East Costilla for old-time ambience.

### La Baguette Downtown

117 E. Pikes Peak Ave.

Colorado Springs, CO 80903

labaguettedowntown.com

Informal and affordable French country dining with authentic French onion soup, crusty baguettes, croissants, and delectable desserts in the heart of Colorado Springs.

### La Casita Mexican Grill

306 S. Eighth St.

4295 N. Nevada Ave.

3725 E. Woodmen Rd.

Colorado Springs, CO

(719) 633-9616; (719) 599-7829; (719) 536-0375

lacasitamexigrill.com

Basic tasty Mexican food with three locations, daily specials, great salsa bar, and patio dining. Muy sabroso!

### Luigi's Homemade Italian Food

947 S. Tejon St.

Colorado Springs, CO 80903

(719) 632-7339

luigiscoloradosprings.com

Luigi's is a popular and traditional Colorado Springs' Italian eatery with red-checkered tablecloths, hearty servings of pasta, and fresh Italian bread.

### Paravicini's Italian Bistro

2802 W. Colorado Ave.

Colorado Springs, CO 80904

(719) 471-8200

paravicinis.com

Paravicini's, located in Old Colorado City, serves perhaps the best Italian food in the Springs with classic dishes and neo-Italian creations along with complementary wines, appetizers, and desserts.

### Penrose Room

Broadmoor Hotel

1 Lake Circle

Colorado Springs, CO 80906

broadmoor.com/penrose-room

Simply the best restaurant in Colorado Springs and the only five-star and Five-Diamond restaurant in Colorado. Dine on the top floor of Broadmoor South with views of the mountains, excellent food, great presentation, huge wine list, superior service, and, of course, prices to match.

### Poor Richard's Restaurant

324½ N. Tejon St.

Colorado Springs, CO 80903

(719) 578-5549

poorrichardsdowntown.com

Longtime downtown restaurant with delicious pizzas, veggie meals, sandwiches, and salads. Sidewalk and patio dining. Next door is Little Richard's Toystore, Rico's Café and Wine Bar, and Poor Richard's Books.

### The Rabbit Hole

101 N. Tejon St.

Colorado Springs, CO 80903

(719) 203-5072

rabbitholedinner.com

This subterranean restaurant, great for late-night eats, offers a hip decor, diverse menu, inventive drinks, super service, and a cool vibe. Try it, you'll like it for an after-hike meal.

### Uchenna

2501 W. Colorado Ave.

Colorado Springs, CO 80904

(719) 634-5070

uchennaalive.com

Uchenna, the only Ethiopian restaurant in the Springs, is also the #1 ranked restaurant out of 1,162 on Trip Advisor (2014). Fabulous African food with great service and ambience; it's not fancy but you're treated like family. Try the rosewater lemonade too.

## BREWPUBS

What better way to celebrate your latest local hike than quaffing a few pints of craft beers in a Colorado Springs brewpub? Colorado Springs is simply one of America's best beer towns with more than twenty local breweries that create exquisite and tasty microbrews for all you trekking hop-heads. There are, of course, award-winning beers like Laughing Lab from Bristol, a mildly sweet, nutty Scottish ale, and the broad beer selection at Phantom Canyon, the Springs' original brewpub started in 1993 by Colorado governor John Hickenlooper. There are also lots of small brewpubs and taprooms scattered around the Pikes Peak region. Sample my favorites below and then try others, including Smiling Toad, Ute Pass, Rocky Mountain, and Bierworks breweries.

### Bristol Brewing Company

1604 S. Cascade Ave.

Colorado Springs, CO 80906

(719) 633-2555

bristolbrewing.com

The brewery, housed in the historic Ivywild School, offers a taproom and restaurants. Their iconic beers are Laughing Lab Scottish Ale and Beehive Honey Wheat.

### Colorado Mountain Brewery at the Roundhouse

600 S. 21st St.

Colorado Springs, CO 80904

(719) 466-8240

cmbrew.com

Colorado Mountain Brewery off US 24 is a convenient stop after a mountain hike. Taste its handcrafted brews and Colorado cuisine and enjoy views of Pikes Peak from the patio.

### Phantom Canyon Brewing Company

2 E. Pikes Peak Ave.

Colorado Springs, CO 80903

(719) 635-2800

phantomcanyon.com

Popular Phantom Canyon, one of the Springs' oldest brewers, is located in the heart of downtown. Classic beers, special releases, small-batch bomber series to wash down pub food. Also pints and pool upstairs.

### Trinity Brewing Company

1466 W. Garden of the Gods Rd.

Colorado Springs, CO 80907

(719) 634-0029

trinitybrew.com

Convenient to the Garden of the Gods, Trinity was a 2014 gold-medal winner at the Great American Beer Fest for its Elektrick Cubumbahh. Eclectic and busy pub with mountain views from its small patio.

## ACCOMMODATIONS

Since its 1871 founding, Colorado Springs has been a destination for travelers and has offered a wide range of accommodations. Visiting hikers will find a broad spectrum of hotels, motels, and bed-and-breakfast inns with an equally wide range of prices. Stay in a basic no-frills hotel like Motel 6 to save cash, or indulge yourself and bed down for a few nights in one of the Pikes Peak region's many B&Bs where you're treated like family. Here's a listing of some of the most popular accommodations. For more B&Bs, visit bedandbreakfast.com, pikespeakarea bnbs.com, and tripadvisor.com for suggestions, reviews, and contact information.

## Bed & Breakfast Inns

### Adobe Inn at Cascade
4675 Hagerman Ave.
Cascade, CO 80809
(719) 684-2194
theinnatcascade.com

### Avenue Hotel Bed and Breakfast
711 Manitou Ave.
Manitou Springs, CO 80829
(719) 685 1277
avenuehotelbandb.com

### Bed & Breakfast at Historic Onaledge
336 El Paso Blvd.
Manitou Springs, CO 80829
(719) 685-4515 or (888) 685-4515
onaledge.net

### Carr Manor
350 E. Carr Ave.
Cripple Creek, CO 80813
(719) 689-3709
carrmanor.com

### Glen Eyrle Castle
3820 N. 30th St.
Colorado Springs, CO 80904
(719) 634-0808
gleneyrie.org

### Holden House—1902 Bed and Breakfast Inn
1102 W. Pikes Peak Ave.
Colorado Springs, CO 80904
(719) 471-3980
holdenhouse.com

### The Hotel St. Nicholas

303 N. Third St.
Cripple Creek, CO 80813
(719) 689-0856 or (888) 786-4257
hotelstnicholas.com

### Hughes Hacienda Bed & Breakfast

12060 Calle Corvo
Colorado Springs, CO 80926
(719) 576-2060
hugheshacienda.com

### Lennox House Bed & Breakfast

1339 N. Nevada Ave.
Colorado Springs, CO 80903
(719) 471-9265
lennoxhouse.com

### Old Town Guest House

115 S. 26th St.
Colorado Springs, CO 80904
(719) 632-9194
oldtown-guesthouse.com

### Red Crags Estates

328 El Paso Blvd.
Manitou Springs, CO 80829
(719) 685-4515
redcragsestates.com

### A Room with a View Bed and Breakfast

528 E. Bijou St.
Colorado Springs, CO 80903
(719) 633-3683
arwav.biz/1.html

### St. Mary's Inn

530 N. Nevada Ave.
Colorado Springs, CO 80903
(719) 540-2222
thestmarysinn.com

### Silver House Bed & Breakfast
355 S. Second St.
Cripple Creek, CO 80813
(719) 689-5558
silverhousebnb.com

## Hotels
Colorado Springs offers lots of hotels for footsore hikers to rest their dusty boots, including all the major chain hotels like Best Western, Comfort Inn, Hilton, Holiday Inn, Hyatt, La Quinta Inn, Marriott, Radisson, and Ramada. Check out your favorite booking site like Orbitz, Expedia, Kayak, or Hotels.com to find accommodations that meet your price and pocketbook. Here are five great Colorado Springs hotels that will not only massage your feet and back but also clean your boots.

### Antlers Hilton Hotel
4 South Cascade
Colorado Springs, CO 80903
(719) 955-5600
antlers.com

### The Broadmoor Hotel
1 Lake Ave.
Colorado Springs, CO 80906
broadmoor.com

### Cheyenne Mountain Resort
3225 Broadmoor Valley Rd.
Colorado Springs, CO 80906
(719) 538-4000
cheyennemountain.com

### The Cliff House at Pikes Peak
306 Canon Ave.
Manitou Springs, CO 80829
thecliffhouse.com

### The Mining Exchange Wyndham Grand Hotel
9 S. Nevada Ave.
Colorado Springs, CO 80903
wyndham.com

## Campgrounds

Despite its easy access to the great outdoors, Colorado Springs is not exactly camping friendly. There are a few local campgrounds but most cater to RVers rather than tenters. The best campground close to the Springs is at Cheyenne Mountain State Park on the southwest edge of the city. It's easy to reach and offers scenic campsites with expansive views. You will have to drive farther away to find more rugged camping options in Pike National Forest north of Woodland Park and at Mueller State Park.

### Cheyenne Mountain State Park
410 JL Ranch Heights
Colorado Springs, CO 80926
(719) 576-2016
cpw.state.co.us/placestogo/Parks/cheyennemountain
61 campsites in five campgrounds

### Echo Canyon Campground
45044 US Hwy. 50
Canon City, CO 81212
(866) 341-7875
echocanyoncampground.com

### Garden of the Gods RV Resort
3704 W. Colorado Ave.
Colorado Springs, CO 80904
(719) 475-9450
rvcoutdoors.com/gardenofthegods

### Mueller State Park
21045 CO Highway 67 South
Divide, CO 80814
(719) 687-2366
cpw.state.co.us/placestogo/parks/Mueller
132 campsites in seven campgrounds; three cabins

### Pike National Forest
601 South Weber
Colorado Springs, CO 80903
(719) 636-1602
fs.usda.gov/main/psicc/home
Campsite reservations at recreation.gov

**Pikes Peak Ranger District**
Colorado Campground, 80 sites
The Crags Campground, 17 sites
Meadow Ridge Campground, 19 sites
Painted Rocks Campground, 18 sites
South Meadows Campground, 64 sites
Springdale Campground, 13 sites
Thunder Ridge Campground, 21 sites
Wye Campground, 21 sites

**South Park Ranger District**
Eleven Mile Canyon Recreation Area
Four campgrounds with 61 sites

# About the Author

Based in Colorado Springs, Stewart M. Green has hiked, climbed, photographed, and traveled across the American West as well as the United States and the world in search of memorable images and experiences to document. Stewart, a contract writer and photographer for Globe Pequot and FalconGuides, has written and photographed more than twenty-five travel and climbing books, including *Best Easy Day Hikes Colorado Springs, Scenic Routes & Byways Colorado, Scenic Routes & Byways California's Pacific Coast, Best Climbs Moab, Best Climbs Denver and Boulder, KNACK Rock Climbing, Rock Climbing Colorado, Rock Climbing Utah, Rock Climbing Arizona,* and *Rock Climbing New England.* His photographs and writing are also published in many magazines, books, catalogs, and ads. Stewart is a professional rock climbing guide with Front Range Climbing Company and the Climbing Expert at climbing.about.com. Visit him at green1109.wix.com/stewartmgreenphoto for images and information.

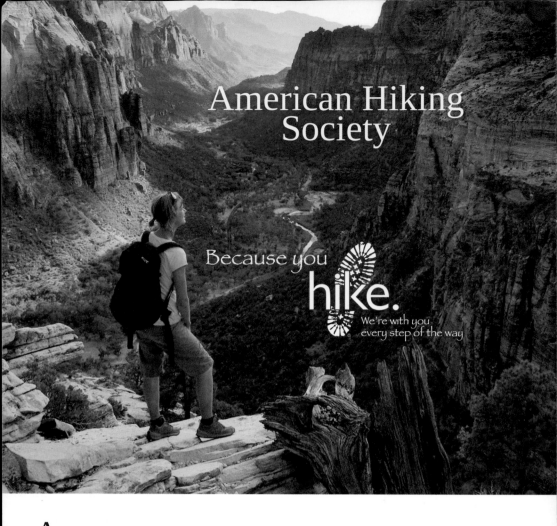

# American Hiking Society

Because you

## hike.

We're with you
every step of the way

$A$s a national voice for hikers, **American Hiking Society** works every day:

- Building and maintaining hiking trails
- Educating and supporting hikers by providing information and resources
- Supporting hiking and trail organizations nationwide
- Speaking for hikers in the halls of Congress and with federal land managers

Whether you're a casual hiker or a seasoned backpacker, become a member of American Hiking Society and join the national hiking community! You'll enjoy great member benefits and help preserve the nation's hiking trails, so tomorrow's hike is even better than today's. We invite you to join us now!

**American
Hiking
Society**